Praise for

ZONE OF ACTION

"Prepare to journey back in time to the Invasion of Iraq from an unusual vantage point: JAG. Colonel Kirk Warner (Ret.) has provided a priceless and the *only* published account of Iraq's invasion and occupation from a JAG's perspective. Warner kept a journal that records the gristle and the meat of daily activity. *Zone of Action's* lively prose and insightful analysis make for a compelling narrative—highlighting an important, yet often overlooked aspect of America's combat operations."

—Patrick K. O'Donnell
Bestselling Author of *Washington's Immortals: The Untold Story of an Elite Regiment Who Changed the Course of the Revolution; The Unknowns: America's Unknown Soldier and WWI's Most Decorated Heroes Who Brought Him Home; and We Were One: Shoulder to Shoulder with the Marines Who Took Fallujah*

"Duty in a combat area is a personal experience to be sure. Kirk Warner, a litigator of national renown, and a citizen soldier, clearly has affirmed that adage with his book, *Zone of Action*. His writing is at times humorous, but mostly he offers earnest and intense observations of a group of dedicated American soldiers, sailors, airmen, and Marines as they went about the incredible task of imbuing the concepts of the rule of law and order among a population who for decades knew only tyranny. It is important for the reader to understand Kirk and his colleagues went about doing their duty while in a war with no clearly defined lines nor easily recognizable enemy. *Zone of Action* is a superb memoir."

—Dan K. McNeill
General, US Army (Ret), Former Commander, Coalition Forces–Afghanistan, XVIII Airborne Corps, US Forces Command, and International Security Assistance Force–Afghanistan (ISAF)

"An on-the-ground, in-the-moment look—not from the battlefront but from the decision-makers' tents and palaces. At times comical, at times insightful and always engaging, Kirk's experiences show the myriad of issues judge advocates face in the zone of action, providing fascinating insight into the tactical, strategic and even political features of modern combat."

—Thomas E. Ayres
Major General, US Army (Ret), Former Deputy Judge Advocate General of the Army

"An illuminating and colorful telling of an Army JAG's contribution to the initial stages of Operation Iraqi Freedom. From battle preparation and targeting constraints, through mishaps and investigations, to identifying war criminals, to prisoner operations of all types and sizes, to efforts to rebuild the Iraqi courts and judicial system, and loads of legal challenges in between, Colonel Warner provides a serious and realistic recounting, tempered with a soldier's humor, on the essential role of his judge advocate team supporting commanders and troops in major combat operations and the early reconstruction in Iraq. Highly recommended."

—Dan Wright
Major General, US Army (Ret), Former Deputy Judge Advocate General of the Army

"The challenges that commanders face in combat today are as diverse as the use of force according to the ROE to the post-combat uncertainties of nation building. Colonel Warner has captured the nature of these complexities in his gritty and often humorous memories in this book. This should be mandatory reading for all JAG students in their service's introductory JAG courses. Well done, soldier!"

—Thomas C. Waskow
Lieutenant General. US Air Force (Ret), Former Commanding General, US Forces Japan, and Commander, 5th Air Force.

"*Zone of Action* is a fantastic and fast-paced read. An entertaining, behind-the-scene, insider report from a man in the arena and about everywhere else in the war rooms, courtrooms, and streets of Iraq. I was not able to put it down as the insightful and witty fact-based stories and observations kept coming. I absolutely loved this book."

—William S. Busby
Major General, US Air Force Reserve (Ret.), Former Commander, 455 Expeditionary Operations Group, Bagram Air Base, Afghanistan

"More than a few firsthand accounts about Iraq have been written by soldiers who were there, but Kirk Warner's memoir is unique in telling the story of what an Army lawyer did in the earliest days of military operations in Iraq. Then Lieutenant Colonel Kirk Warner's participation in Operations Cobra II and Iraqi Freedom illustrate how an Army attorney not only can enhance mission success but sometimes can be critical to achieving the military mission. *Zone of Action* is insightful, humorous, and educational. From the time that Warner arrived at Camp Doha, Kuwait, in March 2003 and then moved to Baghdad the following month, he saw the war unfold. Warner and his fellow judge advocates, legal administrators and paralegal specialists handled legal issues ranging from prisons, piracy, and smuggling to Iraqi governance, justice and Red Cross inspections. If you want to learn about what the early years of US military operations in Iraq were all about, read *Zone of Action*."

—Fred L. Borch
Regimental Historian, Professor of Legal History and Leadership, Judge Advocate General's Corps, US Army

"As someone who never served our country in the armed forces, I have always been in awe of professionals like Kirk Warner, a great lawyer and an American hero, who fought in multiple campaigns with consummate professionalism under the most challenging circumstances. *Zone of Action* taught me so much about the collaboration and mutual respect that knit together those responsible for a complex military operation. I am grateful for the education I received from this outstanding firsthand account of soldier-lawyer's life at the front."

—Martin H. Brinkley
Dean, University of North Carolina at Chapel Hill School of Law

"Kirk Warner has written a marvelous book about the invasion and occupation of Iraq that is a lot more fun to read than to have experienced. Like the author, the book is witty, insightful, and speaks (occasionally irreverently) truth to power. Kirk and his Reserve lawyer cohorts were a critical part of the Coalition invasion force that brought Saddam Hussein and other criminals of the former regime to justice and, through the disciplined use of force, brought justice to many other enemies of peace. His first-person observations are a must-read account for anyone interested in what really happened in the first year of the war, and in what military lawyers do in combat. If ever there were a need to disabuse civilians of the notion that judge advocates are "in the rear with the gear" or have a silk-stocking position in modern war, this book will document the reality that military lawyers, both active and Reserve, are an integral, agile, and essential part of the operating forces."

—Marc Warren
Colonel, US Army (Ret.). Former Staff Judge Advocate, V-Corps and CJTF-7 (Iraq)

"An entertaining and humorous, yet respectfully serious and insightful, front-row seat to the preparation and successful overthrow of the Saddam Hussein regime, and the impossible legal challenges of the aftermath. If Robin Williams and Alan Dershowitz had a lovechild, it would grow up to be Colonel Kirk Warner! A must read for armchair historians of contemporary legal operations in a combat environment."

—David Hayden
Colonel, US Army (Ret.) Former Staff Judge Advocate, NORTHCOM, XVIII Airborne Corps, and 82nd Airborne Division

"Forget sterile SITREPS and official histories. Colonel Kirk Warner's *Zone of Action* captures the sights, sounds and smells of the first installment of Operation Iraqi Freedom from the unique vantage point of a mobilized JAG providing legal advice, counsel and guidance to a variety of senior commanders and officials, both coalition and Iraqi, on issues that simply run the gamut as the mission morphed from conventional combat operations to nascent counter-insurgency and nation building. Structured around detailed contemporaneous chronicles shared with the home front, Colonel Warner pulls no punches and shares a compelling and informative account of the intersection of the rule and role of law in modern combat with keen legal observations and actions wrapped in a devastating wit. Any soldier will appreciate the accounts of the mysteries of securing transportation, billeting, food, and the ever-elusive bearable latrine in any theater of operations."

—James B. Mallory
Major General, US Army Reserve (Ret.), Former Deputy Commanding General, NATO Training Mission–Afghanistan and Commanding General, 108th Training Command

"Colonel Kirk Warner's *Zone of Action* is a masterful recap of Operation Iraqi Freedom and provides insights from all levels of conflict—strategic, operational and tactical. In an age when diaries and the written word are often replaced by texting, his forethought in keeping a detailed journal, coupled with personal and now unclassified emails, brings to light events and activities previously unknown or unreported by the media. It is done in layman's language—not your typical legal jargon but plain English by a soldier first and lawyer second. Colonel Warner brings humor, candor and a firsthand experience to the initial phases of the enduring conflict. An important read, especially for those dealing with the uncertainties of the modern battlefield."

—John Falkenbury
Lieutenant Colonel, US Army (Ret.), Executive Vice President, Congressional Medal of Honor Society

"While in uniform it became more apparent that the more rank and responsibility I attained, the more I depended on the 'soft' skilled functions of my command, i.e. legal, PAO and finance. Kirk hits on the magnitude of issues that face a commander in combat and other operations. Targeting, ROE, friendly fire incidents, handling disparate armed groups, contractors and civilians on the battlefield, detainees, POWs, captured weapons and equipment, war crimes and mass graves are fleshed out robustly in Kirk's *Zone of Action*. These are issues all commanders must deal with every day, and the JAGs are our essential advisors on these critical decisions."

—David L. Grange
Brigadier General, US Army (Ret.), Former Commanding General, 1st Infantry Division ("Big Red One")

"Kirk Warner is a born storyteller! From the descriptions of Saddam's mega palaces, to the daily heroism of our troops, his compelling narratives, balanced with respectful humor, take you inside the war in Iraq, as only a keen-minded observer could. Most importantly, *Zone of Action* is a welcomed reminder of the daily sacrifices the heroic men and women of our military make on our behalf."

—Santo J Costa
Retired Vice Chairman, President and Chief Operating Office, Quintiles Transnational Corp., Author of Humanity at Work

"Like the estimable Harry Flashman, Colonel Kirk Warner seems to have been everywhere and met everyone in newly-liberated Iraq. Yanked from his law office in Raleigh, JAG officer Warner relates with compassion and dark humor the challenges and burdens of reestablishing the rule of law in a land ravaged by Saddam Hussein's brutal tyranny."

—Justice Robert H. Edmunds, Jr.
Retired Justice of the Supreme Court of North Carolina

"*Zone of Action* is a fascinating journey that provides an inside look at an Army Reserve lawyer mobilizing and deploying to Operation Iraqi Freedom. Colonel Kirk Warner takes us into the top echelons of US military and civilian leadership and provides a very humanistic perspective on navigating through the legalities of land warfare. With humor and satire, Colonel Warner's diary and emails of those initial days and months give a vivid and accurate description of not only historic places and events but also the daily interactions of both soldiers and the Iraqi people. He has truly captured the pandemonium and realism of the war in Iraq."

—Rob Stall
Major General, US Army Reserve (Ret.), Former Commanding General, 108th Training Command

"Insightful, instructive, and enjoyable. Colonel Warner's insights and advice served me exceedingly well on my tour in Iraq, and the insights and advice in his book *Zone of Action* will provide future judge advocates and students of history a 'front row' seat as citizen soldiers rose to the challenge of becoming 'One Army' in support of joint operations in Iraq."

—Gill P. Beck
Major General, US Army Reserve (Ret.), Former Commanding General, US Army Reserve Legal Command

Zone of Action:
A JAG's Journey inside Operations Cobra II and
Iraqi Freedom

By Colonel Kirk G. Warner, USAR, Ret.

© Copyright 2020 Colonel Kirk G. Warner, USAR, Ret.

ISBN 978-1-64663-139-1

Library of Congress Control Number: 2020911734

Published by

◀ köehlerbooks™

3705 Shore Drive
Virginia Beach, VA 23452
800–435–4811
www.koehlerbooks.com

Uday's Crib: Outside Uday's Palace gate in the Baghdad Green Zone, April 2003. Uday was an extremely sick twist who terrorized all Iraqis, and even Saddam determined he could not be trusted to lead Iraq in his absence. His lion cages on the palace grounds and his porn stash were legendary. Uday, his brother Qusay, and Qusay's son were finally tracked down and killed by US forces in July 2003.

ZONE
★★★★
OF ACTION
★★★★

A JAG's Journey Inside Operations
Cobra II and Iraqi Freedom

**COLONEL KIRK G. WARNER,
USAR (RET.)**

VIRGINIA BEACH
CAPE CHARLES

Dedicated to my wife, Diane, and all other "household sixes." Your brave perseverance at home enables the courage and humanity of your loved ones serving abroad.

"I've been a Danish prince, a Texas slave-dealer, an Arab sheik, a Cheyenne Dog Soldier, and a Yankee navy lieutenant in my time, among other things, and none of 'em was as hard to sustain as my lifetime's impersonation of a British officer and gentleman."

—George MacDonald Fraser
Flashman in the Great Game (1975)

TABLE OF CONTENTS

NOTE TO READER

Military jargon and acronyms are the vital ingredients of military life. Accordingly, the Glossary of Terms and Acronyms located at the back of this book is an essential resource to appreciating this story and the characters involved.

COMMAND AND CONTROL

For Cobra II and Iraqi Freedom, the U.S. Central Command (CENTCOM) (GEN Franks), established and had command and control of air, land, sea, and special operations component commands. The Combined—or often termed "Coalition"—Forces Land Component Command (CFLCC) had command and control of the operations of all Army, Marine, and coalition ground forces. U.S. Third Army (LTG McKiernan) was designated as the CFLCC. V-Corps (LTG Wallace), 1st Marine Expeditionary Force (1MEF) (LtGen Conway), and coalition land forces and their respective divisions [V-Corps: 3rd Infantry (MG Blount); 4th Infantry (MG Odierno); 101st Airborne (MG Petraeus); and 1MEF: 1st Marine (MajGen Mattis); British 1st Armor (Maj Gen Brims)], brigades, regimental combat teams, air cavalry, and expeditionary units were under the CFLCC. The Combined Forces Air Component Command (CFACC) (Lt. Gen. Moseley) had command and control of air and space forces (save one Marine aircraft wing and Army air cavalry which remained under 1MEF and V-Corps). The Combined Forces Maritime Component Command (CFMCC) (VADM Keating) had command and control of naval forces and the Combined Forces Special Operations Component Command (CFSOCC) (MG Dailey) had command and control of special operations forces.

PHOTOGRAPHS

Uday's Crib

Departure Cigar: Polk AFB

12th JAG, Green Ramp

12th JAG, CFLCC

Camp Doha Bunker

CFLCC War Room

Current Operations and Intelligence Center (COIC)

Camp Bucca EPW Camp

Aw Faw Palace, CFLCC Forward Headquarters

Saddam International Airport

CFLCC EECP

Combined Effects Shelter, CFLCC EECP

Grumpy Old Men with Guns

ICRC Headquarters

Ministry of Health-ORHA

"God Bless the USA"

Emergency Payments

Thumbs Up?

Judicial Reconstruction Assistant Team (JRATS)

SECDEF

Iranian-held Iraqi POWs

Lawyers Union

Judicial Assessment Team Advisors: St. Matthew's Church

Saddam's Throne Chair

Parade Rest

Execution Chamber, Abu Ghraib Prison

US Army Birthday Party with LTG David McKiernan

CCCI Announcement: CPA Administrator J. Paul Bremer

Lion of Babylon

Art 5, Geneva Convention Article 5 Tribunal Panel

MEK Inspection with LTG Ricardo Sanchez, CG CJTF-7

Operation Orphanage Toy Delivery

Golf at Tigris River CC

Abu Ghraib Prison: Bremer and De Mello

NAVSTAR I Special Prosecution Task Force

Operation Sweeney Todd

SPTF—Najaf

CJTF-7/V Corps JAGs

Last Cigar in Iraq

Homebound: 12th JAG Departing APOD

12th JAG: Republican Guard Palace

Pirate Captain

TUESDAY, SEPTEMBER 11, 2001

Tuesday, September 11, 2001, dawned temperate and nearly cloudless in the eastern United States. Millions of men and women readied themselves for work. Some made their way to the Twin Towers, the signature structures of the World Trade Center complex in New York City. Others went to Arlington, Virginia, to the Pentagon. Across the Potomac River, the United States Congress was back in session. At the other end of Pennsylvania Avenue, people began to line up for a White House tour. In Sarasota, Florida, President George W. Bush went for an early morning run. For those heading to the airport, weather conditions could not have been better for a safe and pleasant journey. Among the travelers were Mohamed Atta and Abdul Aziz al Omari, who arrived at the airport in Portland, Maine.

—The 911 Commission Report

After arriving at Boston's Logan Airport, Atta and Omari, along with three others, checked in and boarded American Airlines Flight 11 bound for Los Angeles. Five others checked into United Airlines Flight 175, also bound for Los Angeles.

Hundreds of miles southwest of Boston, at Dulles International Airport in the Virginia suburbs of Washington, DC, five more men were preparing to take their early morning flight. These men checked into American Airlines Flight 77, bound for Los Angeles.

A few hundred miles north, at Newark Airport, four other men checked in at the United Airlines ticket counter between 7:03 and 7:39 a.m. for Flight 93 going to Los Angeles.

Nineteen men were now aboard four transcontinental flights. They were planning to hijack these planes and turn them into large guided missiles, loaded with up to 11,400 gallons of jet fuel. By 8:00 a.m. on the morning of Tuesday, September 11, 2001, they had defeated all the security layers that America's civil aviation security system then had in place to prevent a hijacking.

—The 911 Commission Report

At 7:59 a.m., American Airlines Flight 11 took off from Boston. Its last routine radio transmission occured at 8:14 a.m. Its transponder was turned off seven minutes later. The Northeast Air Defense Sector (NEADS) scrambled fighter jets from Otis Air Force Base in search of AA 11 at 8:46 a.m. Forty seconds later, American Airlines Flight 11 crashed into the North Tower of the World Trade Center.

At 8:14 a.m., United Airlines Flight 175 took off from Boston. Its last radio communication was received at 8:42 a.m. Its transponder code changed at 8:47 a.m. Fifteen minutes and three seconds later, United Airlines Flight 175 crashed into the South Tower of the World Trade Center.

At 8:20 a.m., American Airlines Flight 77 took off from Washington, DC. Its last routine radio communication was received at 8:51 a.m. Five minutes later, its transponder was turned off. At 9:37:46, American Airlines Flight 77 crashed into the Pentagon.

At 8:42 a.m., United Airlines Flight 93 took off from Newark. Its last routine radio communication occured at 9:24 a.m. Its transponder was turned off seventeen minutes later. At 9:57, the passengers of Flight 93 revolt. Six minutes and eleven seconds later, United Airlines Flight 93 was driven into the ground near Shanksville, Pennsylvania.

Thousands of Americans died. With that, we were awakened by evil from our peaceful slumber. We each have our recollections. That unforgettable Tuesday morning, we listened to Warner Wolf on the *Imus in the Morning* radio show tell us about the Monday Night Football game from his apartment near the World Trade Center and then pause and say, "Don, I think a plane has just flown into one of the towers." Several of us were in the break room at our law firm watching the towers collapse with gasps and mutterings of "those bastards." My law partner's friend Todd Beamer yelled, "Let's roll" and helped take United Airlines Flight 93 into the dirt, saving who knows how many lives in our capital. My law partner and good friend Dave Hayden, married the week prior, was the staff judge advocate of the XVIII Airborne Corps, America's ready deployment force, and he knew his honeymoon was over. Our Armed Forces girded loins and puffed up for a fight . . . the long war that has consumed us since. We knew our world had changed.

President Bush's speech on the evening of that tragic day still rings loud and true:

> Today, our fellow citizens, our way of life, our very freedom came under attack in a series of deliberate and deadly terrorist acts. The victims were in airplanes or in their offices: secretaries, business men and women, military and federal workers, moms and dads, friends and neighbors. Thousands of lives were suddenly ended by evil, despicable acts of terror. The pictures of airplanes flying into buildings, fires burning, huge structures collapsing have filled us with disbelief, terrible sadness, and a quiet, unyielding anger. These acts of mass murder were intended to frighten our nation into chaos and retreat. But they have failed. Our country is strong.
>
> A great people has been moved to defend a great nation. Terrorist attacks can shake the foundations of our biggest buildings, but they cannot touch the foundation of America. These acts shatter steel, but they cannot dent the steel of American resolve. America was targeted for attack because we're the brightest beacon for freedom and opportunity in the world. And no one will keep that light from shining. Today, our nation saw evil—the very worst of human nature—and we responded with the best of America. With the daring of our rescue workers, with the caring for strangers and neighbors who came to give blood and help in any way they could.
>
> This is a day when all Americans from every walk of life unite in our resolve for justice and peace. America has stood down enemies before,

and we will do so this time. None of us will ever forget this day, yet we go forward to defend freedom and all that is good and just in our world.
—President George W. Bush, September 11, 2001

Our nation knows how to fight and sacrifice. During the past century, our nation has found itself in many corners of the earth . . . often to the rescue of those who fight for freedom and liberty and against tyranny. No other nation has so consistently stepped to the front lines and run towards fire, not away from it. After 9/11, we ran once more unto the breach and showed who we truly are: the beacon of liberty.

Since that day, we have not escaped the human cost of sustaining freedom and independence. Since that day, our nation's troops have deployed nearly four million times. We owe them and the host of brave responders our full commitment and thanks. This story is inspired by such a commitment and thanks to those who have served and continue to serve our nation.

ZONE OF ACTION

"CFLCC attacks to defeat Iraqi forces and control the zone of action, secure and exploit designated sites, and remove the current regime. CFLCC conducts continuous stability operations to create conditions for transitions to CJTF-Iraq."
—Mission, CLFCC COBRA II EXORD, 190900Z March 2003

"Strike fast and hard!" At 0312 hours on March 19, 2003, the word was given by President Bush. Twenty-six minutes later two stealth F-117 Nighthawks callsign Ram 1 and Ram 2 were launched from Al Udeid Air Base in Qatar and were en route to Dora Farms south of Baghdad to drop 2,000-pound bunker-busting bombs. The aim was to decapitate Saddam Hussein and his dissolute regime in one lightning strike to start and finish the war against Iraq. Our team had cleared the time-sensitive target for the Coalition based on single-source, continued-eye human intelligence (HUMINT) with a time-on-target of no later than 0530. And now we could and would pounce on a sick regime that had for over a decade defied numerous United Nations resolutions and thwarted UN atomic inspectors from doing their work.

HUMINT had supported a strike on the same target the night before, but it was called off as that moment was only twenty-four hours into a forty-eight-hour ultimatum by President Bush to Saddam: Take your sons and get out or else. So, playing by the rules—what Americans do—the best generals in the American inventory waited again for the word to be given. They would become household names for what followed: Franks, Abizaid, McKiernan, Moseley, Wallace, and Conway, as well as division commanders Mattis, Blount, Petraeus, and Odierno. The entire world waited, watching for the showdown as time ticked by on the final forty-eight-hour ultimatum clock. The wait would end a day later with the F-117 Nighthawks dropping their bunker-busters on that same grid at Dora Farms. The war was on.

Zone of Action is the story I lived in action from inside the Coalition Forces Land Component Command (CFLCC) Current Operations Center, in Baghdad, and across Iraq during Operations COBRA II and Iraqi Freedom. But it's also my close observations of heart-and-soul small moments of those who carried out the operations.

The book gathers the war-theater observations from my journal, weekly chronicles in essay form sent homeward, and selected emails that replaced my journal at the end of major combat operations—so some information will be repeated. All of these were written during the build-up, invasion, liberation, and occupation of Iraq in 2003. This story's zone of action begins with Operation COBRA II and transitions into Operation Iraqi Freedom. Because I wore many hats for the Coalition in many places—commander of the 12th JAG Detachment/LSO; senior judge advocate (OIC Night) CFLCC (US Third Army); forward staff judge advocate, CFLCC Early Entry Command Post, Baghdad; and deputy staff judge advocate, Combined Joint Task Force-7 (V Corps–CPA) in Iraq—I learned to use the "unguarded" or "unobserved" moments of my own "Iraqi freedom" as an officer to analyze, compare, contrast, and record the vagaries and "unofficial" thoughts, words, and deeds of "conquerors" striking "fast and hard" up against a strange, unprepared, and unaccountable "enemy." As one British officer quipped to me in a moment of Baghdad chaos, "When you want to fight and win a war, we've learned that it's always best to fight against the French." Maybe next time. The book details my official and inner journeys and those of soldiers and Iraqis I encountered along the way.

PROLOGUE
THE ROAD TO REGIME CHANGE

One of my reporter friends at Camp Doha, Kuwait, and in Iraq early in the war was Michael Gordon, chief military correspondent for *The New York Times*. He was assigned to Coalition Forces Land Component Command (CFLCC) at the start of the war and describes well the road to regime change:

> When the Iraqis were ejected from Kuwait in the 100-hour war [Desert Storm in 1991], President George H. W. Bush calculated that Saddam Hussein might be overthrown by humiliated and disgruntled Iraqi generals. But Saddam proved to be a far more durable figure than the Americans expected. His network of security operatives and internal police was vast. His powerful Tikriti clan enjoyed the trappings of power. His sheer ruthlessness was a potent weapon. Beyond that, enough of his Republican Guard forces, including the critically important corps headquarters, had escaped during the Gulf conflict to help him contend with a spontaneous rebellion in the Shiite-dominated south and resistance in the Kurdish north. Saddam put down the uprisings with extraordinary brutality.[1]

Saddam's regime in Iraq thereafter continued to defy United Nations sanctions and remained in power by means of brutality, Oil-for-Food money, and threats to use weapons of mass destruction. United Nations weapons inspectors were diverted and delayed.

---

1   Gordon, Michael R. and General Bernard E. Trainor, *COBRA II, The Inside Story of the Invasion and Occupation of Iraq*, Pantheon Books (New York, 2006), 11.

Operations in the Post-9/11 Global War on Terror (GWOT) in Afghanistan were coming along and under control of the Coalition forces led by the United States. So the new time and place, Iraq, was ripe for the next phase of the War on Terrorism.

1.
GWOT TO "GEE-WHAT?"
DEPLOYMENT

Striking a "John Wayne" Green Beret poster pose during last cigar in US at the Green Ramp, Pope Air Force Base/Fort Bragg, NC (February 2003)

I threw one of the two levers to the trap doors in the execution building at Abu Ghraib and wondered why they needed dual hanging chambers and why they bothered with the deadly redundancy of making the bodies squirm by simultaneously electrocuting the prisoners as they hung there. UN Special Envoy Sergio de Mello and Ambassador Paul Bremer asked me the same questions as they stood there aghast.

I also wondered why the Iraqis lined up outside Abu Ghraib asking for permission to seek their kin's amputated hands, ears, and feet that must be buried near there. I returned to the Republican Palace just in time to receive 556 teeth from 299 skulls from a mass grave at Musayib during the Shia uprising in 1991. I also wondered, How the hell did I get here? *Just four months ago, I was sitting at a Bruce Springsteen concert in Chapel Hill with my wife and good friends when my cell phone rang.*

★ ★ ★ ★

JOURNAL, 4 FEB 2003

A 4:05 phone call from COL Dan Shearouse ended an eight-week period of suspense and also headed off a growing mid-life crisis that needed resolution. I had been selected to be the leader of a JAG team headed to Kuwait. We were to report to Ft. Jackson, in South Carolina, on 7 Feb., and then to the Ft. Bragg mobilization station in North Carolina on 10 Feb. to start the validation process in anticipation of deployment. I had expected a few days' notice and perhaps a few weeks more time to wrap up affairs at the firm and at home. However, the anticipation had ended, the worry time had been minimized, and the hectic preparation was somehow comforting, though harried.

My first call was to my wife, Diane, or, as usual, to her voicemail. The night was eventful since some yahoo at the Department of the Army (DA) had inadvertently sent activation orders for the entire 12th Legal Services Organization (LSO)—eighty-five folks, rather than the eight-man team intended. As a result, we had to alert the whole unit to be prepared to report on Friday.

Mom was as circumspect and supportive as anyone who had seen four of her brothers go off to WWII would be. Even so, deploying is much more taxing mentally and emotionally than physically. Trying to foresee issues and logistics constantly taxes your present mental state and capacity, even as you try to sleep.

5 FEB 03: US Secretary of State Colin Powell delivers remarks to the United Nations.[2]

---

2   Bolded event entries through 4 May 03 come from 6 May 03 briefing by General Tommy Franks, USCENTCOM commander, to President George W. Bush. Author: CCF6-D USCENTCOM.

JOURNAL, 5–6 FEB 2003

A litigation meeting at the firm was called to implement the contingency case-coverage plan for my caseload. Over twenty attorneys joined in the roster call of cases and the priorities involved. To me the caseload seemed manageable until I realized the number of cases, number of deadlines, and number of items and trials ahead. I had crafted a form letter to the courts/judges and to all of my clients. These totaled over 200 letters. My secretary Erin, as usual, expedited the process, and we pumped out some serious workload in the two days available. Personal issues consumed the remaining time, including a pesky driver's license renewal. Why is it that the DMV is such a moving target? Three locations, no service. It would have to wait.

My packing commenced in an orderly fashion. Just throw anything green or brown into a room, put it in a green sack or ruck, and move it to the car. We had to make sure our yellow Labrador retriever, Rocky, wasn't tucked into a flight bag inadvertently, although the thought crossed my mind that I'd like to have him along. Emotions ran strong with Diane, but she was in the main, as always, strong, stoical, and supportive. Her good German stock usually prevails. I will miss her strength, her love, her brown eyes, and her smile.

JOURNAL, 7 FEB 2003

At 0730, I was on active duty in support of Operation Enduring Freedom (OEF)—the War on Terrorism following 9/11. We were joining the mounting crowd in the Kuwaiti desert that was planning to kick Saddam Hussein's regime out of Iraq. After a conference with COL Dan Shearouse, our team began the tedious administrative and training build-up to war. In addition to attorneys Majors Phil Lenski, Lake Summers, Perry Wadsworth, Craig "Jake" Jacobsen, and Owen Lewis, we were to be joined by two paralegal NCOs— SSG Beverly Smith and SSG Amanda Eisman. This was our team. I signed the assumption of command and the delegation of authority for weapons, ammo, chemical defense equipment, and Class VIII medical supplies. We developed a training plan to do as much as possible at our Ft. Jackson home station to assist us in quickly validating at Ft. Bragg. We tackled the common training and NBC tasks that would be needed for validation in the days ahead. The remainder of the time we spent scrubbing down a packing list and canvassing the area for supplies and needed comforts for the trip ahead.

JOURNAL, 8 FEB 2003

While the team was engaged in NBC train-up, COL Dan Shearouse, LTC Joe Zima, and I placed a secure call to our new boss—COL Richard "Flash" Gordon, Staff Judge Advocate (SJA), US Third Army, Coalition Forces Land Component Command (CFLCC). We were to be an independent JAG shop operating in Iraq with an area legal mission. It was a fantastic mission. We were to remain as a team—the first LSO Reserve team in theater, so we would carry the banner. The CFLCC [US Third Army] was the land component of CENTCOM, and the three-star CFLCC commander LTG David McKiernan answered only to US CENTCOM's GEN Tommy Franks and to SECDEF Donald Rumsfeld. Clearly, this was a choice assignment. We would wear the Third Army patch—Patton's Army that I'd dreamed about since becoming a Patton junkie back in college. I can still remember the Patton speech to his troops by heart and the movie theme song that I hummed before every final in college and law school. On his shoulder was the famous "circled A" patch standing for Occupation Army after WWI. We'd be wearing it, too. CFLCC was home to twenty-four generals.

We commenced our training accordingly, hoisting a few beers to strengthen our arms for saluting. Unfortunately, we'd be well downrange from the brass, and probably from power and water as well. LTC Don Perritt was COL Gordon's deputy SJA. He briefed

me on the details of our mission. A great call and opportunity—
and challenge—was ahead. We were to be living austere and needed
to be able to carry everything on our backs. We'd fortunately have
some solid escorts and compatriots in the Military Police (MPs)
and Civil Affairs (CA) folks who would surely be in our AO (area
of operations). We would see. I briefed the team fittingly after we
finished our NBC gas-chamber training that morning.

JOURNAL, 9 FEB 2003

We continued to train-up and receive equipment and supplies.
A farewell luncheon was held at the Ft. Jackson NCO club. Brig.
Gen. Knighter said a few inspiring words of God, country, and the
American way. Diane made it down, and we met the families of
the South Carolina team members (Lenski, Summers, Smith, and
Eisman). The rest of the 12th would have been jealous of our mission
if they had known of it and of our activation. Most of them would
likely get a chance to serve later on. Diane and I returned to Raleigh
for a last night together before we reported to Ft. Bragg Monday
morning for mobilization and validation.

JOURNAL, 10 FEB 2003

Our new higher command, the 2125 Garrison Support Unit,
was commanded by the Jacobses. COL Jacobs was the commander,
and he turned out to be a really good egg and a major general. LTC
Jacobs was his sidekick. Together, they had the unenviable task of
receiving and validating tens of units and thousands of soldiers.
Being reservists themselves, I'm sure both Jacobses were pissed
at their stateside assignment and felt a natural envy for the units
deploying abroad. They were also pissed while we were there because
several members of the command staff, including the commander
and chaplain, of an attack helicopter unit in the deployment queue
under their charge had been caught streaking in the old division
barracks area. All in all, they tolerated us, though neither had any

idea what to do with a team of lawyers—packing only six 9 mm pistols and two M16 rifles—who had taken over a conference room at the XVIII ABN Corps' SJA shop. At least we weren't streaking . . . yet.

JOURNAL, 11–16 FEB 2003

Our mobilization station was Ft. Bragg, teeming with soldiers. The 82nd was deploying during this time, too, and the C-17s, C-141s, C-5As and other craft were departing Pope AFB every ten minutes or so. It was the place to be, if you're in the Army and into all the signs of high testosterone—noise, speed, and vehicles of land and air amassed and on the move. Some Public Affairs (PAO) genius thought it would be great to have the 82nd ABN troops sent off to Kuwait by Faith Hill. The poor bastards were bused to the stadium in the freezing cold for an 0800 concert, then placed on buses to the Green Ramp at Pope for a relaxing eighteen-hour flight to Kuwait City!

Meanwhile, we were being entertained with smallpox vaccinations that rendered the previous anthrax-shot side-effects warnings trite by comparison. Then the PAO taught us how to be candid to the press, yet be careful not to vary the script: "We're excited to be here; we will do our duty and do it well." Some narcissistic ex-Green Beret gave us an MTV-spot techno-thrill-ride video and a speech in support of Anti-Terrorism and Force Protection. We might've been better motivated, though, had they thought of turning on the heat in the Post Theater, colder inside than out.

We as a team received over 125 shots—averaging more than 15 per person. Smallpox, accounting for 15 sticks for us old-timers who still had a small scar on our arms from the first smallpox shot in the early '60s, my fourth shot against anthrax, PPD, Hep. B, Typhoid, and the list went on. I was fortunate to get only 20 sticks.

We then encountered the dreaded hearing examination. The testing station is a padded room with headsets and a handheld button that you are to depress every time you can discern a tone at various decibels. Jake couldn't hear very well, but we were determined to get him through this station. We told him to just start hitting the button and keep doing it whether he heard anything or not. He agreed. A few minutes later we heard the staff announce, "Stop pressing the damn button; the test has not started yet!" Not that lawyers need to hear well—Jake at least. Lake kept us entertained. We kept the Combat Readiness Center (CRC) and medical staff entertained. Phil just kept passing gas. We kept each other laughing mostly.

On to the range. We lucked out weather-wise and time-wise. Our six 9 mm and two M16s fit in with whatever group was firing, so we could force our way into the range when we wanted to. We moved to a pretty high-priority unit for training based on our NLT [no later than] date, and, by pushing, we were able to clear CTT, security, range fire, TI, T-SIRT, SRC, CIF, and Finance in record time (PDQ!). We also bluffed our way into a DCU (desert camouflage uniform) issue as a priority 3 unit out of fifty or sixty units going OCONUS. This coup landed us ready for validation as early as Saturday, 15 Feb. Now for transport, loading, and movement, we were ready.

Diane and Rocky stopped in on Thursday night in a pre-Valentine's Day celebration at the Sonic drive-in. Rocky ordered a junior cheeseburger. A quiet Sunday afternoon allowed me to review our team's military personnel files and learn more about them. They are a talented crew. We will do well.

On Friday, the tedious march to deployment continued with our daily 0730 training meeting and 1600 commander's briefings with train-up wrapped before, between, and after those daily events. Except for some chemical defense equipment (MOPP gear) and some optical inserts (for gas masks) on order, we'd validate. We were green in all other areas.

25 FEB 03: Red Cross workers build warehouses in three countries adjacent to Iraq in the event of war.

27 FEB 03: United Nations Nuclear Inspection Chief Hans Blix on Iraq: "Still hasn't committed to disarming."

JOURNAL, 17–28 FEB 2003

Although we received valuable training on TOC operations, chemical (CDE and NBC) operations, as well as on detainee operations, we were thwarted in our early validation and travel efforts by supply issues—lack of chemical defense equipment (CDE) and optical inserts for protective masks—throughout the second CRC week. Through some Herculean efforts, we validated by Friday, 21 Feb. Our required CDE arrived at Bragg after we pushed hard for it on Wednesday 19 Feb. but was turned around and headed back to Raleigh when S-4 personnel refused to sign for the stuff. After searching the 308th CA's Conex for our CDE, we realized the screw-up. After I threatened the overnight service with impending death because of their incompetence, they made an immediate rush delivery from Raleigh that arrived at 2115 Weds. night. Optical inserts required an additional push, and we had them manufactured on Ft. Bragg to expedite. Finally, we validated all green on Friday afternoon, took the weekend off, and officially did the validation formation on Sunday afternoon 23 Feb.

Transport to the theater of operations was the next step. We were locking onto a Tuesday morning flight to Kuwait when the ITO advised us that CENTCOM had thrown a hold-in-place code on our unit and a bunch of other units. Friday afternoon, we commenced our efforts to lift this code. USARC, FORSCOM and CFLCC SJAs worked for us, and by Weds. a.m. we were cleared to travel. This suspense nearly killed us as we continued our load plans and property/comfort item acquisitions.

Once the code cleared Weds. morning, we started again pushing for a flight. By Thursday afternoon, we were tracking a Friday (28 Feb.) evening flight to Kuwait. Lake and I scrounged around the

USAF guys at Pope AFB to see if we could strap-hang our eight-packs with the Friday night bird. A one-man show controlled our destiny. SSG Maples was an outstanding load-plan manager for the flight with the 9th PSYOPs unit. By 1500, we were looking good to travel the next night. Unfortunately, we had to palletize by 2130 Thursday night. The adrenaline surged as we had but four hours to finalize the equipment packing and footlocker stenciling, pack our A and B bags and rucks, and get these to ADACG for palletizing by 2100. We made it, but barely. We actually piled our stuff onto the air pallet at the ADACG at Pope on the Green Ramp area in a driving rainstorm.

We nearly froze to death as temperatures approached freezing with a bitter wind. We had to hang out until 2300 while we waited for straps and netting to secure the pallet. Of course, our hardcase—presumably air-droppable—RDLs hit the tarmac twice during the process. Whether they work is still up in the air. Anyway, we were locked on for a 2045 flight through Spain to KCIA on Friday 28 Feb. to meet our NLT date of 1 Mar. Of course, the Air Force is not subject to any on-time departure or arrival statistics or surveys that we could feed the traveling public via the media. And no in-flight movies or peanuts! Oh well.

By early afternoon on Friday, our flight had slipped to Saturday morning at 0930. Still we had no tail number, however. Apparently things were hopping at Rota, Spain—the Air Force guys bitched that the Germans were behind the air-flow problem. Anyway, we stood ready to board the C-5A Galaxy in the morning. Diane and our friends Becky and Gil arrived on Friday afternoon as planned to pick up my car and say good-bye. Diane and I grabbed dinner and hugged farewell. Rocky looked sad. Diane looked sad. Hearts aching as we parted, neither of us had any idea about the length of our separation. March on to March.

I dreamed I was looking down the hole in the palace roof the size of manhole cover and wondering how we could so precisely target the JDAM that could penetrate three stories of the Al Faw palace, leave two perfectly tight circumferential holes, and then blow Saddam Hussein's bedroom and anyone in it to smithereens. Nothing could survive that impressive hit. How in the hell did we do that? I would soon learn how.

2.

PHASE II[3]: SEIZE INITIATIVE
CAMP DOHA AND THE DESERT BUILD-UP TO WAR

A thousand or more hostile Iraqi eyes watched my every move as I waded into the massive traffic jam in the middle of Baghdad in the weeks following our Thunder Run into the heart of the city. But we either needed to carve a way through the crowd or become ducks sitting for revenge. Neither option was a good one, but one opened a door to survival, one left us to a fait accompli. At that point, we cared only about getting through the crowd alive, ironically, so that we could help the very people whose eyes were boring through us with wonder or with contempt, perhaps, or with keen indifference to our plight after weeks of war and suffering.

1 MAR 03: Turkish Parliament votes No to US Troops being based along Iraq border.

---

3   The six phases of Operational Planning are Phase 0 (Shape), Phase I (Deter), Phase II (Seize Initiative), Phase III (Dominate), Phase IV (Stabilize) and Phase V (Enable Civil Authority). COBRA II campaign plan had four phases mirroring the classical Operational Planning phases: Phase I (Preparation), Phase II (Shaping the Battlespace), Phase III (Decisive Offensive Operations), and Phase IV (Post Hostilities).

12th JAG at Green Ramp at Pope AFB, Feb, 2003. (Left to Right: Front Row—MAJ Owen Lewis, MAJ Perry Wadsworth, MAJ Phil Lenski, SFC Beverly Smith, SSG Amanda Eisman; Second Row—MAJ Lake Summers, LTC Kirk Warner and MAJ Craig Jacobson)

JOURNAL, 1 MAR 2003

Change three to our flight started late last night. Although we were bumped another twelve hours, we had a tail number this time and looked like a solid go at 1830 on Saturday. The eight of us planned to meet at 1330 for manifest call at Green Ramp at 1530, picking up our weapons at 1400. We made it smoothly to the Green Ramp at Pope by 1500 hours and were individually weighed. Our equipment minus body armor topped only ninety pounds on average.

After several briefings on the C-5A procedures and readying for the bus to the tarmac, we were advised at 1730 that the flight had slipped four hours. After another three hours, we were told the crew had been grounded by their hours. The Air Force could have at least calculated crew hours correctly before slipping the ramp time back and then canceling. We rousted the armorer, returned our weapons and, fortunately, had the hotel to head back to. But we were dejected and exhausted.

JOURNAL, 2–3 MAR 2003

Our ramp time for Sunday moved at short notice from 1630 to 1200. We went through the same routine at Green Ramp as on 28 Feb. This time by 1600 on 1 March we were beside the C-5A Galaxy, a huge plane. It's the type you drive the vehicles in through the tail and out the nose, thus primarily a cargo flight. Apparently, from Pope the plane can take off only with tanks half full due to the short runway. So . . . we get a mid-Atlantic refueling from a tanker and then fly on to Morón, Spain—an air force strip fifty miles from Gibraltar on the Spanish Riviera. Due to a perceived weight problem, they drew the plane's fuel down an additional 5,000 lbs. The plane was still weighing in at 726,000 lbs. The eight vehicles in its belly did push the weight limits a bit. We were fortunately traveling with the 9th PSYOPs commander and some of his team. LTC Glenn Ayers was a blessing. His team movement NCOs hooked us up for the flight, palletized our small load, and eventually were a godsend once we arrived in theater.

The ascent to the passenger perch is somewhat tricky, particularly in full gear. First you crawl into the door behind the wing and shuffle beside the vehicles and pallets in the belly. Looking forward you see a series of vehicles end to end and side by side throughout the craft. You next climb up a fifteen-foot ladder into the passenger loft that's like an old DC3 without windows and facing aft. After an endless takeoff—the C-5A defies aeronautics—we settled down to an eight-hour flight to Spain.

Around 0300, I moved up and talked awhile to the master sergeant crewman. He, along with the crew, were reservists activated a month ago. The plane was from Westover AFB in Massachusetts. A few hours into flight, we heard some clanking on the roof but didn't think much more about it. Apparently, unbeknownst to us, the air refueling tanker and our plane failed to hook up during the flight and we were coasting into Spain on fumes. The crew were continuously recalculating our fuel and distance. We could drop into a small island off the Portugal coast if needed, into Portugal itself or, if possible, into Morón, Spain.

By 0800, we were bouncing down the runway in Morón, pronounced Morône. The sun was rising on a beautiful day. When we finally shuffled out the door onto the tarmac, we saw six more C-5As and a score of C-17s and C-141s in a line that stretched three abreast for what seemed like a mile. F-15s were parked behind this impressive line. Apparently there are only fifty to sixty C-5As in the entire USAF, yet we saw ten alone at Morón. So Spain was one of the three or four transit points into the Kuwaiti theater. Elements of the 101st ABN were also en route with us to Kuwait International. We laid over for around four hours in a pleasant café/cantina on base near the airstrip. Some troop had heisted the toilet seat in the men's room, so we commenced our squatting routine early.

At noon, we boarded the C-5A again for our last leg—seven and a half hours into KCIA. En route, Glenn Ayers briefed me on the current OPLAN into Iraq. The information was timely and assisted us in our mission analysis. Glenn's PSYOPs boys would work in our sector, so we should hook up with them again. They developed leaflets and used loudspeakers to get enemy troops to surrender or capitulate, preventing them from following orders to blow oil fields, blow bridges, and kill innocents. Glenn was an active-duty LTC six years younger than I with combat experience and over 108 jumps. His team was awesome.

Lights went out an hour or so before we landed at KCIA. We geared up and moved into the belly of the C-5A after touchdown. As vehicles moved out through the nose of the plane, we dodged their wheels and scrambled off the plane at last into the back of several trucks that came off the plane. Looking over the flight line at 2300 hours, 3 Mar., we saw what seemed like miles of aircraft. After moving 200 yards, we disembarked again on Kuwaiti soil and moved again off the marshalling area to Camp Wolf—a tent-city marshalling yard adjacent to KCIA. After a "welcome" briefing with 101st ABN soldiers, we were told that someone would pick us up from the holding tent in the morning and transport us to Camp Doha.

A windstorm kicked up as we arrived and sand was blowing everywhere. We thought we'd not seen the last of the sandstorms and we were right. The 9th PSYOPs again came to our rescue when their boys arrived with our pallet and a convoy heading to Doha—the soldiers were heading on out to Camp Virginia west/north of KCIA in the desert where they were hooking up with the 101st. We and our equipment hopped onto the 9th PSYOP vehicles and cruised on to Doha, arriving at 0330 hrs. The ride was a vivid reminder of how desolate the desert is and how little it had changed in the three years since I had been here in Kuwait for a warfighter exercise.

After passing through three security points, we at last made it into Doha. We fortunately hooked up with SGM Zaworsky of the CFLCC SJA office, and he, along with MSG Davis and SP4 Ortiz, assisted in getting us into a warehouse barracks/bay. We turned in our weapons and went to the 0500 chow line. Doha was an old port warehouse complex on the Persian Sea, a.k.a. the Arabian Sea, and our bay is simply a portion of one warehouse. The bays are concrete pads with chain-link fences topped with concertina. We hit the cots with gusto. We had arrived in the combat theater, unharmed, with our equipment and bags. We had pushed, pulled, and pressured our way into Kuwait to follow our orders in anticipation of carrying out our mission. Everyone here was amazed at how we had scrounged our rides and our flights and how aggressively we had pursued our mission step-by-step.

JOURNAL, 4 MAR 2003

An hour after lying down on our cots, I was escorted through security into the CFLCC operations center and on to the SJA office where I met LTC Don Perritt and COL Dick "Flash" Gordon at long last. The 0900 staff call involved all the SJA JAGs. I was a zombie throughout the introductions. We "meeted and greeted," and then collapsed back to our Bay 3 Warehouse 6 home, a slab of concrete encircled by concertina. We weren't sure whether it was to keep folks in or out.

Sleep was soon easy; then the Morale, Welfare, and Recreation (MWR) watercraft division attacked. We were in a MWR section that let you sign out watercraft for recreation. Where they'd use the things was not clear, since the Arabian Sea was near but not accessible from Doha—although it is a marine warehouse facility.

Anyway, these yahoos fired up a 225 Mercury motor dry. The fumes about killed half a dozen soldiers bedded down by the dividing fence. This lasted several minutes; then they fired up the jet skis. I was close to calling Doug Wilson, litigation counsel at Kawasaki, but thought better of it. We also had a company of 101st ABN (AASLT) beside us who specialized in noise. We started drinking the "heavy" water placed in every corner of Doha. As a result, I constantly had to pee. The port-o-lets next to Bay 3 were reserved for the Aussies. A sign on each declared the dunnies theirs and ended with a joyful "Cheers Mates." I pissed there anyway. My forty-five-year-old bladder revolted against the longer stroll, over 200 yards, to the trailer facilities.

We made it through the day, reported back to the SJA shop and continued to meet JAGs there, but the rest of the day was a blur. We did take a stroll around central Doha, saw the library, PX, and food court. The carpet shop was still there from three years ago. Lines at the PX and food court were "bleeding-awful," according to a few dejected Brits. The Czechs took things in stride and piled up the pogey bait that I'm sure was like filet mignon to them. A pile of Germans were here, although they were non-grata since their current führer—Schroeder—was a puss. Anyway, night and sleep came early.

12th JAG DET at CFLCC HQS, Camp Doha, Kuwait, March 2003 (Leftt to Right: MAJ Owen Lewis, MAJ Craig "Jake" Jacobsen, MAJ Lake Summers, SFC Beverly Smith, SSG Amanda Eisman, MAJ Perry Wadsworth, LTC Warner, and MAJ Phil Lenski)

JOURNAL, 5 MAR 2003

Just past midnight, and I'm at the gym since my sleep cycles are off. The gym, as before, is the center of activity at Doha. MTV more popular than CNN. They courteously put a few TVs in an alcove with CNN on for the over-forty crowd. Fifty or so TVs are for the hip, MTV crowd. Music is curfewed at 2300 for unknown reasons, though no one tries to sleep in the gym.

We reported on time Wednesday to the SJA shop to discuss our mission and the timetable to war. Learned we'd have to wait it out until things got hot and we could head north. Until then, we were tasked to CFLCC SJA and other subordinate shops. We were to integrate into ARCENT-KU here (Owen, Beverly, and Phil), two (Jake and Perry) to Arifjan in southern Kuwait (CFLCC-Rear and 377th

Theater Support Command (TSC)) and Amanda to 3rd Medical Command (MEDCOM) at Arifjan. This was effective Thursday.

We continued our orientation to CFLCC, Doha, and to the technology at our disposal, and keenly to the wind. After some time in the gym after dinner, sand and wind flew. I sneaked back to Bay 3 just in time. The wind warnings had come over a FRAGO at the Current Operations Center (COPS) at CFLCC. By the time I got back to the bay around 2200, it was wicked. We six battened down in our cots for a long night. Although the lights were on, the entire warehouse was a dust cloud. The light barely made it through, though the wind, on the other hand, had no trouble. Metal from several warehouse roofs and from separate covers were ripped from their moorings. Marine major Kevin Chenail, a JAG in our shop, trotted home barely in front of pieces of metal and roof supports. The boys in the desert cabals (camps) had to be taking it hard. We later learned one sergeant with the 82nd ABN at All-American City held onto a tent strap as he flew thirty feet into the air before crashing down to earth. Some ride. Camp Victory lost four mess tents, and I MEF took a beating as well. We were concerned but thankful we weren't further out in the sand.

JOURNAL, 6 MAR 2003

We were part of a two-vehicle caravan heading to Arifjan to drop off Perry, Jake, and Amanda. First, we went back to the ammo/arms room to load up and get back into our body armor/flak vests. They must've thought we were a bunch of Barney Fifes back in Mayberry, NC, because we were issued only two clips of 9 mm bullets and one clip of 5.6 mm bullets per person, as we trekked around Kuwait to Arifjan.

Little has changed since I was last here, mostly camel herds, shepherds, and Bedouins, their tents parked in the desert with their Mercedes. We entered the dusty logistics base Arifjan around 1130. We met COL Griffiths and the 377th JAGs. A neat young attorney

(CPT Saloom) from Lafayette, LA, who had held down the JAG shop at Arifjan for the past three months, was now getting a bit of help. Looked like they needed it. Arifjan was bustling, as construction was underway to make it the permanent US camp in Kuwait. They had talked of moving Camp Doha for years, but Arifjan was the ultimate answer. The mess hall held over 2,000 soldiers at a time. Of course, they can never push enough soldiers through the line to fill it up at any one time. I spent some time with the 377th TSC and 3rd MEDCOM JAs who were going to work with our guys and slept on the way back.

When I returned to Doha, I went to the CFLCC COIC. The War Room overlooks a sea of SIPRNet computers, microphones, consoles and three massive multi-paneled screens. All are connected by networks, speakers, headphones, and CNN/Fox. We could watch (USAF/USN) Southern Watch strikes on Iraqi targets on the screens. Amazing. NASA Control at Houston has nothing on the CFLCC COPS, and here is where I work. I am to operate as the OIC of the twelve-hour night shift when we go to twenty-four-hour operations. A case of Saddam's Revenge set in on Thursday night and fought me all day Friday. Again, not much sleep when you're trotting to the gym in search of porcelain.

KUWAIT, CHRONICLE #1
7 MARCH 2003

After two and a half weeks at Ft. Bragg's Combat Readiness Center, an average among us of fifteen needle sticks for smallpox, anthrax, etc., and successfully—i.e. not killing anyone or anything—firing at the range, my team validated and loaded a C-5A for Kuwait via, appropriately, "Moron," Spain. As important as we thought we were, the primary load was ten vehicles in the belly and some other soldiers perched above for the seventeen hours of flight. We could only take off with half a tank of JP8 fuel because of the short runway at Pope AFB, so things were a bit tense when we missed the tanker aircraft that was to refuel us over the Atlantic. We coasted by two other landing points and fumed our way into Morón, arriving in Kuwait early Tuesday morning. Danger was immediate as they drove the vehicles off the plane through the nose and almost over our toes. We arrived with tons of 101st ABN soldiers and were almost lost in the shuffle.

Some kind PSYOPs folks gave us a lift to Camp Doha, helping the eight of us avoid another day of waiting. Unusual to see embedded reporters with the 101st troops. They were having a bad day after twenty-six hours of travel. We particularly enjoyed seeing them try to get out a story while weathering the sandstorm that kicked up just as their feet hit the ground. We are doing well here in Doha at present. While we wait to start our mission, we are temporarily assigned to the Coalition Forces Land Component Command SJA shop. I'm the CFLCC SJA night-shift OIC in the Command Operations Center. It is dramatically high-tech, a lot like Caesar's Palace in Vegas or the control room on the Starship *Enterprise*. All things are warming up here, notably weather and operations.

We may discontinue connectivity and commo out of here in the near future for security reasons, so silence means merely that. You should be proud of the men and women here, especially the young Marines and soldiers I see run by here for an hour's respite from the tents out in the sand. They are America's finest, they are motivated, and they are doing us all proud. I've never seen a more dedicated set of patriots anywhere, anytime.

JOURNAL, 7 MAR 2003

Meeting with the ARCENT-KU SJA. He is going nutty— probably for good cause as he was the JAG stuck at GITMO with the detainees late in 2001 and 2002. He's been here eight months—eight months too long, seems like. Phil and Owen finally met him after I forced my way into his office. We actually hit it off well, but it helped that COL Gordon blew him out when he hadn't bothered to meet Owen and Phil earlier that morning. The rest of the day was getting familiar with the current operations (COPS), etc. I attended a Phase IV meeting in FUOPS to discuss issues following combat operations in Iraq. The planning cell had an impossible task since the end state was totally variable. Several specific goals were discussed, and the civilian/military division of chores was on the table. Friday night was movie night (*The Outlaw Josey Wales*).

E-mail to CPT Sean Delaney, 8 Mar 03: *No sunscreen yet but wind protection needed. Sand storm last night nearly killed us. Saved some costs on dermabrasion, so, if I say so myself, resemble Brad Pitt now. As long as saltpeter is still working, sexual assault charges not imminent for anyone. Saving Korea for you and James* [Oliver]. *Don't do kimchi too well; gives me gas. Speaking of which, Lenski is a gassy man.*

JOURNAL, 8–9 MAR 2003

We're more settled in . . . for now. I am operating the night COPS SJA desk. Lake and I were briefed on targeting analysis and other issues so we can run the desk. We continued our involvement in preparing for our mission. Perry and Jake had hooked up with representatives of the 800th MP BDE. By Sunday we were somewhat in the groove. We took most of Sunday off, doing nothing, hanging around the SJA shop and the gym until we could start our night shift. Lake and Phil had obtained rooms, and Owen and I were the sole team-survivors of Bay 3.

COL Karl Goetzke—the incoming CFLCC SJA—dropped an AR [Army Regulation] 15-6 investigation legal review in my lap this evening. It involved a HMMVW MP patrol accident rollover when a twenty-three-year-old National Guardsman (1-293rd INF) from Ft. Wayne, Indiana, decided to do a donut in the sand but furrowed, tripped, and rolled the vehicle, ejecting and trapping the turret gunner under the vehicle, killing him. The nineteen-year-old decedent was just a kid from Indiana. Sad story. I had to provide the legal review for ultimate publication to the kid's mother. With almost two decades of experience defending auto manufacturers in rollover accidents in my civil law practice, this was a familiar bit of legal work for my first nonoperational law work this time around.

It was a long night at COPS. My system had just gotten used to the time change and suddenly I had to change it again. Things have loosened up here since the UN/US deadline was moved back to March 17. Until then, we were sure we were kicking off earlier. Based on some briefings, we faced a significant potential for a chemical attack once we launched our attack to Baghdad. We started carrying our JSLIST chemical suits with us at all times. We had always carried our protective masks, but now carried the suits, boots and gloves as well. We received a FRAGO to start carrying them Friday night.

We bet on when the air war and ground war would start. My money was on Sunday night until the US/Britain deadline was extended. The forces looked ready and poised for action at any time now. By the time our shift ended after the 0900 meeting Monday morning, Lake and I were stumbling a bit. Then Lake had the unique experience of being grabbed in the hall and suddenly told he was the JAG representative to a planning group responding to some inquiry from SECDEF on how we were tackling ROE issues on Shia Muslims and mosques. This stuff was already in the ROE, so Lake just surfaced the plan, and the group forwarded a summary up to Rumsfeld. Typical night at COPS.

JOURNAL, 10–11 MAR 2003

Sitting here at COPS in JSLIST. Fortunately, a rehearsal only. The Joint Services Lightweight Integrated Suit Technology (JSLIST) is the new NBC gear. Lightweight it is not. Hot and uncomfortable it is, covering your body and face with a hood that fits onto/over your mask. I suspect it is not all that effective either as a sealer around the mask. And some sadist invented "the crotch strap" that attaches/ cinches the top to the bottom—severing your testicles in the process. This so-called "integration" technology has forced the folks wearing the JSLIST back to walking like early primates once the crotch strap is fastened and cinched.

The desk tonight was slow, just a couple of classic Air Force gripes over defending the Brits and the Aussies who want to blow captured enemy weapons/vehicles in place. Uh, probably not a great idea, but seemed like good fun. Ended shift around 0930 and hit the sack for few deep minutes. The list of sounds that can awaken you in Bay 3 is endless: a spirited night baseball game in the next bay; a platoon or two of the 101st ABN (AA) who specialize in busting our chops; a 225-hp Mercury Marine motor firing dry; six jet skis firing dry; a forklift that only knows reverse; a huge metal garage-type door that opens more than a New Orleans whore (so I have heard!); the nefarious extra end poles from endless cots assembled in the dark hitting the concrete a few inches from your head; a giant roof-ripping sand-and-wind storm; and now the latest mid-morning enema—the SCUD alarm. This lifesaving ball-buster can ring out day or night— particularly daytime just when you've hit the sack. The imposing siren and mechanical "This SCUD's for you" blasts into every square inch of Doha and throughout the Kuwaiti theater.

The result is simple chaos and self-mutilation. You go to MOPP 4 immediately donning mask, JSLIST pants, JSLIST top, boots, glove liners, gloves, mask carrier, helmet, body armor, and LCE, all this while you sprint to the blast shelters positioned throughout beautiful downtown Doha. There you complete your ensemble by "sardining" with twenty or so similarly bewildered compatriots into an 8' x 10' bunker, surrounded and covered by sandbags. This will wake you up from even the best and deepest sleep, then keep you from sleeping for at least the remainder of your time off. It is a great way to lose weight and pulse. So went our first SCUD alert—again, fortunately just a test. Kevin Chenail about suffocated as the SJA gang were in the middle of breaking down their masks when the alarm went off. He inserted two filter bleachers backward and could barely get any air into his mask. An hour later "the attack" is over. Even so, you needed to keep your mask on for some time afterward. This SCUD drill taught me that when you are tired enough, you can sleep in your mask.

After a spell at the gym, I returned to find I had over a hundred new bay mates. The cots were now side-to-side, end-to-end over the entire bay. I was probably Bay 3's oldest resident—at least by duration. Fortunately, the night shift spared me from joining the comforts of sleep among my new and many guests.

My legal review and recommendations concerning the rollover accident investigation apparently drew good marks, so they were adopted wholesale by LTG McKiernan and his deputy chief of staff; particularly satisfying since it brought some closure to a high-profile needless death in theater. The task for the evening was scrubbing and commenting on a Phase IV ROE, following tactical operations. Lake covered an Art. 32 hearing all day after last night's shift, so he is sacking-out now. I'll hold down the fort.

E-mail to Maggie Alston, 11 MAR 03: *Been here, not done this, however. Kind of cool stuff here at battle central. Lots of sand, lots of camel, lots of troops, lots of nervous camels, no beer. Pretty much sums it up.*

E-mail to Alex Warner, 11 MAR 03: *Just waiting on George to shove things up Saddam's butt, not surprised if Chirac is already up there . . . Rousted from hour's sleep with a SCUD rehearsal today. Hell of an alarm clock. Spent a few hours in full NBC gear and masks, first in the bunker then on my bunk trying to sleep. Almost made it to sleep when 100-plus troops moved into my bay with their cots, then set them up—all at once. Made enough noise for an Army!*

JOURNAL, 12–13 MAR 2003

Sand: The sandstorm is a nasty thing. It darkens the sky, it darkens the room. It gets into everything, everywhere. Tonight it grounded all movements. Most of the night, Ollie North reported on Fox out with I MEF. He could hardly talk except to get out something about the awesome sandstorm and its effect on men and machines. My cot, the office and the COPS was coated in sand, so we heartily endorsed his news. This was the third or fourth sandstorm since we arrived.

Working on several issues tonight in addition to the standard OPNS desk work. The legal problem of Kuwaiti traffic tickets issued to rental car companies triggered by stop sign and speeding cameras is interesting. Also, I'm writing a tax article for the local newspaper/ magazine. We learned targeting analysis tonight on the impressive ADOCs (targeting) software. It is awesome. We vet targets for conflicts by searching for "no-strike" targets or "restricted" targets to avoid, check the satellite shots and weapons impact/effects radius, and comment on any problems to the Fire Support folks after doing a collateral-damage assessment. ADOCs plots the target on the satellite photo, then allows you to sight the "conflicts" within one km or more and zoom in or out on a map or satellite photo. It is remarkable.

Another technology that's cool is the target and guidance systems. We watch air strike missions in process and then the resulting impacts. The next day the same stuff appears during the Rumsfeld/Myers briefings to the media. I monitor all FRAGOs, warning orders, OPLANs, OPORDs and messages for JAG issues, and significant/serious incident reports for murders, accidental discharges of weapons and other military-justice issues. Interpreting the rules of engagement for Phases III and IV and responding to inquiries keep the rest of my evening full of action.

Wednesday night is "surf and turf" night, though it's really neither. No way is a hockey puck a steak. A camel's hoof would be tenderer. It is difficult to mess up a steak, but you must first start with one. The surf is a slang term for "anti-beef." The lobster tail is okay, the crab legs suck. They cook these bad boys so long that they bend but don't crack. The universal Leatherman's tool does not help. A sharpened axe for cutting the legs open is the only way into this barely edible sea morsel. Steak! I dream of a juicy Sullivan's cowboy ribeye. My taste buds are rapidly degenerating—and we're in the food mecca here—Camp Doha. Wait until we get into the sand up north. Yum.

The news is ambiguous, as the UN again proves its irrelevance. The picture of the US courting Guinea, Mexico, and other "swing nations" is laughable. And then there are the French. I believe the French would veto fries with a combo meal. The momentum appears to be simply to ignore the UN and march on with protecting US security. The boys here are ready, and things are moving fast apace. Everyone is eager to get on with it. I guarantee that the boys in the sand are ready to roll north. The 101st ABN is now off-loaded and ready. With Turkey not yet on board, 4th ID and 1st CAV will have to back-fill. The southern option is the only option at present. It still is a good plan, provided 3rd ID can do their job and the JSLIST NBC suit will do its job of protecting us. Remember, too, that equipment and men will eventually degrade in the sand unless we get going. Everyone is honed and ready.

Bet Diane's as lonely as I am, despite my cheek-by-jowl 130 fellow bay rats. These guys kill me. They don't bitch or moan. They snore, like me, and can sleep anytime, anywhere. They are also still young and bright-eyed. They are technologically savvy. They enjoy working a Playstation and DVDs in a bay in a warehouse in the middle of nowhere. They laugh, clean weapons, again sleep despite the lights, the forklifts, the noise and their ambiguous future. They are awesome. Yet they are the same age, or younger than, my nieces and nephews. Can't imagine them here now at this age. Guess I am the old man in the bay of youth. They are secretly counting how many times I have to get up each night to pee.

Email to COL Dan Shearouse, 12 MAR 03: *Yes, in Bay 3 I'm senior in all ways. So much for rank hath its privilege. On the plus side, I do somewhat enjoy seeing all the resilient and creative young folks in the bay. They don't bitch or moan. Perhaps they do some snoring, but they are all energetic, motivated cut-ups who are ready to roll north. Torpedo ready to launch!*

KUWAIT, CHRONICLE #2
14 MARCH 2003

I've always loved sand. Good thing. We've been getting it air-delivered to us. Sand in your toes is one thing. Sand in your nose, eyes, mouth, lungs, coffee, food, ears . . . is another. We were hit by sandstorms three times this week. These brutal storms come suddenly and rip up everything from tents to port-o-lets. 82nd ABN lost all four mess tents, probably a blessing. One sergeant held onto the tent straps and reportedly flew thirty feet up and did a not-so-satisfactory parachute landing fall resulting in a few broken bones.

We're still temporarily assigned to the Coalition Forces Land Component Command. The twelve-hour night shift has become pretty active as op-tempo increases. I'm doing target vetting, responding to rules of engagement inquiries, giving legal input to serious accident/inadvertent weapons discharges investigations and the like.

I'm now the old man in the bay (warehouse-type) for now. My bay mates are a rotating company of young Marines or soldiers from the villages in the sand, coming in for a night of "magic"—a shower, no embedded reporter, an hour's wait in line at the post exchange to buy the last Q-tips and baby wipes in theater, and a chance to sleep next to me and the 10K forklift that only backs up, accompanied by the harmony of snorers in our dust bin strung with concertina we call the "bay." I am particularly delighted to see the embedded reporters. They don't look so GQ now they have been in the sand for a few weeks. The best one I've heard was the Doonesbury-cartoon soldier asking for permission to embed "Ashley Banfield!" Otherwise, the operations continue apace. The folks here are ready. The young troops here are great.

Able to use my old Jeep CJ/Bronco II training this week while reviewing the investigation of an unfortunate death in a HMMWV rollover accident. (Note to self: Do not recommend placement of open turret in commercially available HMMWV II—it will ruin your day every time.)

Everyone on my team has adjusted well and is ready to tackle our mission soon. Miss everyone back home and do wish you were here!

JOURNAL, 14 MAR 2003

I am getting into a routine now. Sleep came easy this morning as the hajis took today off from driving the reverse-only forklift in the next bay. Hajis are Pakastani or Indian workers stuck cleaning the restrooms, repairing and maintaining things, serving food, delivering water, doing laundry, serving Hardee's burgers, and so much more. "Smurf" hajis wear blue jumpsuits, and their lot is the worst. You simply cannot pay anyone enough to constantly mop, flush, re-paper, and clean the camp's restrooms and shower trailers. Food in—food out: "Saddam's Revenge" is rampant. Salmonella hit Arifjan and damn near killed folks down there. The food has no taste going in— but man does it "flavor up" on the way out. Several times I've donned my protective mask to keep from vomiting on the crapper.

Back in the COPS things are warming up. The G2 reports chemical warfare units of Saddam's army moving south and positioning containers of chemicals with explosives. Also, satellites show Saddam burying missiles in some construction sites. Don't understand why the president doesn't reveal some of this intel to the world. If they knew more about these moves, surely the Hollywood gang would temper their objections and protests to our being here, but, then again, probably not. They know more than everyone else about everything else. Amazing I haven't seen one anti-Saddam sign at any anti-war protest. Makes you wonder who the protestors are pulling for.

We get some interesting intel here, though I'd better hold off writing some stuff, but the truth is that CNN seems to know most of the US and Coalition movements before we do. Last night at 0320, SECDEF ordered the fleet in the Eastern Mediterranean to the Red Sea, since Turkey has not allowed Tomahawk overflights. A few hours later, CNN had already reported the movement of our ships. Amazing. That said, the poor embedded reporters do not know what they're in for. Ollie North, Rick Atkinson and the others better be ready for the sand, for chemicals, for sweat, and especially for sudden bloody deaths on the battlefields.

The Brits today were classic. After being with us, then hinting they may not be with us, today they led the charge and then found themselves north of the southern berms. Of course, they were lost! The command repeatedly reminded the major commanders not to have their forces any closer than 10 kms south of the berms. In a way, the Brits were in compliance, since they were north of the berms. Berm-clearing is ongoing and the rolling troops/units have been practicing. They are ready. The 101st ABN is now offloaded and ready. 82nd ABN is good to go. I MEF is trigger-happy and ready. One of their Marines sadly shot himself in the port-o-let. Hell of a way to die. That dunny must have been nasty to cause someone to go that far. Out in the sand, the dunny is the only place anyone has any privacy. Two Marines in adjacent dunnies heard the poor guy chamber a round. Depression is a tough enemy. That said, the sand will do it to you if the food doesn't already!

The Brits were also testing the "Oswald single-bullet theory" yesterday. They were in the equivalent of our Bradley Fighting Vehicle when one accidently discharged his weapon. The bullet ricocheted throughout the interior of the armor-clad vehicle, injuring five soldiers, one through the neck, one in the knee and god knows where else. Yet another instance of chaos.

Saw my old Medical Service Corps pal MAJ Mike Bachman this week. He's with 3rd MEDCOM now. We were together in the 312th EVAC in Greensboro and went to Ft. Sam Houston for a few weeks in PAD training. Poor Mike. He was mobilized for Desert Storm, mobilized last November (2001) for a year here and to Atlanta, returned home this past November for forty-five days, then activated again for a year.

Ops tempo is increasing here. We loaded ADOCs onto our SIPR computers at the COPS desk last night. ADOCs allows us to vet target request by using satellite imagery and map overlays and to evaluate whether there are any conflicts within the effective bug-splat range of the selected weapon system and to assess collateral damage. A remarkable system. We can locate the targets and the no-strike areas (e.g., mosques, prisons, power towers, and schools) on satellite photos and overlay maps all on the same screen. It does all the work, warning you of conflicts within a certain radius of the target.

Target descriptions include tracing security guards of DIA black-listed persons—Saddam's sons and key leaders. Time-sensitive targets are assessed and vetted continually within the time parameters. We chiefly point out ROE issues to the Fire Support guys and remind them of problems/issues relating to non-strike and restricted-strike targets within the weapons' effective range. Sometimes if the collateral damage looks too high or the approach direction or weapon ordnance selection is not appropriate, they stop the targeting or adjust fire. All commands are looking at the same target and providing input to make sure it is a green target. SOF makes sure it doesn't have operators in the danger zone, hazmat problems, etc. That's good vetting.

Hep. B shot today. Also purchased a cool native Kuwaiti head shawl and woman's veil (hijab). Should be entertaining at Halloween. Can't wait to see (or not) Diane in the classic veil showing only her beautiful eyes. Fat chance!

Almost forgot, the Albanians and Romanians are here! We can now sleep soundly in the knowledge that we really have a coalition. Unfortunately, we are the meat. They are more likely the dressing.

Owen did a classic Owen today. Our Marine JAGs are great. One is Maj Jim Carbury. Jim's a prankster and rooms with Owen. He dropped a pair of black panties on the floor in the room and acted like he had found them there. He questioned Owen about the panties and what he'd been doing in the room.

Owen's face flushed and he reported that they had to have come from the laundry that day when a female major suddenly had to borrow Owens PT shorts, so she stripped in front of him to put her uniform in the washer and put his PT shorts on while they washed. Owen expected that somehow she must have had her panties in his PT shorts when she returned them. Great story, especially to Carbury, who was merely playing a joke on Owen.

E-mail to Becky Steadman, 15 MAR 03: *Fortunately working during last sandstorm. It blew in fast and scattered everything, especially thoughts . . . Surf and turf? More like carp and camel. The food sucks. No way what they serve us ever stood on four hooves. . .*

17 MAR 03: United Nations orders all UN personnel out of Iraq

17 MAR 03: President Bush addresses nation, setting a forty-eight-hour ultimatum for Saddam Hussein.

Email to Mark Warner, 17 MAR 03: *Ironic you will be in Normandy. Take a lengthy piss anywhere and everywhere in France. As Stormin Norman Swartzkopf said, "Going to war without the French is like going hunting without your accordion."*

Email to Diane, 17 Mar 03: *Beautiful full moon here tonight. I look at it and talk to you, hope you hear me.*

JOURNAL, 15–19 MAR 2003

I'm settling into the CFLCC COPS night shift. Targeting nominations (joint time-sensitive targets) are getting more interesting. We had one RO (response option) on Sunday that got some attention. An Iraqi missile battery had moved into the southern zone down close in range to the boys on the berm. Despite some close ROE calls, CENTCOM sent it up to SECDEF for final approval. It was nixed at the last moment, maybe on the heels of the summit in the Azores with Bush, Blair, and the Spanish president. Everyone waited anxiously for the Azores meeting speeches. The Coalition was going to give the UN Security Council twenty-four hours to put up or shut up. Finally, the ball is moving forward again.

Water at Doha apparently is hit or miss. Off as much as on lately. I've been lucky most of the time. Fewer showers taken in the afternoon, I guess.

Still stuck in Bay 3 as a bay rat. This morning (19 Mar.) brought a new twist. The dust blower. This nasty creature is comprised of a haji on top of a scissors lift with an air hose blowing sand/dust down: death from above, then dusted again. After three hours of the sound of powered air creating an artificially-made dust storm, I finally gave up and started to the gym. As I left Bay 3, my haji friend with the air-hose departed Bay 2. I think he must have been watching—once I gave up, it was no longer any fun for him to annoy me.

The night C3 battle captain (COL Forrest) is a Vince Carterlookalike. He is awesome. I'm keeping a separate list of his Forrestisms. We have a night shift change brief every night at 2300. He has, amazingly, used "Rhino snot" (a form of asphalt glue) and that useful verb "undick" in the same sentence. "Folks, we need to undick the commo situation"; or my personal favorite, "I need a no-shit commo answer." After Monday night's Bush speech giving Saddam forty-eight hours to defect or else, Forrest mumbled into the COPS mike, "Fire in the belly!" You can't make this stuff up. Forrest also has that unique, and obnoxious, Army trait of asking for a "hooah"[4] after every statement. To hear someone casually use "undick" in front of you is one thing. To hear it over the COPS speaker in front of a hundred folks is another. Hooah!

We are moving to a pre-war readiness level soon. Tomorrow (20 Mar.) we start wearing full "battle rattle"—Kevlar, body armor, LCE at all times unless you are doing PT. Also no more civilian clothes allowed. By Friday (21 Mar.) we get to put on the JSLIST—fashionable woodlands green for the 12th JAG!—under the battle rattle. Mess halls close by Friday night. Hajis were given appropriate NBC gear and gas masks yesterday. They deserve it. Hope Kayani, the ice cream haji, weathers the war.

One of the most disappointing turns of events is the blocking of a bunch of internet sites from our eyes. The bastards! They closed off the sports connections, though fortunately not until after Duke won the ACC tourney. We couldn't access the NCAA tourney selections or the brackets. War is hell!

Everyone here seems ready to get on with the war, and I sense that time is ticking down to it. We were briefed on the conversion of the OPLAN COBRA II to OPORD COBRA II tonight. It's pretty aggressive, but with complete air supremacy, most desired results are possible. With the tension in the air now palpable, Bush's speech this morning (18 Mar. 0400 here) got everyone revved up. The boys

---

4   There was also a splattering of "oorahs" from the Jarheads in the room. Oorah is the guttural battle cry common in the US Marine Corps since the mid-twentieth century. It is comparable to the Army's own "Hooah" and the Navy's pathetic "Hooyah."

in the sand I'm sure are just ready to do something, anything, other than to sit and train anymore. Frankly, they'd lose their edge soon if we didn't go.

The intelligence FRAGOs coming in are amazing. Underground facility, Al Qaeda, buried weaponry, and conniving, worthless UN inspectors among the reports. Apparently several of the famous UN arms inspectors have mistresses and sneak away in the afternoon to accommodate rather than inspect. Tonight we lost an interesting possible target. Saddam was reported to be at his first wife's farm, Dora Farms, just outside of Baghdad for the evening.[5] We were given the target to work up a firing solution: a TLAM (Tomahawk) package of twenty-four missiles. An opportunity for regime decapitation. But we were still inside President Bush's forty-eight-hour ultimatum to Saddam. D-Day was to be tomorrow. Everyone cleared the target when POTUS/CENTCOM/SECDEF canceled the launch. So, no joy tonight. Too bad. If Saddam had been there, this thing would have ended before it started.

Back to just another day at the office. Jake is working on the 800th MP, our potential future hosts, to secure support logistics and coordinate our mission details. I'm working COL Gordon to get the go-ahead. If so, we'd move up sometime D+20 or so into Iraq. We'll see. I may have a front row seat here in COPS for A- and G-day and then a great seat on the course for later events. Not bad for a guy who was stuck behind a desk in Raleigh only six weeks ago.

As tomorrow approached, we received word that the Dora Farms complex likely included a reinforced-concrete bunker.[6] This intelligence demanded a different firing solution: Two F-117 Stealth Nighthawk fighter-bombers took off from Al Udeid in Qatar as a result. Game on!

---

5   Based on HUMINT sources, the CIA reports a probable meeting of Saddam Hussein and his sons Tuesday night, 18 March 2003, at a complex called Dora Farms in the southern part of Baghdad on property belonging to Saddam's wife, Sajida. Franks, Tommy, *American Soldier*, Harper-Collins Publishing (New York, 2004), 450-451.
6   *Ibid*, 453. *Cobra II*, 169-176.

3.

PHASE III: DOMINATE
THE ATTACK AND MAJOR COMBAT OPERATIONS

19 MAR 03: (D-DAY)—OIF War Begins

- **Special Operations Forces (SOF)/Other Governmental Agencies (OGA) recon Iraqi units along Green Line**
- **SOF/OGA infiltrates, and link-ups continue in the south**
- **Coalition Forces Air Component Command (CFACC) initiates counter-TBM operations**
- **Special Forces destroy visual observer stations (VISOBS) and assault into western Iraq (S-DAY)**
- **Task Force 20 (TF 20) destroys western VISOBS and moves into Iraq**
- **Ground forces recon into southern oil fields with SOF/OGA**
- **I Marine Expeditionary Force (I MEF) conducts relief in place (RIP) with Kuwait forces**

CLFCC EXORD: CFLCC COBRA II OPLAN Conversion to CFLCC COBRA II OPORD, 190900Z March 2003:

"Mission. CFLCC attacks to defeat Iraqi forces and control the zone of action, secure and exploit designated sites, and remove the current regime. CFLCC conducts continuous stability operations to create conditions for transitions to CJTF-Iraq."

★ ★ ★ ★

JOURNAL, 19–20 MAR 2003

On 19 March, the war begins. LTG McKiernan issued his "Strike Fast and Hard" message to the 200,000-plus troops under CFLCC. Iraqi Freedom was thereby launched with the execution of OPORD COBRA II: tonight is D-Day. Iraqis surrendering at the berms were the first ROE struggle for the I MEF, the Kuwaitis and me. Targeting was pretty hot. We tracked the missiles and bombs—saw them on CNN/FOX with the air-raid sirens going off in Baghdad. Two F-117s dropped their bombs on regime leadership at Saddam's first wife's farm, Dora Farms. An interesting question of capitulations and another on repatriation of POWs from Desert Storm have arisen that I weighed in on.

We're approaching our last dining hall (DFAC) meal and weighing in thirty pounds heavier with our body armor/flak vest, Kevlar, LCE and hauling our JSLIST around. I'll probably be sleeping in JSLIST soon. After nearly three weeks of waiting, it was an invigorating feeling to hear the words "D-Day before a Kick-Off," as MG J. D. Thurman (OPNS) announced at our 1900 BUA in the COPS. We go to twenty-four-hour full operations, so tomorrow I'll have company in the COPS at the desk. Schweiger, Whitman, and Ortez will join me. We also worked today on our follow-on mission (EPWs, JTF-Iraq) and how we'll staff it. The barrage soon will be intense to accomplish "shock and awe" as scripted in the OPLAN/OPORD (A-Day). Life in the COPS' high-tech world seems remote from the fight—at least for now. A few MREs, however, and the entire body-armor weight will remind us we're now in a war zone.

20 MAR 03 (D+1):
- **TF 20 raid on Ar Rutbah**
- **Time sensitive target (TST) with two F-117s and twenty-four TLAMs attack leadership target**
- **Air operations conducted to shape the battlespace: 537 air strike sorties, 34 TLAMs, 143 PGMs**
- **SOF forces attack to seize Tallil AB and Euphrates River crossings**

JOURNAL, 20–21 MAR 2003

The stealth and Tomahawk strike starting the war apparently struck hard. Although the damage assessment is still open, word is that it caught the Iraqi leadership asleep and may have shaken, even killed, Saddam. After a long night of real excitement, I, too, was shakened awake by the first real SCUD alert. The sirens are caustic shrieks, the confusion extreme. In my rush—and perhaps the sleep funk I was in—it led to some real comedy. By the time I got my boots on and laced, JSLIST pants and blouse on overboots, and looked for my gloves—all with my mask on in relative darkness—I was frustrated by not finding my gloves and glove inserts, which I was sure were in my JSLIST bag.

Anyway the Marine chief in the cot next to me came to my rescue with his extra set—medium, not large. We ran to the bunker and helped others in putting their stuff on. The helmet cover is also a tricky and frustrating item to get on. It is a huge shower cap for your helmet. The problem is, of course, that you have to put it on with seriously thick butyl rubber gloves. It's a mess. The funny thing is that my boots felt cramped indeed—as boots would if you had gloves lining them! That's where the gloves went to!

The second SCUD alert came a few minutes after the first "all clear." When I ran out of the bay, a nearby Patriot battery fired two shots. The Patriot sends an eight-foot missile at a SCUD and tries to intercept it before it intercepts us with prejudice. Our missiles sound like jets going by as they fire off. The sound also means that a SCUD is incoming. By the end of the day, the Patriot boys were our best new friends. They were three for three with two other SCUDs. These incoming TSMs—Ababil 100/Al Sarroud missiles—fell way off course in the desert or in the gulf. We went to MOPP 4 for sirened SCUDs/NBC alert nine times on Thursday. In case we didn't feel that we had enough SCUD alerts, one gas alarm also triggered at the front gate.

One of over twenty SCUD alerts at Camp Doha, Kuwait, after commencement of combat operations. Warner (front left) in Joint Services Lightweight Integrated Suit Technology (JSLIST) worn to protect against NBC attack, March 2003. I was plotting how to get Kayani, our ice cream haji, one of these protective outfits.

Wearing the JSLIST, body armor, and MOPP 4 is brutal. Lessons learned: (1) Pee when you can; (2) Pee whenever you can. We got somewhat passive in our response by the seventh or eighth SCUD drill. As I took my first bite of stewed okra at our last supper at the mess, yet another SCUD alert boomed. My cynical mind somehow fixated on how funny it was that after all the great food and wine I've had in my life, my last morsel on earth would be stewed okra! After the alert ended, I skipped the rest of the meal and, taking no chances, went to see Kayani, the ice cream man.

While all soldiers were in MOPP4 protections, Kayani and the other Pakistanis workers had no protection from NBC attack, standing resolute while everyone else was squatting along the wall in full protective gear. I did notice a bus of hajis waiting out an earlier alert. Their vulnerability, frankly, was sad. I noticed after that, at least some of the workers on post were receiving chemical protective gear and using it.

Back at my desk, things were intense. G-Day was moved up to 21 0300Z MAR—D+2. Recon from 3ID/V Corps' cavalry was launched hours earlier to be 3ID's eyes. I MEF sent a task force to secure the Rumaylah oil fields before Saddam could burn them. Unfortunately, nine wells had been torched by Saddam before I MEF's TF could get there. We keep wondering why we don't schwack the Iraqis now, especially the SCUD launchers. Key events of the night included a miracle and an accident.

The miracle was a friendly-fire/fratricide incident where a Marine Cobra attack chopper fired a Hellcat missile into the turret of a M1A1 Abrams tank from the 1 BN, 7th RTC. Amazingly, though the turret was blown off, only one crew member was injured and then only slightly. The tank was destroyed, but I couldn't help think of Telly Savalas in the *Battle of the Bulge* driving that turret-less tank around France.

Later a Chinook CH46E chopper dropped out of the sky with four Marines and twelve British commandos killed—apparently a mechanical/fire. The commandos were following up the good work of the Navy SEALs to capture the GOPLATs (oil platforms) at the Iraqi gulf entrance. COL Gordon and I were tasked to prepare the fratricide/friendly-fire report on the turret shot, having to get info from I MEF—who were still smarting from losing the men in the chopper, yet getting ready to roll through the berm at the line of departure.

I MEF and 3ID did exactly that at 0300Z on Friday morning, G-Day. Attacks continued throughout the night in the air and on the ground. First, they had to clear the berms. These monster berms of sand and electric fences were breached at several lanes by Kuwaiti bulldozers and follow-on engineers. A few minefields later, you're in Iraq. Simple indeed, unless you're the one in the sand.

One comical law of war issue arose with the poor Iraqi soldiers assigned near the berms. Seeing the entire heavy 3ID lined up to breach the berm and attack, several of the soldiers attempted to surrender before the war commenced. Who wouldn't when facing an entire division by themselves? We recommended that they be told to hold off until the war started before officially surrendering.

21 MAR 03 (D+2) (G-Day)
- **I MEF seizes western Rumaylah oil fields. Accepts surrender of senior leadership of 51st Iraqi Mech. Inf. Div.**
- **Initiate strategic air operations (A-Day); 832 air strike sorties, 381 TLAMs, 124 CALCMs, 231 PGMs**

Email to Erin Malcolm, 20 MAR 03: *We're okay here. Four scud alarms, no hits. Our guys on the Patriots are batting 100%. A hell of a wakeup call, however. First three while asleep in old Bay 3, the last while just sitting down at the table for last mess hall meal. Great! My last taste of food was stewed okra. When sirens ended, I bellied up for some ice cream and am much better prepared now. I will admit these get a more vigorous response than the fire drills back at the office.*

Email to Diane, 20 MAR 03: *. . . Got a shower today. Ten minutes later, another siren and I started sweating again. So it goes.*

22 MAR 03 (D+3):
- **V corps seizes Tallil AB; controls Euphrates River crossings; establishes a forward ammo and resupply point (FARP) south of An Nasiriyah**
- **TF Tarawa conducts RIP with 3rd ID to secure Euphrates crossing sites**
- **Civil Affairs (CA) teams begin food and water deliveries and restoring local governance**
- **Continue air operations; 878 air sorties, 45 TLAMs, 3 CALCMs, 644 PGMs, 15 ATACMS**

23 MAR 03 (D+4)

- **Ground forces attack toward Baghdad**
- **Twelve soldiers assigned to the 507th Maintenance Company, 3rd ID missing near An Nasiriyah. PFC Lynch and five other soldiers taken prisoner by Iraqis.**
- **Conducted strategic air operations: 827 air strike sorties, 72 TLAMs, 690 PGMs**
- **Weather, especially dust storms, impacts operations**

KUWAIT, CHRONICLE #3
22 MARCH 2003

On Wednesday evening, March 19, our forces indeed struck hard and fast. CFLCC commander, LTG McKiernan, sent electronically the 200,000 or so of us a letter stating, in part,

> Your task will not be an easy one, but it is just and you will triumph. You are a member of the best trained and equipped military force in history. This campaign will place extraordinary demands on individual soldiers, sailors, marines, airmen and small unit leaders who must be prepared to fight as they have been trained, while, at the same time, providing a helping hand to those Iraqis who welcome the coalition as liberators. Your courage, training and determination, backed by the will of all freedom-loving peoples, ensures your victory. Within this force, each of us has a job to do, and each of us serves the whole. Every single CFLCC unit is important in the campaign to remove this dictator and restore Iraq to the people of Iraq.
>
> Likewise, we are part of a larger joint and coalition team under COMCENT [Commander CENTCOM]. Each of us has a duty to our unit, our service, and our country, but we have an equally important duty to each other. Your courage will be tested but you will draw strength from those on your left and right. You will not falter. I know that all of you will represent yourselves, your units and your respective countries with honor and valor

in the days ahead. We will fight as a team and will be victorious as a team that is fighting for a common and just goal. I have total confidence in you. There is no finer team gathered anywhere in the world; no team more capable of addressing the task at hand. We are comrades in arms and I have unbounded pride in leading you. Trust your instincts, training and leadership in the days ahead. You are warriors in a historic campaign that will benefit our families, loved ones and our countries, as well as the people of Iraq. Strike fast and hard!
—McKiernan.

The word was given and it began in earnest. A similar letter came to us from GEN Franks on behalf of the commander in chief. McKiernan's letter was special because it was on point, and was largely written by COL Goetzke from our SJA office!

I am fortunate to be working for now at the JAG desk of the CFLCC Operations Center. The war is right in front of us and we sit just below the CFLCC commander and his staff in the war room. It is exciting to be ahead of the curve, most of the time, or at least ahead of Fox News, which is at times hard to do. Again, the targeting issues are challenging, but our new technology helps us keep ahead of our problems.

The rules of engagement issues are many. Although our rules of engagement belong to the commander, they wisely seek our interpretations and guidance: what and who we can target; how we are supposed to fight against the enemy; how we must protect civilians and protected structures like hospitals and schools; where and when we can fire and see what we hit; how the enemy is supposed to act; and what we can do if they violate the code of war. The bottom line is that we are bound by the rules of armed conflict no matter how hard the enemy fails to abide by those same rules. The ROE are simple in concept, yet often complex in execution.

The CFLCC War Room during the attack into Iraq, March 2003. LTG David McKiernan, CFLCC commander, is on the phone. CFLCC comprised over 200,000 troops from the USA and thirty-eight other countries. Primary elements included the US V Corps and I Marine Expeditionary Force and the 1st UK Division. In the category of small world, at back right in the photo is CPT Hansbarger, aide-de-camp to Deputy Commander MG William Webster. His family was from my tiny hometown in Ohio. [Photo courtesy of Global Security.org, public domain]

We have now had ten or eleven alerts for inbound SCUDs and Ababil 100 missiles. We don masks, protective trousers, tops, overboots, two sets of gloves, Kevlar helmet cover and helmet, body armor, and load-carrying equipment, all while sprinting to a nearby bunker! This wake-up call is most irritating . . . and terrifying, particularly when you see and hear a Mach-speed Patriot missile or two taking off to try to intercept. These SCUD alerts occur at the most inopportune times: when you are sleeping; when you are going, but have not gone, to the latrine; when you take your first but hopefully not your last bite of food. You get the point. Fortunately our Patriot anti-air defense batteries have been batting 1000—a good seven for seven so far, plus a few SCUDs falling out into the desert or into the Arabian Sea. The problem seems to be that unlike a missed catch in baseball, a miss here means you head to the big bench in the sky. For now, however, we persevere.

Current Operations and Intelligence Center (COIC) of the Coalition Forces Land Component Command (CFLCC) at Camp Doha, Kuwait, in March 2003. "Lightening, lightening, lightening" sounds and protective masks and gear were worn during the twenty missile attacks on the headquarters during the early days of the war. The US Patriot batteries saved countless troops by intercepting most of the inbound attacks but also shot down a RAF Torando pilot whose "friend or foe" signal was inactivated. JAGs were the legal advisors and reviewers for the subsequent investigations [Photo Courtesy of CNN, public domain]

Our team is doing well under the circumstances and doing their duty (perhaps occasionally in their trousers, but doing it all the same without complaint!). Of course, it's hard to complain when you are speechless. With luck, our troops will continue to drive to Baghdad without significant casualties.

Email to Diane, 23 MAR 03: *Busy night last night as you can imagine with the explosion/attack on the 101st ABN by one of its own sergeants, a converted Muslim; a British Tornado shot down by our Patriot guys; and other problems encountered with the Iraqis because they're not following any rules of war. Another SCUD alert*

tonight after midnight meal. Everyone here is pissed about the rough treatment of our US POWs, including evidence of physical abuse—especially Jessica Lynch—and then parading them on television in clear violation of the Geneva Convention. The troops' anger will help them press on with more resolve now.

JOURNAL, 22–23 MAR 2003

Smoke from the burning Rumaylah oil fields moved down with the northern winds to Camp Doha, darkening the sky and filling the nose. Another few SCUD attacks through the day and night. I believe we are up to twelve or thirteen by now. Our Patriot guys are doing great—seven for seven. Serious consequences if they fail to intercept the SCUDs and Ababil 100s Saddam has been sending. The biggest question on everyone's mind is whether Saddam is still alive. Who knows? He has completely disappeared and doesn't appear to be meaningfully communicating with his leadership, so I believe he's either dead or deathly ill of lead poisoning.

We had a busy night on the 22–23rd. We started off with war-crime reports—3ID reported Fedayeen soldiers herding women and children in front of their tanks and artillery as human shields; dressing up civilians with uniforms and weapons, including an envelope with instruction on how to disseminate anthrax; POWs from a lost US maintenance unit shot and paraded in front of Al Jazira television and exploited; search and rescue by spraying the reeds with bullets . . . And the list of war crimes just keeps on coming.

While we were dealing with those issues, keeping track of our forces driving north, and monitoring capitulations, property destruction and EPW activities, some idiotic criminal, a SGT Hassan Akbar from the engineering section/company of the 101st ABN, threw grenades into the brigade command tent and an officers' tent, killing at least two and wounding twelve others, including the 1st BDE CO, XO, SGM . . . and one of our JAG captains. This villainy was apparently in the name of Allah, Akbar being a recent convert to Islam. PAO immediately needed our input on how to tackle the Muslim question/issue and the fact that he had confessed to the S2. CID had secured him. I was getting casualty and situation updates from the BDE CJA.

CNN/Fox already were reporting that he was a recently converted Muslim. Of course, our concerns were his prosecution and preventing retaliation against the rising number of Muslims in our army. While I was tackling that nightmare for MajGen Blackmon and completing a FRAGO for the I MEF friendly-fire Cobra-on-Abrams incident, a US Patriot shot down a British Tornado, killing two Brit pilots. Not a good night for the home team.

A-Day did start the night before, and targets across Iraq were continuously hit, along with the artillery and close air support to the 3ID/11 ACR and 1 MEF Regimental Combat juggernauts that were rocking up highways 1 (Tampa), 6 and 7 toward Baghdad. On the lighter side, the G1 reported that I MEF had captured the 51st Mech. Inf. Division of the Iraqi Regular Army, and their weapons. Amazingly, the first three rounds in their magazines were blanks. I suspect that their "handlers" from Baghdad wanted to at least have a fighting chance of shooting them if they happened to turn and fire on the handlers!

Diane's birthday came eight hours earlier here than in Wilmington. I was able to call her and wish her happy birthday . . . and just hear her voice. I've been talking to her through the moon since I arrived here. She has been doing the same, so we have been able to chat and understand each other. This ritual was practiced during WWII, and I suspect from the dawn of man and woman and war. It is comforting and so it is done.

A message from GEN Franks on behalf of the commander in chief was, like LTG McKiernan's, sent to the troops electronically. I have been sleeping some since Friday when I finally moved from Bay 3 into a pod with two other LTCs. Bay 3 has served me well and, frankly, I will miss the constant interaction with the troops rotating through. On the other hand, a good day's sleep is welcome. Bay 3 held up as well as it could. As we were moving my stuff and cot out of it, the SCUD siren went off again and I hustled off to my favorite bunker once more.

The new pod is fascinating. Apparently, some genius came up with an idea to put a trailer park under a roof. I imagine that these pods—an 8' x 14' self-contained room set side by side and on top of each other—make for a curious feel: a cocoon of metal and darkness that all but soundproofs Camp Doha—even, almost, the sounds of the sirens. My first two hours of sleep were still interrupted by yet another SCUD alert. But the pod structure actually appears pretty sturdy, and the resulting honeycomb effect seems protective against any incoming missile.

24 MAR 03 (D+5)
- **CFLCC continues attack toward Baghdad; holds Euphrates crossing sites and attacks north towards Al Kut with I MEF**
- **US SOF and OGA insert assets into An Najaf**
- **11th AHR attacks RG Medina DIV south of Baghdad; one AH-64 shot down; two POWs**
- **"Boots and Coots" begin oil field fire-fighting**

25 MAR 03 (D+6)
- **1st UK Armored DIV secures Al Faw southern oil fields**
- **Blacklist issued to components**
- **US V Corps seizes An Najaf, continues ops to secure city**

JOURNAL, 24–25 MAR 2003

Another four SCUD alerts, and the last one was a close call. On his way to midnight chow COL Davis from the ADA command witnessed two Patriot missiles strike the Ababil 100 in the direction of the desalination plant. The desalination plant has two towering smokestacks that resemble a football goalpost. We call them "SCUD uprights" because if Saddam could kick a missile through them, he would definitely score his goal, our headquarters. All of this before the alert went active. I was, of course, just sitting down to eat, but first had to order some punk Marine private to put his mask on: "I didn't give a shit if you don't care if you live, but your death would mean someone else would have to take your place, plus a bunch of medics and Mortuary-Affairs folks would have to spend needless time over you." That and a direct order made that smart-ass put his mask on.

COL Goetzke, who came here from Fort Bliss, was put in as the legal advisor to the investigating board for the downing of the British Tornado. BG Lennox arrived this evening from the Pentagon to head the board. It should be interesting.

Weather up north was grinding ground operations to a halt, canceling two major assault operations—16th AA British and 101st ABN. The 101st ABN had jumped to FARP Shell for the operation and was ready to get into the fight as a way of shaking off the grenade incident and death of one of their MI captains yesterday before moving to Shell. Some idiot, lacking sound judgment, came up with an idea to name several of the FARPs (forward area resupply points) after the names of oil companies, e.g., Exxon, Shell, BP.

We lost a new AH64 Longbow attack chopper in fighting north of Objective Ram in the Medina sector. The pilots were alive but unfortunately were captured and then paraded shamelessly on Al Jazeera television Sunday, clouding everyone's mind with anger and remorse. COMCENTCOM wisely directed an operation to be mounted by SOF and TF 20, with CFLCC FUOPS in charge of planning the rescue. First, they had to locate the pilots.

Meanwhile, our own enemy prisoner of war–holding facilities were being constructed—first in the I MEF area as a holding area, then an internment facility. I figured we were going to be tasked for tribunals at these camps—Theater Internment Facility (TIF) 1 and TIF 2, later at LSA Bushmaster up north in the 3ID area. Jake and Perry were working the angles with the 800th MP BDE—the ultimate EPW MP BDE tasked to grapple with the EPWs.

The Fedayeen, those human kamikazes, were at it again in the south. They dressed in black or in civilian clothes and randomly threw themselves into pickup trucks, buses, taxis, whatever, first feigning surrender, then attacking as Coalition forces were cheering them on. These bastards were Saddam's henchmen—handlers for regular army soldiers who fought at gunpoint for Saddam's regime.

All in all, though, we had in five days driven on three different axes of advance to within 100 km of Baghdad; captured the southern oil fields virtually intact; secured the vital Basrah port and terminal facilities intact; and held the bridges over the Euphrates and Tigris. Not bad . . . and probably killed Saddam on the first night of the war. Despite news of some problems, a few accidents, and the captured pilots and lost convoy, we were kicking ass.

At home, daily letters and emails are rarely read twice. Here, however, letters and emails from home get many readings and are scoured over time and again for comfort, no longer for news. Reading Diane's voice into emails is very seductive and satisfying. I'm fortunate to have email for now and appreciate this luxury while I can.

Speaking of luxuries, none of the hajis who support us has been assigned a gas mask yet. We needed to remedy this for at least one of the key hajis in our life: Kayani, our Pakistani ice cream man. Last night Lake was breaking us up with his new plan of action for the mess hall when the next SCUD alert siren came. Kayani, who serves us ice cream with a playful glint in his eye, as if to ask "Is this enough?" had no gas mask. Lake suggested that after his twelve years of friendly ice cream service, Kayani was an essential person and needed to be kept safe. So, Lake plans to "buddy-breathe" with

Kayani next time—in return for which Kayani would probably be Lake's man Friday, bringing him ice cream at the snap of his fingers. As Lake snapped his fingers, we all applauded his plan.

COL Forrest came up with a great line over the speaker tonight. "Let's stop dick-dancing around on this issue." MG Thurman added a little spice to the 377th TSC commander's statement that 3 POL companies would "provide self-service protection," meaning an assistant driver with a M16 en route to logistics base (LSA) Adder. Thurman—a bear of a man—boomed "Son, that dog won't hunt." A full MP convoy escort was soon in place.

★ ★ ★ ★

26 MAR 03 (D+7)

- 4th INF DIV decision made to move to Kuwait
- 1st UK Armored DIV isolates Basrah
- 173rd ABN BDE executes airborne assault into Bashur airfield via fifteen C-17s
- Umm Qasr port open and ready for humanitarian (HA) delivery
- V Corps defeats enemy forces vicinity An Najaf and As Samawah

★ ★ ★ ★

JOURNAL, 26–27 MAR 2003

A close one Tuesday afternoon. Two incoming missiles were met by four Patriots. The Patriots were a hell of a wake-up call! On the whole, I'd rather buy an alarm clock. The 1600 siren wake-up got everyone's blood pumping again. At the same time, the weather was seriously nasty. Huge sand/windstorms in the north drove land and rotary air forces to a halt. Despite that, 3/7 CAV engaged north of OBJ Ram and inflicted death and mayhem on the enemy, estimated at over 500 KIAs. I MEF captured a school that the Fedayeen bastards were using as a headquarters. The haul included 170 persons captured, a bunch of weapons and over 3,000 chemical suits—a harbinger of their nasty plans to come. Every SCUD brings heightened fears of inbound chemical weapons. I am tackling EPW issues, war-crimes issues, and working with the PAO to address media concerns.

Our gloves will soon come off as the Iraqis continue to fight dirty; for example, dressing as US soldiers and shooting their own surrendering soldiers or striking markets with their own bombs and blaming us. We served a Ba'ath Party headquarters in Basrah notice with a JDAM that ended their party. Uprisings in Basrah motivated the British 7th Group to help quash the Fedayeen who were firing mortars on their own citizens.

When the environment in southern Iraq becomes more permissive, COL Ralph Sabatino—and probably I—will escort the ICRC to a site visit at the I MEF holding facility. There is a concern that the holding area is not yet constructed, but some serious fighting there is still ongoing, so no complaints from me.

Combat parachute drop successfully inserted the 173rd ABN BDE into northern Iraq this evening. 82nd and 101st are ready for action. The attack on the Iraqi Medina Division south of Baghdad is gearing up—our forces taking advantage of the opportunity to shape the battlefield.

New targeting issues continue to absorb my time throughout the night shift. The collateral damage assessments are becoming more permissive as target lists move from restricted to green as the hard push continues to Baghdad. I still believe that Saddam is either dead or incapacitated. The remaining leadership and the Fedayeen are "dead-enders." They will meet their makers one way or another very soon. We are evaluating the use of military tribunals for these thugs, and are looking forward to instituting them.

The field shower is an impressive one-handed exercise. Start with a dollop of shampoo on your head and move, shower shoes on feet and soap in hand, to the luke-cold shower, drizzle head to toe, avoiding the smallpox vaccination sores, until you are done—less than a minute, max. You are, in principle, squeaky clean.

JOURNAL, 28–29 MAR 2003

A silkworm or seersucker missile flew in under the radar at 0145C 28 MAR and hit the stylish City Mall in Kuwait City. Saddam must have been targeting the Starbucks at the mall. Fortunately, the missile fell short into the water but caused a ruckus in the city and a blast back here in Camp Doha across the bay that seemed to lift the roof off the office, shake the cement floor, and cause CPT Wittman to adjourn his quest for midnight chow and opt for the laundry to tackle his newly soiled drawers. The missile is thought to have been a low flyer under the radar or perhaps was launched from a tugboat or close to the shore on the Al Faw peninsula. Add "exploding mall" to the things-that-wake-you-up-in-the-night list. We continued to shape the battlefield and demolish Iraq's Medina and Baghdad Divisions guarding the approach to Baghdad.

The *Times* writer Michael Gordon, author of *COBRA II*, who has been seeking guidance on the television-transmitter target issue, again drops by and shares his rebuttal to Human Watch. War crimes head the short list of actions on the front burner. Car bombs, shallow graves in Al Nasiriya, suicide bombers and gliders are the latest trends for the I-will-meet-Allah-now crowd. The Fedayeen have gone from paramilitary to regime death squads. The British air liaison is entertaining at the night BUA, reporting that the evening's plans are to implement "robust air sorties without respite." Love the Brits. One of their armored vehicles was unfortunately engaged by one of our passing A10s, calling for another friendly-fire investigation. The Brits have had some bad luck lately.

Some observed items of interest: dolphins serving as mine detectors in the port approaches doing a surprisingly good job, a toilet paper dispenser in the latrine labeled "Saddam Voting Ballots," the free laundry that has a temporary 1700 hours closing that's become permanent—or a close-when-they-see-me attitude. My sixth meal interrupted by SCUD siren tonight has forced me to eat dessert first and otherwise prioritize my meals.

Our JAG team may be soon focusing on war-crimes forensics and documentation assistance; both we hope to take on as follow-on war-crimes commission work. EPW facilities construction is way behind—we first scoped out a land-mine field to build one on. The boys up front cleaned up the southern sector and are running down the bad guys on the fringe. The air campaign is indeed robust, so that the Medina Division is believed to be reduced to 50% strength.

Nice flood of emails from all over poured in when Erin gave them the okay. An email from Mom left me sad and concerned about Dad, though. He's such a great guy. Mom seems to be holding up well. Diane and Rocky, as always, are always on my mind. No new mail. Boxes apparently in the mail zone. Duke out of tourney, ACC teams completely finished this year.

Email to Diane, 28 MAR 03: *All okay here, though a blast boom just rattled the ceiling of the office like a large sonic boom. Couple captains in our shop about crapped their pants. It did seem pretty darn close. It apparently hit the city mall downtown, no one but a night janitor hurt. One SCUD must have slipped under the radar.*

Email to Mom, 29 MAR 03: *Our guys on the night shift merely added the blast to the list of crazy things that wake you up over here. My entry: "Exploding Mall."*

KUWAIT, CHRONICLE #4
28 MARCH 2003

At D+8 we have our jaws set and teeth clenched as we get report after report of Iraqi violations of the laws of war. It is all too easy to get complacent in thinking our enemies will follow the rules of war established over 3,000 years of civilization. Perhaps it's easy to expect proper conduct and compliance with the rules when you are the one generally kicking their butts. Such is the general opinion here. The troops are angry and their anger is raised a degree with each SITREP and SPOT report of Iraqi atrocities. Our team may well be tasked to assist in the forensics, documentation of evidence, and eventual disposition of these crimes—putting into action the pen that may here be mightier than the sword. These crimes range from the bizarre to the sadistic to the horrible. There will be a day of retribution, with the JAGs serving as the clean-up crews for those Fedayeen, first termed "paramilitary" and now "regime death squads," who have survived the brunt of our offensive so far.

Operations continue to be unbelievably successful with relatively miniscule casualties under the circumstances, despite what you may read in the *Times* or hear on CNN. The boys up front are tough professionals. They are real heroes with raw courage. These might be high-tech times, but our men up front are high-time heroes. We are working ridiculous hours here on targeting issues, all patterned to avoid friendly-fire incidents and avoid civilian collateral damage. Often—in the face of the atrocities—you want to remove the gloves and hit back hard, but you remind yourself that we are Americans and must take the high road.

It is a deadly game we play as we watch live Predator feeds on several moving targets that disappear before our eyes as our weapons home in. EPW and law-of-war issues along with friendly-fire or collateral-death investigations grab up the rest of our long hours. Of course, we are motivated by the boys up front who are going on fewer, if any, hours of sleep and are continuously both on guard and on the attack. Remember them in your prayers, for they do the work for all of us to their rear.

The technology is remarkable in every aspect of the war. For instance, global-positioning systems allow us to precisely direct ordnance and follow from here individual tanks and Bradley Fighting Vehicles on the battlefield. My roommate is with Bradley, and they can remotely monitor the maintenance status and specific location of each of these fighting vehicles from the battlefield to here. Another technological advance is the video teleconferencing capability. VTC capacity allows commanders in the field to link up face-to-face remotely. Staff secretly communicate vital missions and operate in electronic chat rooms. Radar-directed Patriot missiles launched daily intercept incoming SCUDS/missiles by some miracle algorithm of physics. All this is remarkable stuff in the middle of a fight. We have seen the bizarre, as in the case where the first three rounds in each of one enemy unit's rifle magazines were blanks, and the amazing, as when the Fedayeen ran suicide missions south in a convoy of Chevy trucks only to get robustly crushed by our cavalry. To this latter development, MG Thurman declared, "Thank god they weren't in Fords, for then we would have had a serious fight on our hands!"

Quotes from the Command Operations Center are equally entertaining. Last night, the British air component liaison officer dryly reported that they will implement "robust air accommodations, prosecuted without respite throughout the evening." One of my favorites is instructions from our night operations G3 extolling folks to quit "dick-dancing around on this issue." and "Y'all need to undick this"—funny enough in private conversation, but hysterical when you hear a senior officer say it over the loudspeaker.

If we weren't at war, it would make a great script for a future *Law & Order* or an old *Hogan's Heroes* show. Unfortunately, it's not a game but a deadly engagement—where rules of engagement are turned on their heads when the enemy dresses in US uniforms to commit atrocities, executes its own citizens, holds children at gunpoint for shields or blackmail, or feigns surrender. Days are running together here on the twelve-to-fourteen-hour night shift as we adapt to the continuous war tempo and pressure. We continue to dream of home, families, the beach, fishing, and sports. The closest we get are letters and e-mails from home that we read time and time over just to keep something soft in our minds.

All in all, though, thanks to low-high humor and infusions of ice cream, we are doing well, persevering and continuing to be amazed by the good work done in front of us by those who are the edge of the spear. Again, do keep them in your prayers.

29 MAR 03 (D+10)

- **101st Air Assault DIV conducts deep attack vicinity Karbala**

30 MAR 03 (D+11)

- **V (US) Corps and I MEF occupy attack positions vicinity Karbala and Al Kut**

JOURNAL, 30–31 MAR 2003

We started off the evening with another siren. Nothing but a false alarm though. The Kuwaitis put a series of low-level radar and counter-missile screens up. The British air evac chopper had to reroute as a result. Problems abound. The war atrocities continue. A well outside Al Nasir was found to have cyanide in it. The Iraqis lined up women and children in front of them as they crossed a bridge over the Euphrates—no worries; 101st Air Assault took out the vehicles, scattering the women and children.

82nd Airborne is into the fight now and kicking ass. Classic entry, coming into the fight and immediately tallying several scores of KIAs inflicted. They are very good. 3ID, 101st, and I MEF are pressing the fight and fixing the Medina and Baghdad Divisions with aggressive reconnaissance in force to maintain contact with the enemy, aiming to draw him out. LTG McKiernan put out need for "aggressive application of ROE." EPW camps going up slow, and our mission keeps slipping calendar to the right. The Marine colonel at the night BUA relayed the reaction of MajGen Mattis, 1st MARDIV commander (and future secretary of defense), to problems with snipers along MSR Tampa—"We don't need a f**king FRAGO, just tell us where they are and we will kill them."

The Red Zone—as in football—is the area of approach to Baghdad, i.e. from the twenty-yard line to the goal line. Operations at this juncture are—according to J3 MG Thurman—"setting conditions for the Red Zone fight." One of our convoys hit a child as he was coming south on Tampa, watching an old man on the side of the road. Of course, the driver pressed on to avoid an ambush. We're still trying to determine what happened to the child. The British air captain reported that they were continuing to "rain destruction, disruption, and neutralization of the Medina and Baghdad" in order to "well and truly set conditions for the destruction of the Al Nida and Medina [Divisions] with strikes that deliver full CFLCC support with unremitting pressure."

The British 1st DIV commander reported that Iraqi forces reinforcing the southeast, around Basrah, were struck hard as the enemy keeps reinforcing failure. COL Forrest chastised the laser pointers used during last night's briefing and admonished the wielders to "quit measuring the size of your lasers!" Tonight we worked with FUOPS (Future Operations) to develop a plan to bring 600 to 700 Iraqis from the Iraqi National Congress into the south for the fight and a publicity shoot. We'll see. A billion legal obstacles and problems to integrating, arming, and trusting this bunch.

A war-crimes meeting with Mortuary Affairs, forensic science officers, CID, and a pathologist was held at 1300 on my birthday—hell of a birthday. Kick it in with working 12 to 7 a.m., sleeping a couple of hours, discussing war crimes and other villainy, sleeping a couple of hours, and starting back to work from 5 to 12 p.m. Happy Birthday!

I did have a couple of nice surprises, though. One was a call and chat with Diane at the beach. It was great just to hear her voice. We promised not to miss each other's birthdays again. Emails came pouring in from the firm, several cards from folks back at the church in Greenville, one from Kathy Joyner's friends from Texas, and one from the Hensleys—a classic cleavage-to-butt-crack card. Also, four boxes of stuff showed up from the firm. Enough pogey bait for an army . . . and a slice of birthday cake that held up all right. Reminded me of the scene in the *Battle of the Bulge* where Robert Shaw captures a fresh chocolate cake sent across the ocean to US soldiers. Excellent. Best among the goodies were the notes, cards and letters, particularly the cards and drawings from the third-grade class at Harnett Elementary School. Classic kid stuff—good for the soul. The emails are also a boost—touching and heartfelt.

All in all, a memorable birthday. The troops are continuing to march to Baghdad. The fight will soon be in the face of Baghdad in the Red Zone and, I hope, the beginning of the end. We shall see.

Email to Diane, 31 MAR 03: *I've had birthdays in some strange places but none so strange as here. . . . After a long night last night, I barely got to sleep before I had to get up to attend a 1:00 p.m. meeting on war crimes with Mortuary Affairs, forensic investigation MPs, special agents and pathologists to discuss the scene investigations, etc. Lake will be providing a bunch of advice for now and look to expand our team involvement later. . . . Bunch of wild stuff tonight. Van ran a checkpoint and our guys properly tried to stop it by shooting the engine, then when it still didn't stop, properly engaged the occupants . . . unfortunately thirteen women and children . . . seven killed. Why would they refuse to stop on order and with warning? Cannot understand it. Other issues demanding attention, too. You'd think there was a war on! Again the routine is a grind 24/7, but I have to remind myself that the boys up front have it worse. . . . Just heard two booms, will email you back.*

1 APR 03 (D+13):
- **PFC Lynch rescued and remains of eleven soldiers recovered**
- **3 ID attacks north through Karbala Gap to secure Baghdad**
- **I MEF attacks north towards Al Kut to secure Baghdad**

2 APR 03 (D+14)

- **3 ID secures Euphrates crossing site seventeen miles south of Baghdad**

3 APR 03 (D+15)

- **1st UK DIV begins Phase IV transition vicinity Umm Qasr**
- **I MEF cuts Hwy 6 to isolate Baghdad from southeast**

JOURNAL, 1–3 APRIL 2003

April Fool's Day! Some day for it! We rescued a young soldier, a nineteen-year old named Jessica Lynch, from the confines—and probable torture—at a hospital in An Nasiriya. It was a beautiful operation combining Air Force, I MEF, SEAL, and other SOF elements. The girl was, in fact, young—just a girl. I'm sure she was scared to death. It pisses you off that the RDS thugs could have tortured her. A battery was found beside her bed, as well as eleven bodies, nine US soldiers in various forms of mutilation and decomposition—some probably from shallow graves. The two Iraqis may well have been a couple—one was pregnant. A female US soldier among them.

The euphoria of the Jessica Lynch rescue—based on tips from Iraqi women who described her being held at the hospital and related tales of torture there—were dampened by Aviation and Mortuary Affairs' coordination to pick up bodies first thing in the morning. The MET/CID team up there investigating the "shallow-grave" reports were held over to begin the investigation of the dead bodies located near or in the hospital. Lake viewed the bodies here at Doha. He said it was rough as bloating/decomp. had set in. He also believed that several had been executed by the Iraqis.

The middle-aged generals were mood-swinging between joy and sorrow as these developments unfolded. News the following night of an AH-60 Blackhawk hard landing, mechanical trouble suspected, killing six. Also, another Patriot missile friendly-fire kill on a FA-18 west of Karbala, along with two other friendly-fire events: (1) a 3ID captain dismounted his command vehicle to look at a destroyed T72 tank and was engaged and killed by a Bradley in an adjacent unit; (2) a soldier killed when the SAW (squad automatic weapon) he was sleeping with went off; and (3) a soldier and an embedded reporter drowned when their HUMMV slipped into the Euphrates' Saddam Canal. This was similar to the Abrams hitting the river, drowning several on board. These are the perils and sidebar tragedies of war.

Perry and Jake were going on Thursday to Umm Qasr to the EPW internment facility to witness some British Article 5 EPW status tribunals. The Brits started their tribunals early for prisoners they captured and were releasing civilians captured. The Brits continued the fun as they played soccer outside Basrah with a group of Iraqi school kids and looked to be having a ball.

EPW Internment Facility in full capacity, Camp Bucca, Umm Qasr, Iraq, principal Coalition EPW internment facility, April 2003. [Photo Courtesy of MAJ Perry Wadsworth]

Someone back in D.C. came up with a novel plan to use 700 to 800 Iraqis now fighting in the north under the Iraqi National Congress, soon to be named the Free Iraqi Fighting Force or FIFF, in the south. This required getting them here, arming and clothing them, training them and getting them into the fight. Great. All in two to four days. The FIFF as originally intended had in several months died on the vine when they found out all they had were criminals and thugs. Here was a way to better spend the remainder of the $92 million allocated by Congress to the FIFF. I was the JAG rep at the FUOPS cell trying to figure out how and if these could be incorporated into the force. Someone from on high really wanted these guys in for a publicity shoot. I frankly thought there were some serious risks in having Iraqis bent on vengeance wearing strange uniforms and fielding AK-47s—in our perimeter. Sounded like a recipe for fratricide. Others had the same concern. However, our concerns were met by news that the first two C-130s were arriving Friday, 4 Apr., to Tallil Airfield/LSA Adder. Tough!

My first brush with MajGen Blackman—a great Marine and CFLCC chief of staff—today. Secretary of State Powell was to visit CENTCOM forward in Qatar this morning and needed information on the death of a British journalist in Basrah on 22 MAR. The investigation was apparently halted when the 1st MARDIV SJA was shot twice investigating the death. Apparently the journalists were following two reported cases of Fedayeen suicide trucks and got in between the trucks and a I MEF armor shell. MajGen Blackman ended up having the only information, so we missed the two-hour suspense—but he had the ball all this time.

Box from Diane dated in early March finally arrived. It was great, although I had finally given in and bought some socks an hour before at the PX! Of course, the box had three additional pair in it. Murphy has struck again!

Email to COL Dan Shearouse, 2 APR 03: *We're fine, the days are so routine now—sleep work eat work—that we can't keep up with the passage of time. We mark time with "How long has it been since the last siren?" Lake is working with CID/Forensics teams on war crimes for now. Jake and Perry still at Arifjan doing legal assistance and some operations, but will head up to recon the Joint Internment Facility in Iraq very soon. Looks more like we will also be heading up behind them soon enough. Phil spending more time in MIL Justice with CFLCC now, and Amanda is there as well. Owen and Beverly still plugging away at ARCENT-KU, and I'm still running the night shift for CFLCC-SJA at the Command Center. Bunch of war-crime, ROE and targeting issues. Boys up front moving fast and kicking butt. We're on our twenty-fifth or twenty-sixth SCUD alert, sixteen to seventeen effectively knocked down, a couple misdirected, a few close enough for discomfort.*

KUWAIT, CHRONICLE #5
3 APRIL 2003

War is indeed a young man's game. The stamina and unfailing motivation of the boys of the 3rd Infantry ("Marne") Division and the Marines of the 1st Marine Division can only be summoned when you're twenty years old. It is a good thing, however, that generals and their staff are older men—fathers and parents. Despite their hard exterior, these seasoned leaders die some with each reported US and British KIA and POW. Their souls ache when the reports of treachery and perfidy by the regime death squads come back to us at the Command Center. But the toughest moments of all are the mood swings involved when young women—really still girls—are taken as POWs and then rescued. These nail-chewing generals like MG Thurman deal with the loss of young men in battle as part of the warrior's rite of passage—horrid but accepted in a war.

On the other hand, the rescue of Private Jessica Lynch tore their hearts apart. The joyous news of her daring rescue almost choked up these he-men, perhaps because they saw her as one of their own daughters. We held our breaths as the rescue was conducted by Special Operations' task forces. The resulting success was indeed inspirational, yet tempered by the horrors of finding the bodies of other soldiers who weren't so fortunate. The bravery of the rescuers was surpassed only by the remarkable coordination between the forces involved. On the lighter side, COL Forrest proudly announced the rescue of [sultry actress] Jessica "Lange" instead of Jessica Lynch, followed by some tittering by the older men in the Command Center and the stray comments that it had indeed been a long eight months over here for COL Forrest.

At D+15, we are in the "beginning-of-the-end" mode as elements of the 3rd Infantry Division and the I Marine Expeditionary Force rush to the outskirts of Baghdad, leaving three of Saddam's vaunted Republican Guard divisions in its wake and left to their own wakes. A few days of close air support, ATTACMs and well-placed ordnance certainly softened them up.

The 101st ABN (Air Assault) is at the Baghdad International Airport, probably booking the first flight home, and the 82nd ABN is cleaning up the approaches to the city. The Iraqi information ministers seem almost cartoonish narrating how they are kicking our butts. They are, in fact, living in a cartoon world. As they send armor south to Basrah night after night, the British blocking-force commander enthusiastically notes that "they are vigorously reinforcing failure" as the 1st British Tanks destroy them by air and by land.

Events are flying by here at the CFLCC Command Center. Every night, we have scores of events that require JAG input—myriad events that can be good, bad, or ugly. Again, the war crimes surface hourly: bayonets shaped as stars, citizens forced to run checkpoints to their death for media value, and other sordid war crimes rampant from the so-called Fedayeen thugs. Yesterday, it was reported that two young men wired with explosives approached a checkpoint, gave up, and told our soldiers that they were wired by the Fedayeen and forced to commit suicide. On top of that insanity, their families were being held as cruel blackmail to ensure they carried it through. Thugs all.

In contrast, the British are classic good sports. Today they played soccer with Iraqi kids outside of Basrah. Reminds me that during the trench-warfare years of WWI, a company of British troops, kicking a soccer ball back and forth, went over the wall into the no-man's land—directly into the face of a machine gun barrage and certain death from the unamused Germans. The British air liaison officer continues to provide an enthusiastic air report during the many night briefings. Last night, the air officer reported that "we will well and truly set conditions for destruction of the Al Nida Divisions" and "the full weight of our fire will be brought to bear and will be focused on the continued destruction and deep attrition of the remnants of the Medina and Baghdad Divisions."

Good old COL Forrest again unwittingly entertains us at the Command Center. After hearing someone reporting on today's criminal activities of the Fedayeen, he declared to the combined audience that "these shits are not freedom fighters, they are death-squad peckerheads." I followed this up the next evening reporting to the same audience that "the SJA is tracking down and bringing the peckerheads to justice." Hooah!

The fog of war takes its own toll. We have had a slew of friendly-fire accidents on our huge, complex battlefield. Most incidents are caused by natural human error: an inverted grid number typed into the targeting computer, rather than the old-fashioned stubby-pencil method, or an automatically engaging Patriot missile battery that misidentifies a plane for a missile. Others are a product of a hyper-technical battlefield: young men and women trying to decide whether a blip on the radar rapidly approaching at night is a jet or a missile, and, in the ten seconds allowed, making the wrong call—thereby going from hero to goat as the first three counter-missiles knock down SCUDs and the last knocks down a passing

British Tornado or a FA-18. Most errors are more basic—a trigger pulled while sleeping with your SAW machine gun, or a mistaken identity made in a sandstorm. All produce sad tales. Each requires JAG investigation and a legal review . . . and many explanations to grieving spouses and parents. Welcome to war.

On the crazier side, I've noticed that most soldiers watch birds and animals more intently here. They actually notice the sparrow and the cat and watch them intensely. Perhaps it is because they are contemplating their involvement in this war. The birds that seem to fly into our SJA area are welcomed. Not for beauty or curiosity, but mainly because someday that bird will serve as a good chemical detector. That's warped, but it's how crazy things can get here. The cat is another story. Fortunately they don't serve Chinese much here!

Instead of the sports section, placards posted over the urinals describe "Rollover Procedures" if your Abrams tank or Bradley Fighting Vehicle rolls. This seems preposterous, but we've had tanks roll over on berms, drive off bridges and into rivers, and pitch into sixty-foot depressions. The predominant safety tip on the placard is "Hang on!" That we are.

4 APR (D+16)

- **Operation Mountain Thunder—air strikes against Iraqi V Corps in the north**
- **3 ID attacks to seize Al Hillah (Medina DIV) and Baghdad International Airport (BIAP)**
- **I MEF attacks to seize Al Kut (Baghdad DIV)**
- **82nd ABN attacks north of As Samawah**

5 APR (D+17)

- **FIFF moves from northern Iraq to southern Iraq**
- **First "Thunder Run" into central Baghdad by 3 ID**
- **I MEF isolates Baghdad from the southeast**

6 APR (D+18)

- **1st UK DIV executes attack into Basrah**

Email to Maggie Alston, 4 APR 03: *The boys to our front are really giving it to the Iraqi peckerheads. Don't know what kind of crack the Iraqi information minister is smoking but it has him delusional at best. Labotomal at worst. The scene here is hectic, as you'd expect. The war crimes mounting, so we have plenty to work on as well as operational issues.*

Email to Lauren Warner, 4 APR 03: *We have plenty of sand here but volleyball sucks due to the camel poop everywhere. Aside from those few inconveniences and the fact that we're in a war, everything is cool here, but not for long. Expecting a balmy 105 degrees tomorrow. I'm working the 5 p.m. to 8 a.m. shift, so my godlike tan may suffer. It is also somewhat tough for the sun to pierce through my Kevlar helmet, chemical suit, body armor and protective mask. My chin(s) is well tanned, however.*

JOURNAL, 4–8 APRIL 2003

The 3rd ID brigade combat teams pushed into Baghdad and showed the information minister who is boss. He is an incredibly cartoonish character. I need to ask Diane to videotape *Saturday Night Live* this week as surely they will have a skit on this clown. Jake and Perry got back from Umm Qasr and the Joint Internment Facility [at Camp] Freddy. They did some pre-Article 5 tribunal screenings. We hope to be there to conduct our own tribunals soon enough. Owen and Phil met with COL Gordon to see if there is any alternative to working at ARCENT with the looney command JAG there. Owen will start back here at CFLCC working on Phase IV issues—post-hostility stabilization and security.

I am amazed at the number of countries and uniforms hanging out here at Doha. Thirty countries have troops here now. Everyone seems to get along fine. We're still working on the legal and LOW/ROE training issues for the new FIFF. I've been point man for CFLCC SJA on this issue. Hard to believe that there are almost no translators here at Doha . . . and even fewer Arabic typists. We finally got the agreements to be bound by our ROE . . . documents translated and out by chopper to Tallil Airfield tonight, 8 Apr.

Barrels of what appear to be blister (mustard) GA and GB gas located near Karbala. Our night FUOPS meetings have been focusing on use of 4ID in the north to seize Tikrit and Kirkuk and figuring out what to do with prisons and inmates when we find them. Quite a mess.

However, grim findings of JSLIST at a Baghdad military prison with holes and blood dampen the lighter moments. Scenes of Saddam's statue on a horse crumbling with our tanks makes us smile. Scenes of the Brits playing soccer in Basrah means their progress is going well.

The mix in our own services is remarkable. Although Doha is somewhat top-heavy, there are still fresh faces, young as our nieces and nephews—hard to believe they are grown soldiers. Amazing what the young nineteen-year-old, typical of those fighting for twenty-one straight days, can accomplish. Remarkable. They are now men proper. Mark's note at how the high-school class was somber at the US cemeteries in France was a reminder that these eighteen to twenty-two-year-old warriors are the first in battle. Those college kids at home need to shut up and look at the tombstones and the heroes here. They will be changed people if they do.

I am feeling the team cohesion slip away, and will correct this if I can. We're glad to help, but we should not be replacement soldiers. I'm sure we'll be used meaningfully as a team soon. I need some patience.

Talked to Diane Sunday night—a highlight. Trip to JIF at Umm Qasr canceled for me when bumped by COL Goetzke. I'll get there soon enough.

For now, the kids act like grown men; grown men act like kids. We endeavor to persevere. The big work lies ahead.

8 APR 03 (D+20)
- **I MEF raids Rasheed District**
- **3 ID completes outer cordon of Baghdad from Tigris north to south**
- **Second "Thunder Run" into central Baghdad by 3 ID**
- **TF 20 commences Hwy 1 interdiction ops north of Baghdad**

9 APR 03 (D+21)
- **I MEF secures Al Rasheed complex southeast Baghdad**

10 APR 03 (D+22)
- **Regime fractured; Saddam statue toppled by people of Baghdad**
- **3 ID holds BIAP**
- **Kirkuk and northern oil fields secured by JSOTF-N**

KUWAIT, CHRONICLE #6
9 APRIL 2003

For centuries, soldiers have been communicating with loved ones using the tools and technology of the day. On the modern battlefield, we communicate instantly through the magic of electrons and satellite phones. For me, and a few other soldiers in on the secret, we talk to our loved ones through the moon. This may seem crazy, but dogs and coyotes have done it, too, and howled about it forever. Only soldiers in the foxhole, in the jungle, and in the desert have listened and learned.

Diane and I have a pact to talk to each other every night through the moon. We look at the same moon and talk. It may be in our imagination, but it seems so real. It makes us realize that we aren't so far apart—we are both looking at the same moon on the same night. We share our thoughts and dreams and thereby cement our love. The desert moon is magical that way. It's good for the soul(s).

At D+21, elements of the I Marine Expeditionary Force and the 3rd Infantry Division met at a bridge over the Tigris River in the center of Baghdad—Saddam's heart. Thus ended twenty-one days of fighting and hell for those Marines and soldiers. Although it wasn't over, it felt good from here, and I'm sure from up the road. My good colleague, the British air liaison, proudly announced last night, "If the [Coalition land forces] continue to put the noose around the enemy's neck, air power will kick the stool out from under his feet," and tonight: "If the regime cannot hide, then it will run, and if it runs, it can be found and it will be destroyed."

Is it just me, or does Saddam look like Joseph Stalin's love child? We watched in awe as monuments to Saddam came tumbling down like his regime has. Scenes of enthusiastic grunts wrapping an American flag around Saddam's neck caused LTG McKiernan to pick up the red phone—yes, there is a red phone in the war room that I plan to use to order pizza when no one is watching—and immediately order that no US flags be permitted to be flown by US forces in those circumstances and no monument is to be destroyed.

This is, of course, the correct implementation of the rules of engagement and politically savvy, not to mention a physiologically safe move; you can hurt yourself crawling around on those monuments—just ask any UNC student who clamors over a goalpost celebrating a payback win on the gridiron over William & Mary! It certainly seemed to me, though, to be sort of a spoilsport order under these circumstances. You might as well have ordered the sailor not to kiss the nurse at Times Square. Anyway, that's why McKiernan is the boss.

Unfortunately, there is still much to do here to prepare for our next operations. This is the arena of Future Operations or FUOPS— so much fun to say. I'm the night FUOPS JAG representative.

Our group brainstorms and develops courses of action and plans for future operations, including the continued fight, the security, stabilization, and occupation of Iraq. We plan for whether and how to carry the fight north of Baghdad, how to get Iraqi Freedom Fighters into the fight, and generally what to do with Iraq once we've caught it. Running a country, even just until you can hand it back to the Iraqis, is an endless task. We try to figure out how to sort and repatriate prisoners of war, how to run the prisons, the asylums and the trains, what to do with war criminals we are investigating and how to best conduct basic governance. It's a blast. No worries, it should be easy . . . not.

Many think that the Army is a social dinosaur. They would be wrong. The armed forces is a wonderful melting pot. Our mess hall is the world's best social brew. Servicemen and women of all shapes, sizes, colors, and nationalities mingle easily. Thirty countries in all comprised the Coalition in this war, with folks from Albania to the Ukraine. The uniforms make a patchwork: Czechs in shorts, Aussies in polka dots, Koreans in checks, our Marines in digitized camo, and Estonians, Macedonians, Lithuanians, Bulgarians, Latvians, Romanians, Emirates, Koreans, Georgians, Slovakians, and Polish in various shades of desert flora. They all get along famously, though you have to be *en garde* against the good ethnic joke tossed here or there, or you'll get your ass whooped!

A twenty-year-old Czech private speaking a blend of sign language and a form of English casually discusses whether tonight's meat was ever on hoof with a fifty-year-old National Guard private from Tennessee speaking a blend of sign language and a completely different form of English. Generals and privates sit and converse as family, sharing news of the front, of family and of home. These quite varied men and women merge here by a unity of purpose and resolve.

Mail call has long been the highlight of a soldier's day, and that still holds true. Soldiers love mail, any mail. They're getting a bunch here. Yesterday, 242,000 pounds were delivered in the theater; today

350,000 pounds. That's a lot of nuts, candy, cards, letters, photos, and a whole lot of lovin'. It is amazing what people send us here—and some of it is even legal! The look on soldiers' faces when they get mail is fantastic. Some open the boxes in front of everyone and announce the contents like presenting an Academy Award; others slink away to open their box in private—here generally in the privy, the only private place in the field, hence "privy." Cards from so-and-so's third-grade class, letters from Scouts, churches, friends, friends of friends, firms, families and fiancées; then, food, sundries and crazy stuff, some from folks we don't even know. We love the smell of the envelopes and the feel of something that was once in the hands of family and friends—in every sense reminding us of home. We just love it! We send a bunch of the mail a few miles north to the boys who have toughed it out for twenty-one days of hell. It is they who most deserve the whole lot of lovin'.

Email to Sean Delaney, 10 APR 03: *Yes, we will still need you and James over here soon. I've put in my recommendation to COL Shearouse to send the rest of Team 2 over in thirty days . . . Despite what others here may think, I don't think you'll look like a tumbleweed in your DCUs.*

4.
BAGHDAD
THE MAN IN THE BIG CHAIR

"Who is this man?" Upon learning that the man on the five-dollar bill was Abraham Lincoln, the elderly Iraqi chief engineer's eyes got big and he exclaimed, "He is the man who sits in the big chair!"

11 APR 03 (D+23)
- **JSOTF-N accepts surrender from Iraqi V Corps**
- **CFLCC Early Entry Command Post flows to Baghdad**
- **CENTCOM releases "playing cards" displaying the fifty-five most-wanted members of the Iraqi regime**

12 APR 03 (D+24)
- **I MEF attacks north toward Baqubah and Tikrit**
- **Civilian authorities turn Mosul over to Coalition**

JOURNAL, 9–12 APRIL 2003

The war continues. Scenes of Saddam monuments torn down, Basrah's boys riding on the broken head of Saddam down streets. In addition, the calming and policing of Baghdad and northern operations to take Tikrit and Kirkuk are in progress. Most of the northern defenses against us are crumbling. Stories of attempts of regime leadership to escape are investigated. My favorite, and one that SJA input was sought on, was that some leadership were reported to be trying to slip out of Baghdad in caskets or wrapped as corpses. We advised that corpses be verified at checkpoints.

Another team (4th LSO) arrived on Friday. Three went down to Arifjan today, Saturday, to work war crimes with Lake. Another (153rd LSO) team arrived tonight. Who knows where they go? I hope that Phase IV will kick in and everyone will head north. Owen is working on Phase IV planning.

The early entry command post—EECP—left Thursday night and was established by Friday at BIAP. The EECP is pretty cool, basically six Conexes on wheels, attached together with almost everything you need to run a command. The Boss headed up yesterday trying to get into the action. I can't imagine there is anything he can do there better than here at Doha.

Our Future Operations work at night is dealing with courses of action in the north, governance, prison administration, and the use of the crazy FIFF forces. Scrubbed the Tornado friendly-fire accident investigation report for COL Goetzke. Called to see the deputy commanding general, MG William "Fuzzy" Webster, and J3 MG J. D. Thurman last night to advise on the age needed for FIFF fighters to fight because they have some thirteen-year-olds in their "force." Waited Friday morning on call to ramp up our repatriation team in anticipation of TF 20 mission trying to seize back our POWs. No luck by our guys, however, but I hope we'll get them back soon. We're trying to get our hands on a deck of the "Blacklist Wanted" playing cards for a great souvenir. No luck so far, but I'm pumping the IO (information) and C2 (intelligence) guys for a few decks.

Perry and Jake went Friday to Umm Qasr to start in on some Article 5 tribunals. We want to rotate up there weekly to join in the fun. Otherwise, we press on at night keeping up with current operations and the wartime routine. We were finally secure enough to stop wearing our body armor and helmets and stop carrying our MOPP/JSLIST and even the mask, though now we feel naked.

Reports of war crimes are still filtering in. They should increase once we get people to rat others out. Speaking of rat, the night FUOPS battle captain is a Marine LtCol named Willard; yes, his nickname is "Rat." He's from the Bronx and sounds like Marlon Brando in *On the Waterfront.*

Mail keeps chugging in. Thursday, 350,000 lbs. in theater; today, 550,000 lbs. Cigs a problem up front since they smoke more under stress, yet they aren't in the pipeline anymore. Erin, my secretary, is on a personal mission to support the smokers. All the Easter candy streaming in to everyone. We'll all have diabetes if this keeps up.

The routine and hours are killing my music, movie and reading practices. I'll have to change my routine somehow to accommodate. Hard to do when you're a pod rat when not working—which is almost never.

13 APR 03 (D+25)
- **Ar Ramadi surrenders to OGA and Tribals**
- **4th ID starts movement into Iraq**
- **Seven POWs recovered vicinity Tikrit**

JOURNAL, 13–16 APRIL 2003

A heads-up that something special was coming my way appeared as my pod-mate Johan burst out "Yes!" as I slept at about 1400 hours Sunday. Our seven POWs were recovered by lead elements of the 7th Marine LAR near Al Samara south of Tikrit. I phoned COL Gordon from the Building 11 phone to advise him that I was aware of the situation and that I was ready for any repatriation team action. When I came around 1600 to the SJA pod, CPT Jim Pietrangelo and I were tasked to go to the TMC to meet up with the POWs and commence the repatriation process. Once there, we were advised that they were en route from KCIA to the Doha TMC. Depending on the level of care required, we needed to be prepared to move to another Level III facility—either Landstuhl Medical Center in Germany, Kuwaiti Armed Forces Hospital or the Navy hospital ship *Comfort.*

I swiftly packed gear for several days and reported back. We eventually departed Doha in a heavily armed military police convoy with the "special packages"—the "Lucky Seven." By 0300, I was sitting on the porch and balcony of KAFH fifth floor, joking and talking with these special folks. The absolute and colossal relief on the faces of these young kids was clear. They wanted to talk to someone, to tell their tale of captivity.

Warrant Officers Ron Young and David Williams—the aviators from 1-227/1st CAV—were the leaders of the Lucky Seven once they met up. The remaining five were from Ft. Bliss with the 507th Maintenance Company—a Patriot missile system maintenance crew. They were young, scared, and not well trained for battle. Their leaders were worth squat—having just recently taken charge—and their 1SGT was dead as a result of his basic incompetence.

The five—along with PVT Jessica Lynch—and their friends were ambushed when the wily Iraqi army turned the MSR Tampa road signs, directing them into the deadly city of An Nasiriyah. Their column crossed a bridge over the Euphrates and realized their error—too late in the game, much too late in a war. They suffered the consequences—predictably, an ambush when they turned around.

To compound the mistake, the 1SGT had allowed their weapons to remain uncleaned, so the weapons jammed as they received fire and could not return it. Seems the 1SGT had them remove their cleaning kits from the stock of their M16s to travel to theater—keeping them in a box, which, of course, did not catch up with the unit. So, without supplies, the weapons went dirty. The result was the difference between fighting through an ambush and catching the brunt of the kill zone.

They were hit hard. A rocket propelled grenade (RPG) into the lead vehicle killed the driver instantly—and severely injured PVT Lynch and others in the resulting crash. They tried to circle together, but, as SGT Riley told us, "It was Custer's last stand . . . and our weapons were worthless. We thought they'd kill us then and there." They were roughed up and groped a bit until they were taken to authorities, then entered into a twenty-three-day touch-and-go captive ordeal, running from An Nasiriyah to locations in Baghdad and north, traveling in ambulances. At night, artillery was fired from the roof of the prisons and the guns hidden during the day in adjacent cells.

They were always in harm's way. They heard shell casings from our A-10 attack planes hitting the roofs of the prisons while they were left locked like rats in their cells as their guards cowered in shelters. They were interrogated sloppily by cartoonish Iraqi thugs, made to piss on another captive in the dark in a warped ruse to create disorientation and disgust. They gave it back when they could. Williams and Young had some SERE (survival, evasion, resistance, and escape) training that they passed onto the rest of the seven. They kept the guards up responding to their requests to use the bathroom—attempting to tire them out. Naturally, the seven bonded in carrying out their own ruses.

SPC Shoshana Johnson was the most injured, having been shot through both feet. The shell severed most of her right Achilles tendon, then continued on to her left, fracturing her lower fibula. They tried to care for it, but kept infection barely at bay. SPC Joseph Hudson took a clean shot through his ass cheeks and some shrapnel in his lower back. He was a superb soldier and held up bravely through it all. SPC Edgar Hernandez was a quiet, dedicated soldier who spoke limited English. He took a clean shot through his right arm with some residual nerve damage to his hand. Fortunately, the POWs were in good spirits, having witnessed no executions, only the battle deaths of their comrades.

Williams and Young were Black Hawk pilots with 1st CAV on the horrendous assault of Karbala on 24 March. The unit dropped to 30% strength in choppers in a mere hour or so of the fight—the first test for their Longbow missile systems. They were not given appropriate close air support when they cleared the horizon, and thus took massive small arms and RPG fire. All but their bird hobbled home from their first hot strike, so they were relegated to V Corps Reserve for the remainder of the hot portion of the war. Altogether, the fight knocked twenty-six of thirty-one birds out of action.

Williams and Young spun their bird into the ground in a hard landing, zeroed their comms, and slipped out to evade their enemies. They swam and glided across a creek, made a dash across a 1,000-yard field to the woods, but were silhouetted in a full moon as clouds cleared. Farmers wielding AK-47s and muskets roughed them up a bit, put a knife to their throats and paraded them around a bit before getting them to local police/army. Blindfolded and threatened with the sound of a slide seating a bullet, they were awkwardly interrogated—using the language and translation problems to their advantage. Then they were rushed to Baghdad in an ambulance and paraded for photos of the group in front of one of Saddam's portraits/monuments.

Thus combined, the group of seven moved constantly just ahead of the 3ID and I MEF elements as the battle raged around them. They grew tired of milk with bread, chicken boiled to toughness, and rice. Once safely returned to us, they gobbled up pizza and burgers. They were shocked that Syracuse had won the NCAA tourney. They were upbriefed on the war, the fighting and their unit members, PVT Lynch, the damaged choppers and their buddies. We brought escorts for them into the hospital from their own units. The pilots wanted to see their commander; the 507th soldiers didn't. Their unit-member escorts were as nervous as the five were happy to see familiar faces. They and we cried, laughed, and listened to their stories. The SERE folks brought in teams to debrief the Lucky Seven, then the Combat Intelligence and Criminal Investigation Division (CID) debriefers were next. I advised them all, particularly the CID on war-crimes issues, the team on the intelligence-gathering protections, and on gifts, life stories, and code-of-conduct issues. I talked and hugged these guys as they decompressed with combat psychologists, nurses, surgeons, and quiet hours on their own, possibly the hardest conversations of all for them.

We spent almost three full and great days together before they pushed on to Germany for more debriefings and then home for Easter. This morning, Easter Sunday, I sit here in Camp Doha watching them on CNN arrive at Ft. Hood and Ft. Bliss. They are heroes, but they are more . . . they are average Americans in the best sense. I now remember that the SERE guys on the repatriation team wear the greatest unit patch: a silhouette of Elvis, surrounded by "If he's out there, we will find him."[7] The 7th LAR Marines missed Elvis this time, but not these seven special packages.

15 APR 03 (D+27)
- **MEK signs "Cease Fire" agreement**
- **Interim Iraqi Authority conference held at Tallil**

16 APR 03 (D+28)
- **3/7 CAV secures Ar Ramadi**

KUWAIT, CHRONICLE #7
17 APRIL 2003

Southwest Asia and the Middle East have fomented, then endured almost constant warfare since the dawn of man. The reason is simple. No, it's not silk, slave trade, undue religious fervor, trade routes, dominion and conquest, or, most recently, oil. Their chronic warfare derives from irritability at the universal lack of sleep compounded by a lack of cold beer. The mosques around here continually trumpet a yodel-like chant that sounds like a man with his you-know-whats in a vise. This aggrieved solo blares out at the most bizarre hours of the day, including 3, 4 and 4:30 a.m., rousting anyone within earshot.

---

7   Speaking of cool patches, our targeting brothers at CFACC wear shoulder patches featuring the Grim Reaper with his scythe. I'd kill for one of those patches!

And when the chanting ends, the silence rousts the roosters, who in turn crow, again rousting anyone within earshot.

No wonder everyone here is always mad at each other. I damn-near shot the loudspeaker, then tracked down and terminated the man who recorded the chant—as if the vise wasn't enough torture for him—and finally went rooster-hunting. Add a complete absence of cold beer to this anger and you have an explosive Arab brew! Thank god they don't have any fast-food drive-thru or there'd be no break at all in the wars hereabouts. As to the lack of beer, we Americans have fought over much less.

Despite the irritating sirens from the mosques and the fowl response, some assignments here make it all worthwhile. Last Sunday, I was tapped to be a member of the CFLCC repatriation team when we received word that elements of the Marine 7th LAR had rescued the remaining seven US POWs. I'm not sure if anyone has ever de-patriated, but we "repatriate" nonetheless. The beauty of this mission is that it means we've recovered our POWs.

I was the JAG assigned to the small, nine-person team of combat shrinks, medical and intelligence officers charged with receiving these courageous heroes and spending time with them as we get them back mentally and emotionally into the fold. We secrete ourselves at an "undisclosed location" with these great soldiers, well away from the media and the bigwigs that want a photo-op, so these soldiers can decompress, recuperate and be debriefed. That third step is where the JAG comes into play. Of course, we cry, we laugh, we hug, we talk—man, do we talk! The biggest shock for the released prisoners of war, of course, is that "Syracuse won the national championship?"

But there's nothing surprising in burgers and pizza being the first requests—anything but chicken and rice or something reported to be chicken and rice. Maybe that's where the damned roosters end up! This emotional return makes you realize what it's like to be an American and what it's like to have them try to take that away from you by force. These recovered POWs have done us proud again.

Coupled with the highly cycling emotions at the POW repatriation retreat, it is good that our generals are parents and good men. The Boss, LTG McKiernan, was the one bigwig we allowed to talk to these young men and one woman. He, as were we all, was at times speechless—choked up in awe of their spirit, bolstered by their never-ending hope of rescue and faith that we'd find them and free them so they'd still be Americans. Our team repatriated them all, but these courageous heroes were always patriots. Perceiving that was why this job and this war make you realize it is worth the fuss. As with my magical-moon talks with Diane, this effort was good for my soul.

At D+27 the war goes well. We now shift to a new phase—stabilization and security. Our team is fairly dispersed but gainfully employed. Two are in Iraq at the internment facilities doing prisoner of war (Third Geneva Convention, Article 5) status review tribunals[8] and sending home some of those merely caught up in the war. One is in charge of war-crimes investigations for now, one is the chief of criminal law for CFLCC, and another team member is the lead JAG planner for the next phase of operations. Not bad for a bunch of good-old Carolina boys and girls moonlighting over here for a while!

With the change of operations comes a change of venue for me, though. I have been tapped to move to Baghdad in the next few days with CFLCC Forward as the senior JAG. Two of us will be living the high life there—no power, no water but plenty of prayer calls and roosters—oh, boy! Well, life is a journey. Though I could do without the roosters.

JOURNAL, 17–20 APRIL 2003

I returned to Camp Doha on Wednesday afternoon and was apprised that I was tapped to go and lead the SJA Forward contingent

---

8   Status review tribunals under Article 5 of Geneva Convention (III) relative to the treatment of prisoners of war, 12 August 1949, are required when there is any doubt as to whether the prisoner is a combatant or other enumerated category of persons entitled to the protection of the Geneva Convention.

in Baghdad. I could have gone to Landstuhl with our POWs, but I was selected to head north to be the senior JAG for CFLCC in Iraq, so am glad I returned. Finally, real front-line action, in Baghdad. I hope to bring our team along behind me.

But getting there isn't all that easy. Seems the CFLCC support battalion's vehicles had been poorly maintained, and as a result needed to be flown to Baghdad rather than driven. The manifest on Thursday night dropped to only me when transport of CLFCC Forward personnel were streamlined to none. So, I was scheduled for one of the later chalks.[9] Sadly, CFLCC and the air boys got into it about the vehicle status—Air Force thinking with some merit that this convoy should be heading north on the ground, not in the air. Regardless, we were bumped a few days. I'm in Chalk 3, heading out Tuesday. I used the time productively and now am ready with bags packed for immediate departure.

I'm going to join up with Marine major Kevin Chenial, who went up last week with the early entry command post (EECP) in anticipation of an early, early regime collapse (EERC?). They were at Baghdad International Airport, formerly Saddam International Airport, but have recently moved to the Al Faw Palace just east of BIAP on Route Green. Neither place had any electricity. However, the area around the palace had promise . . . the promise of more soft turf for more linear feet of slip trench for the needed "class 2 download." Funny how the basics of life in the field remain constant despite the technological revolution of the battlefield.

Jake and Perry are now well entrenched at the internment facility at Umm Qasr—now named Camp Bucca after a Reserve MP killed on 9/11. Both teammates were part of the first Army EPW/civilian detainee screenings and eventual Article 5 tribunals. Lake is still at Arifjan with the 3rd MP (CID) advising on war-crimes

---

9   During Operation Overlord in World War II, the Allied invasion of Europe, aircraft flight numbers were placed on the airborne troops' backs with chalk. In current military terminology a "chalk" may mean either passengers or equipment loaded as cargo. Equipment is loaded in the order it will be needed on arrival.

investigations. Owen is tackling Phase IV planning and Phil acting as chief of criminal law preparing to try several court martials. We are doing well and proving we are value-added to this fight despite the team's physical separation.

On Friday, I attended the major JAG Phase IV planning session. We discussed EPW handling, repatriation, civil and criminal justice systems, law and order and property claims adjudication for a new Iraq. I am excited to get in on the ground floor of creating a new constitution, vetting judges, running tribunals, and crafting basic due-process procedures.

The Marines and soldiers are finding huge weapons and money caches—"cash-caches"? $325 million US dollars were stacked in metal boxes 18" x 18" x 8" behind a false wall in one palace; a $1-billion estimate in gold bricks was found at another location. We must find ways to move and secure this treasure for use by the Iraqi people. This proves how little Saddam cares for his people. For me, the discoveries suggest that he is dead. We are also bringing money in as well to pay the civil servants. $20 million initially with $15 million in $1 bills so they can jump-start the economy there one dollar at a time. Folks, that is a lot of money—and space.

In rooting through the SJA Conex on Saturday, I had to slip around some concertina barricading the parking lot. I had been there the day before and it wasn't there. I didn't think anything about it until I was hip-deep in foot lockers in the darkness of the Conex, and some sergeant yelled, "Are you aware this area is off limits since the Argentinian ambassador is here looking at the remains of an Argentine journalist killed up north?"

I was having a hard time locating the AAA batteries I was seeking and hollered back, "Once the ambassador is finished looking at the body at the Mortuary Affairs Office, he could come over here and help me look for my f**king batteries!" The sergeant just laughed, then asked, "Can I help you, sir?" I guess I was making enough noise grunting and cursing to waken the dead in the next bay across from the Conex.

Lake came up from Arifjan last night, and I took advantage of coming off the night shift to have a great dinner with the boys sans Jake and Perry, share stories, watch part of *Austin Powers,* and drink some near-beers. We pretend these beers are real, but all they do is taste marginal and make you piss three or four times a night.

Email to Diane, 20 APR 03: *Here's word from Perry and Jake about their mission* [EPW Camp, Umm Qasr, IZ]. *As you can see* [in Perry's email below], *we are all doing something worthwhile here and we can be proud that we are doing good stuff.*

Email from Perry Wadsworth, 20 APR 03: *It isn't often you get to interview Iraqi prisoners to decide whether they should be released or detained in prison camp. I heard some stories that were just heartbreaking and some that made me mad. One story I think you'll like was both. I interviewed a young Bedouin sheepherder who was in his early twenties.*

All Iraqi men have an obligation to serve three years in the military unless they buy their way out of it, which is legal, or they get a waiver for things like school or for work in some other form of public service—like police officer. Well, this fella was the oldest of several brothers. His father didn't want him to serve in the military, which isn't unusual for Bedouins, who are basically modern-day nomads. Usually, folks like them and some of the more well-off farming families want their sons to work on the farm and not take three years for military. So, they sell farm animals to come up with the money. If they sell between 50-100 sheep, they can get enough dinars [$500-750 US dollars] to pay off the service. .

If what the Bedouin told me is true, his father sold his daughter (the prisoner's sister) for [the equivalent of] *about $60 US dollars. So I grilled him about this for a while. He saw nothing wrong with it. When I asked him if his father could sell him for cash, he said, "No, men can't be sold, only women."*

I almost kept him in prison just for that. I ended up letting him go because despite his cultural offensiveness to me, he was not involved in belligerent acts against us and didn't appear to be a threat in the future. He was simply a civilian rounded up when troops were trying to eliminate potential threats by people who they couldn't be sure were civilians or military/paramilitary dressed as civilians. . .

I feel comfortable in saying that these were probably the first formal tribunals with a hearing since the Vietnam War. Desert Storm allegedly had tribunals, but they were really paper reviews by a screening officer. We have a lot of lessons learned that we need to put on paper.

21 APR 03 (D+33)

- **Office of Reconstruction and Humanitarian Assistance (ORHA) headed by LTG (Ret.) Jay Garner commences authority in Iraq and begins insertion into Baghdad**

ORHA Mission Statement:
The role of ORHA is to: help alleviate dependence on Humanitarian Assistance; assist in the rejuvenation of a broad-based Iraqi economy by supporting the recovery and repair of critical infrastructure; underpin the creation of effective Governance based on Iraq's rich and diverse cultural, ethnic and religious heritage; so as to assist the Iraqi people to build their own future.

JOURNAL, 20–21 APRIL 2003
Easter Sunday. We've had an annual ritual of sunrise service on the beach at Wrightsville Beach, North Carolina. We always had plenty of sand and the sun breaking over the ocean—stunning. Sunrise service in the PX parking lot at Camp Doha less so, but inspirational nonetheless. Took it somewhat easy this morning

with my first break since we arrived here. I'm preparing for CFLCC Forward's move to Baghdad. Our chalk was bumped to Tuesday morning. Evidently there was some pissing match between the two-stars in the USAF and Army. The Air Force constantly bitching that the Army should be able to drive its vehicles to Baghdad. For me a convoy ride to Baghdad would have been fantastic.

Money continues to drive some issues here. All the generals want to spend the captured money now. Perhaps with good intention but a lousy game plan. My suggestion is to invest it and create a huge Iraqi Trust to educate the Iraqi people.

Phase IV (Eclipse II) OPORD released tonight converting many operations from hostilities to security/stabilization phase. Perhaps the beginning of the end, or better yet, the end of the beginning. I'm communicating with Marine major Kevin Chenail, who will be my partner in Baghdad. He's been there nearly two weeks with the early entry command post.

Received four of thirteen boxes of goodies from Smith Anderson. Unbelievable stuff. The packing list was similar to one from a Ducks Unlimited Banquet. Features were golf balls, seven Victoria Secret catalogues, a pile of *News & Observer* papers—we were short on toilet paper, so we could put these pages to good use—and a convenience-store's-worth of pogey bait. COL Gordon dubbed me the Pogey Bait King. I am. The best, however, was four tubs of homemade tollhouse cookies from Kathy Joyner. They lasted about ten minutes. All the manufactured food in the world can't beat good homemade cookies. It's not the taste alone, but the taste-memory of home that makes the cookies special.

Talked to Diane tonight. Always nice to hear her voice and about her day. Don't know the commo up in Baghdad, so am not sure whether electrons are available there to talk to home like I have been. Continue to fine-tune packing and prepping for move forward. Drew my 9 mm and 45 cal. ammo basic load on Monday night to avoid the 0300 rush. Lowered the 12th JAG guidon and packed it with the South Carolina flag—Palmetto—that Phil was given by the South Carolina Legislature.

22 APR 03 (D+34)

- **101st air assaults into Mosul**
- **First Shia pilgrimage in twenty-five years commences between Karbala and An Najaf; 82nd ABN provides security**

JOURNAL, 22 APRIL 2003

After an 0500 manifest at the Camp Doha theater, we boarded a commercial bus for the Air Pod (APOD) out in the desert of Western Kuwait. We packed in like sardines for the trip. I was buddies with the chalk leader, so I got special treatment and was driven to the departure passenger terminal while they readied the vehicles. The chalk leader suddenly grabbed me and said we had to run. Apparently the vehicles weren't ready to ship, but we could send some passengers on the first C-130 heading north.

We drove across the KCIA/APOD tarmac to Hercules Alley—the C-130s. We drove up to the tail of a revving plane as they were raising the bay hatch. I swung onto the plane, and grabbed a cargo seat as the hydraulic rear hatch closed. A minute later we were airborne. Only then did I realize that I had been thrown onto LTG McKiernan's plane.

I feel like Forrest Gump—falling into the right place at the right time. The only person in CFLCC Forward to make the flight, and not only that—suddenly seated with the Boss. Can't wait for arrival when I'm treated like some sort of bigwig. Funny how things like this happen to me constantly.

The two-hour flight to Baghdad was fairly uneventful. I asked whether we could move about, but the airman advised against it, reminding me that we were still flying into a combat zone. The last flight he had been on took some random AA fire and had to do a little dodging. When they did dodge, one passenger who was moving about fell into some sharp, hard cargo and was severely injured.

I slept most of the flight, apparently on LTG McKiernan's shoulder! We landed at Baghdad International (BIAP) at 1150 and quickly taxied to a secure area. As the ramp dropped, we hustled off with our bags while the C-130 kept its props turning. We shuffled at right turns to an MP escort. Some MP sergeant grabbed my bags, assuming I was with the general and his staff, and threw them onto the general's HUMMV. An aide asked where I was headed. Once he knew we were headed to the same spot, I was in like Flynn. I rode in the HUMMV behind the general a roundabout way to the palace command post. We proceeded what seemed about 10 km to the palace. This fantastic edifice must be the lake palace. So much for the Oil-for-Food program. Instead, it has been an Oil-for-Palace program.

USMC Maj Kevin Chenail in front of our home at CFLCC Forward Headquarters in the Al Faw Palace, Baghdad. (April 2003)

We pulled past several Bradleys securing the palace perimeter, past several cars that had been on the wrong end of the Bradleys, and drove on to the palace. It was symmetrical, three stories tall and decadent. The entrance doors were two-storied and grossly ornate. The surrounding columns were of black marble, and the entrance foyer had a spectacular two-story chandelier and dome.

One of the wings had been hit by a precision JDAM (smart bomb) strike. From the roof—which Kevin Chenail and I climbed to through the kitchen access stairs—was a man-hole size hole where the JDAM hit, penetrating through two more floors, leaving a similar-circumference hole, until it detonated on the first floor in Saddam's bedroom. The blast had exploded the walls outward with unbelievable force. Marble and pieces of a chandelier and just about everything else was in shards everywhere. What remained through the rest of the house was huge furniture and ornate columns and chandeliers and a conference/dining room the size of Raleigh's Memorial Auditorium.

The CFLCC EECP, established in one of the quads outside, was the center of activity. SJA had a station in the combined effects shelter with IO, Aviation, FSE, and the air liaison. ORHA and CSB/CA were inside the palace, with the general's quarters, furnished with complete lack of water and power. Surrounding the wide moat-lake were about fifteen other beautiful mansions, each appearing to have bomb damage, too. These housed regime leadership. The main bridge to Baghdad's inner city had been bombed. Several sheep—brown-faced, supposedly delicious, and black-faced, not so—grazed domestically around the palace on the few strips of grass in Baghdad.

I was assigned a cot in a large bedroom for O-5s. A handful of other O-5s were ahead of me and claimed some of the palace furniture. Many from O-4 and below claimed space in another room and on the heavily columned balconies around the palace.

Sporadic gunfire and explosions came to us from a distance. Attack helicopters, C-130s, Chinooks hauling Conexes, Bradleys, and tank columns surrounded us intermittently. Bradleys patrolled the area. A few officers stole some time and a boat to shoot around the lake. The boathouse and the remaining bridges make the palace look like Pharaoh's digs from a Hollywood movie set. Apparently, the Presidential Palace downtown is more spectacular in size if not in design. I grabbed some marble pieces as paperweights outside the JDAM strike and found several chandelier beads in the debris that would make an interesting necklace, bracelet, or earrings. Quite a conversation piece.

The lack of power and water were an inconvenience. We had to make do with a slit- trench latrine tent. It was unisex depending on what direction the sign was facing. The sleep room was on the third floor. It promised a long, difficult path for my nighttime overactive and undersized bladder. Most peed in bottles or bags, but that got somewhat difficult at night. I took a bunch of pictures, including the obligatory toilet shot for Diane's dad, who often regaled us with his WWII photo of Hitler's toilet at the Eagle's Nest—also captured by elements of the 101st ABN and Third Army.

We were issued brand-new cots. Some warped idiot conceived the army cot. No human can put an army cot together properly. The two end pieces—which unavoidably hit the deck like a dinner bell upon every assembly and disassembly—are impossible to place on the end of the cot by even the most tremendous force. There are many techniques for putting these end pieces on, but the process defies both physics and material science.

One technique is to use another couple of end pieces as levers to attempt to slip the pieces over the end of the cot. Great idea but flawed when you're flying solo. The second way is either to kick your foot hard against it like a jackhammer or invert the cot and stand on the end piece. Neither works, so everyone ends up putting the piece underneath the prongs or one on and one off. Mosquito netting is another exercise in futility. I rigged my netting up between some sort of easel found lying in the bomb debris and a screened window. It worked, but it was fragile where it integrated with the cot. If the gust is big enough, my cot, the netting assembly, and me are going somewhere as one.

IRAQ, CHRONICLE #8
23 APRIL 2003

I've often said, "When you enter Iraq, enter in style." All right, so this is the first time I've said it. I did it, however. Even so, it made for a crazy twist in this journey. I was supposed to be in the first chalk in the (CLFCC) Forward move to Baghdad on Tuesday 22 April. I had buddied up to the movement leader and he was taking care of me. I was one of several who would move with some of the equipment and vehicles in the first C-130 Hercules Aircraft out of the Air Pod (APOD).

After dropping me off alone at the passenger wait area, some captain grabbed me and said I needed to run with them to Hercules Alley, a series of C-130s lined up down on the tarmac. Our SUV dodged several planes across the runway to the first Hercules in line. It was fired up and the rear ramp was coming up ready for takeoff. We stopped directly behind the plane and I sprinted onto the closing ramp, my bags thrown in behind me. I helped the crew strap my stuff down, wiped the sweat off my brow and plopped down on the cargo netting seat, beside LTG McKiernan, the Boss. I apparently had jumped on the wrong plane and was now an unofficial member of the general's personal staff en route to Baghdad! Figures.

We arrived in Baghdad before noon and were met by an MP convoy. They grabbed my bags, thinking I was part of the general's entourage, and threw them into the Boss's HMMWV, and away we went with our mounted .50 caliber escort to Saddam's lake palace north of Baghdad International Airport. We passed the remnants of the Iraqi Airlines Fleet—they had a new option, moon-roof seating—

out of the terminal still marked "Saddam International Airport." We passed mosaic signs of Saddam, one sans moustache that was removed, shaved off by an earlier passing mounted .50 cal. gun.

Flight Delay! Destroyed plane at Saddam International Airport (renamed Baghdad International Airport, or "BIAP") upon arrival of CFLCC Early Entry Command Post (EECP) in April 2003, Baghdad, Iraq.

The palace is on an island, or at least the biggest moat I've ever seen. It is, or was, impressive. Marble columns, three-story chandeliers, gold mirrors and mosaic ceilings. The LTC quarters are on the third floor—eighty-two steps up, sixty-two steps down!—in an ornate yet starkly bare room the size of a basketball court.

The palace has four symmetrical wings, though the wing housing Saddam's bedroom isn't so symmetrical anymore. A JDAM-guided bomb penetrated the roof and down through two floors until bursting in Saddam's bedroom on the first floor. The hole in the roof is the size of a manhole cover, although no item larger than a manhole cover remains on the first floor!

The EECP (early entry command post) is set up in command trailers outside one corner of the palace. I'm in the combined effects shelter that includes Fire Support, Special Operations, Information Operations and Aviation stations. Each of these six trailers is connected by catwalks and contains ten stations with all the bells and whistles (VTCs, Fox News, monitors and commo beyond belief), all in a twelve-foot-by-fourteen-foot pod on wheels that also collapses into a seven-by-fourteen-foot trailer. No, you can't pick one up at your local RV dealer. Not that even Bill Gates could afford one. These things are otherworldly, almost as much as the palace itself is.

CFLCC Early Entry Command Post (EECP) shelters at the Aw Faw Palace, April 2003. The EECP was comprised of connected high-tech, expandable, and air-deployable trailers with all the bells and whistles, except a decent coffee maker.

The palace is posh. Unfortunately, it has no power or water. As such, it's a long trip in the dark at night to respond to my forty-five-year-old overactive and undersized bladder. Here's where it gets interesting. Chem lights mark the path through the palace to a slit-trench, mixed-gender latrine tent outside. A slit-trench, for those unfamiliar with the term, is six pipes stuck in the ground for the men and a three-hole seater over a trench for females and class 2 downloads. The "mixed-gender" is deceiving, because it depends which side of the sign is turned up. Posh? We don't need no stinkin' posh . . . we have a stinkin' latrine! We also have sheep. Fortunately, we only have a few Marines, so the sheep are not quite as nervous as usual! I'm sure that it's only a matter of days, now, before we are offered a mutton MRE selection.

The war around us expresses itself in sporadic gunfire and explosions. Attack choppers patrol the skies; Bradleys and Abrams patrol the ground. We remain locked but not loaded. Settling in for the show, several of us smoked some cigars and watched the sunset over the surrounding lakeside mansions of the regime leadership. We sat in Saddam's sofas and chairs on the balcony. As in the Mastercard commercial, cigars $8; antique sofa and chair, $8,000; smoking a cigar in Saddam's chair in his crib? Priceless!

Tomorrow I head downtown to sample the Presidential Palace and try to figure out how to get the Iraqi courts up and running. I just hope I'm not the one up and running.

JOURNAL, 23 APRIL 2003

Woke up staring at a mosaic ceiling and chandelier seen through the light filter of my mosquito netting. I took a bottle of water down to a marble sink on a boat dock around the palace and shaved and shampooed. Baby wipes completed the shower, and I was lovely and scented. For unknown reasons, MREs were declared optional for breakfast, lunch and dinner—optional if you didn't want to eat. The night before, Kevin and I had sat in our foldout chairs watching the sun set over the palace and lake from one of the huge third-floor balcony walkways, enjoying our MREs, some coffee mocha—a coffee packet and a cocoa packet—and some cigars. We overlooked BIAP and the desert night sky. Since there was no power anywhere we could see, the sky was spectacular.

The EECP shelters are pretty phenomenal. Each shelter has ten work stations embedded in a ten-by-eight movable room—prewired and computer-, monitor- and commo-ready. These collapse even further if needed, and are on wheels. Six of these are joined by a walkway, and together they are a powerful, compact command post. To facilitate targeting decisions, the SJA station is with the other combined-effects Aviation and Fire Support guys. As most targeting was completed, the shelter Command Post (CP) was more of a troubleshooting cell. The coffee maker quickly became the centerpiece of the action, along with the Miller-Lite swimsuit-beauty foldout from *Sports Illustrated* that decorated the shelter's wall.

SJA station in combined effects shelter, CFLCC EECP, Al Faw Palace, Baghdad, Iraq, April 2003. Putting the pilots and PSYOPs guys with the JAG was gutsy. Leaving them without a coffee grinder was nuts.

I am trying to serve as the CFLCC Forward SJA as well as the ORHA legal Liason Officer (LNO), and plan to hook a ride into downtown Baghdad for the latter mission. As the environment was still not permissive, we remained armed with pistols locked and loaded. Some knuckleheads with the MEF tried to fire off an Iraqi RPG this morning, killing three Marines and wounding seven. FRAGOs were issued immediately not to test-fire any captured weapons. Another soldier somehow managed to fall off a convoy vehicle and wasn't missed for several hours until he was found dead by the side of the road by a later column of Marines. We have to remind folks that there is still a war on here.

JOURNAL, 24 APRIL 2003

What a wild day! A Greek Orthodox Navy chaplain and I set off to hook a ride to visit Civil Military Operations Center (CMOC) and ORHA in downtown Baghdad at 0700. We were ready and waiting in our battle rattle—but no ride. While we waited around for a lift, one of the former US ambassadors strolled up. We introduced ourselves, but I lost his name and hated to ask. He was one of the folks in charge of ORHA. They had some press briefing to attend downtown and took off with their MP escort and armor-plated Suburban. A while later I hooked us up a ride with Col Mike Williams, "the Duke," chief of staff to JTF-4 that was soon renamed Task Force Fajr, meaning "new dawn." He was a bull colonel Marine who chewed on his subordinates for breakfast. His sidekick is an internal medicine physician from the Cleveland Clinic named Chuck "Doc" Fisher. Doc was part of the Civil Affairs (CA) surgeon shop who went to wars just for kicks, and indeed, was having a ball! We hit it off. When we saddled up, Doc gave us a rundown on how to fire out a small crack in the windows while moving through an ambush. The MP vehicle was armored everywhere with bullet-proof glass. A mounted M60 machine gun was on top and an MP sergeant driver below.

We took off to the Duke's pointing finger and a "Tallyho!" After clearing the gate, we crossed over a tank trap and down the highway hell-bent for leather. We passed ten to twenty bombed shells of cars along and in the roadway. A few vehicles were on the road beside ours—mainly Bradleys and Abrams. These guys commanded the road in every respect.

We started to see a bunch of Saddam pictures, posters, mosaics, paintings and monuments. Each had been destroyed, tangled, twisted, defaced, or obliterated in some way. We passed a few checkpoints— the end of an Abrams' peashooter—and mainly had the highway to ourselves. We passed the Tomb of the Unknown Soldier and a parade ground with the crossed-swords entranceways. At the base of each was a hand holding a gigantic sword and hundreds of army helmets piled twenty feet or more in cargo nets and across the road as speed bumps. Those were Iranian helmets from the Iraqi–Iran War of 1980-1988, and the hands were said to be modeled after Saddam's. Just down the road, we saw Saddam on his horse, toppled over on the ground.

We dropped off a reporter hitching a ride with us at the conference center in the city where ORHA's chief, LTG Garner, was holding a public town meeting. Then, we went on to CMOC to drop off the chaplain and me. We passed through huge columns and arches with nonfunctioning AA pieces on top before finally arriving at the ORHA headquarters. After learning that my lawyer counterparts at ORHA were out until the afternoon, I sprinted back out and barely caught my convoy with Doc and the Duke. Off we went to the Ministry of Health for a meeting, crossing over the Tigris and into the heart of the city.

The city was a huge mess, with people everywhere in the streets, herding together, watching us intently—some just staring, some giving us the thumbs-up indicating either the Western "Great job" or the Arab "Screw you." The streets were congested with every imaginable car from the '70s and '80s, all small; all barely running. The lines to a gas station ran three to four blocks, two cars wide. The street vendors plied cheap and awful goods—7-UP, cigs, rugs, electronic crap, microwaves, whatever you didn't need. The markets were a free-for-all flea market. The buildings were either bombed out or, more commonly, just poverty stricken and poorly maintained.

We had a few hairy moments when our convoy either got lost or bogged down in traffic and we took significant fire—any fire is significant if you are the one taking it, of course. Fortunately, we survived a few close shots and some soiled pants. We eventually controlled the road, assisted by the glimmer and dint of 7.62 cal. bullets from our mounted M60. The driver, a great sergeant from San Antonio, kept telling our specialist sitting on top in the mount to keep situational awareness (SA). I for one had my eyes on the crowd and my hand on my pistol.

At one juncture we were stopped and vehicles jammed our route. The busy street congealed around us, as did the crowd: Ah, we're likely screwed. The sergeant told us to chamber and ready all we had and go red—hot, off safe—and close all windows in readiness for a real fight. We eventually drove through without too much incident—although I know the two MPs were really nervous, most likely because they had a JAG in the vehicle with a loaded pistol.

The kids were all brown-eyed and smiling. The smaller the cuter, as always. They all gave us the real thumbs-up. The other drivers were less friendly but all curious. We drew a lot of stares. We stared as well and smiled, while keeping SA. Almost no women were about. Those out were older women, principally in their traditional black-robed garb. We continued on to find the Ministry of Health, which was intact structurally but missing windows. We could see it ahead but had a difficult time driving to it. We circled some military statue at a traffic circle at least five times. We finally parked on the street at a bus stop and Doc, the Duke, CAPT Denny Ammundson—a Navy physician—and I took to the streets to walk to the ministry.

We passed donkeys, panhandlers—I exchanged a couple US dollars for five 250-IZ (Iraqi) dinars, of course getting ripped off, but I wanted some dinars with Saddam's face on them—and moved into a huge crowd that had gathered at the ministry. I'm not sure what they were all doing there. Doc remained outside trying to call in our location by grid from a handheld GPS and a cell phone. When it became clear that he didn't know how to use either one, I gave the cell phone a try but to no avail. Calls kept coming in, but we couldn't even figure out how to answer them. We were products of a different generation, I suppose. So there we were, stuck by ourselves and surrounded by hundreds of Iraqis.

Appropriate wheels for Task Force Fajr, a HMMWV named "Grumpy Old Men with Guns"; Warner, "Doc" Fisher, and CAPT Dennis Ammundson, USN (pictured), were, indeed, the grumpiest of men.

Finally, we went in up to the conference with the ministers. I stood over in the corner and just watched. On one side of the table were the Iraqi Ministry of Health representatives—about eight or nine physicians. On the other side was Steve Browning, the ORHA ambassador who had the night before been asked to tackle healthcare as well as power engineering, his real forte. The Duke and the V-Corp surgeon and his entire staff, along with Doc and me, were the rest of the US contingent. International Committee of the Red Cross (ICRC) and Cooperative for Assistance and Relief Everywhere (CARE) had representatives there as well. The meeting seemed to be cast under the shadow of the largest decoration in the room—a large mural of

Saddam helping the sick and injured. His head was painted over in blood-red paint to obliterate or comment on his tenure. The meeting was interesting in part because these ministers had all been appointed to their post by Saddam. After Browning introduced everyone at the head table and went through the obligatory gestures in thanking the ministers for coming, he got to the point.

"We are the occupying power and we will get the system up and running first, then fine-tune it, working with you. But first we have to have security so that employees will come back, and then power, water, and sewer so that they have something to come back to."

The look of relief in the ministers' eyes and faces was profound. Their primary interest was whether they still had jobs. They had jobs now until vetted for competence and allegiance. Earlier, a tremendous power struggle had ensued when the regime collapsed—the ministry and the physicians and administrators at several hospitals still opposed each other, so the room was tense. The meeting lasted about an hour. Interviews with the few press reporters present were conducted, and off we went through the streets to our convoy vehicles.

The Duke, of course, never wore his Kevlar, just his Marine soft-cap. We were bombarded by panhandlers—just boys, really, who had wads of 250-dinar bills to exchange. I have no idea where they came from and did not ask. The group headed back into the noontime traffic locked and loaded. We passed the Palestine Hotel where the journalists hung out, now surrounded by concertina and my favorite twins—Bradley and Abrams. We moved quickly by a few protesters with signs into a rough area that eventually opened into a handsome cul-de-sac housing the ICRC.

We left our arms with our MP buddies and headed in. Dr. Chris Giannou, a Greek-born, Toronto-trained cancer surgeon, was the head ICRC surgeon and our host. We went through a garden into Chris's room in the back. We discussed the current state of the healthcare system in Iraq and the payment tiers for patients similar to Canada's system. We discussed how to get doctors back to work and away from the primary care provided on an emergency basis from the mosques. A danger was that the mosques and religious leaders could unduly influence the plan.

Chris was an interesting sort. He had survived many wars, civil and international, and some harrowing experiences. He had recently been running a hospital in a 200 x 200-meter compound under constant attack for fifteen months. The hospital was underground and each one there was down to 500 to 600 calories a day since the UN relief couldn't make it through.

We then went on a great cruise to Uday's palace and the barracks of Saddam's Republican Guards. The palace and grounds were unbelievable, housing cheetahs and other wild animals. At the barracks, we ran into a bunch of Special Forces guys who showed off some great Special Operations weapons obtained from the Aussies. We proceeded on to the Republican Guard Palace—a gigantic palace with four gigantic busts of Saddam wearing a pharaoh-type helmet. These busts were fifteen feet tall and eight feet across. Hence the nickname "Four Seasons" Palace that ORHA had made its base of operations. A grand old time in Baghdad today!

We ended the day watching a perfect sunset and smoking some cigars, even though it only made us miss home that much more.

IRAQ, CHRONICLE #9
25 APRIL 2003

The Australian ANZAC Day is akin to our Memorial Day. Aussies around the world celebrate the day they landed on the beaches and fought against the Turks and their German allies in the trenches and on the cliffs of the Gallipoli Peninsula in the WWI Dardanelles Campaign of 1915. The Aussies mark this loss as the moment when they came of age. They started the assault with a predawn shot of rum and then attacked the beaches at 0600.

This morning at 0550 the Aussies, chiefly special forces groups that had fought so terrifically in western Iraq, invited us to join the celebration and remembrance. They poured us a shot of rum in our Joe—a "shotgun breakfast" that we drank as the sun rose over a combat HMMWV draped with the British, Aussie, and American flags. The Coalition generals, British Maj Gen Whitley, LTG McKiernan and an Aussie BG, assembled before our little group of twenty or so and gave a few words of praise to the boys of 1915 and their descendants here today.

Taps played from across the lake as they read the same prayer of eighty-eight years ago before so many Aussies hit the beaches. Not many Victoria Crosses were given out, however, as the action had to be witnessed by an officer when the valiant Aussies died there or later in the bloody trenches and cliffs above Gallipoli. Few men or officers survived the campaign as they charged over the trench berms into streams of enemy bullets.

The dawn service was inspirational not just for the remembrance of the ANZACs (Australian–New Zealand Army Corps) but for the reminder that wherever Americans have fought in any sizable engagement since WWI, the Aussies have been beside us. I commented to one of the Brits next to me that it took many Americans 225 years to realize our common bond. He responded, "Yes, it's true, the US has finally realized a basic truth: When in doubt, attack France . . . you will always be victorious!" We Americans are sometimes slow learners!

My lucky habit of being in the right place at the right time continued yesterday. A Navy chaplain and I were trying to hitch a ride downtown to talk to some folks at the Office of Reconstruction and Humanitarian Assistance (ORHA), which is the "interim government" of Iraq, when our original ride fell through and we hopped on a convoy heading in that direction. I joined a convoy headed by a strange group comprised of a Special Forces physician from the Cleveland Clinic and a crusty Marine colonel from Philly, the Duke. These guys must have been sent direct from Central Casting.

Doc Fisher gave me the ambush SOP and detailed how two days ago they had to blast their way out of one in the middle of downtown Baghdad. The Duke did the standard twirl of the finger above his head to mount up and then gave the "Tallyho," and off we went hell-bent for leather.

There must be hundreds if not thousands of mosaics, posters, statues and columns dedicated to Saddam in Baghdad, though not many are still recognizable or still standing. The Abrams and Bradleys of 3rd Infantry Division controlled most of the major streets. After dropping off the chaplain at ORHA, where he headed off seeking Greek Orthodox converts—ice to Eskimos—we headed out to the streets and across the Tigris. I missed some of the folks I was seeking and decided to hang around the Doc and the Duke. Good choice. A few minutes later the MP sergeant driving our armored HMMWV mentioned in a guttural voice, "Sir, I'd appreciate it if you'd chamber a round and raise your [bullet-proof] window. Things are looking a little testy ahead." The traffic and the crowd had pressed in on us, and we were stuck in a jam. I'm not sure what was more frightening to those in the rest of the vehicle, the situation or the fact I was locked and loaded. I'm pretty sure it was the latter. This happened four or five times as our two-vehicle convoy, armed with only our mounted M60 machine guns in the turret and our pistols, pressed ahead.

At the Ministry of Health a few minutes later, we arrived for the first meeting of ORHA and the Board of Ministers of Health. A painting of Saddam loomed over the conference room, his face painted over in blood red. I'm glad I made it to this meeting because it was a huge deal—trying to get the hospitals and medical system up and running. Legal issues arose, so being the only lawyer at the meeting, I was soon called into action. The US ORHA ambassador leading the meeting suddenly became my best friend.

We left the meeting and went from there to the headquarters of the ICRC (Red Cross) compound and had tea—after a cold beverage out of diplomatic necessity, of course—with the head surgeon, a

Greek-born, Toronto-trained cutter who had endured many tribal, civil, and international wars in the trenches, plus the guts and gore of hospitals for the last thirty years. As we sipped on tea, the staccato of gunfire and thunder of explosions rang out from up the street. My teacup shook a little, but no one seemed to notice. The Duke turned and yelled out the window, "Hey, keep it down out there!" By that time our MP escorts were out in the street taking up fighting positions. But the surgeon didn't miss a beat, asking whether we needed to sweeten our tea.

Outside the Baghdad headquarters of the International Committee of the Red Cross (ICRC) in April 2003. I became the uniformed liaison of the Coalition to the ICRC for prisoner of war and security detainee issues as well as for the return of Iraqi POWs from the Iran–Iraq War. We worked well together on many tough issues and under severe conditions. I became a real fan of the ICRC and its dedicated personnel and leaders.

From there we went on a grand tour/patrol of the city's decay and decadence, usually adjacent to one another. Uday's palace was not open for business—closed for some serious remodeling! Funny what a few Tomahawks can do to rearrange the furniture, ceiling, and floor a bit. The barracks around Uday's pad was a peculiar blend of Special

Operations folks carrying every weapon imaginable. It looked like the bar scene from *Star Wars*. We returned with the same flourish, escorted by a column of Bradleys.

Baghdad is a city devastated in equal portion by Saddam, bombings, and poverty. The lack of power has driven everyone into the streets. The gas lines are a four-block, double-wide, bad used-car parking lot winding around the central streets. A donkey and cart moving along beside a rusted-out 1978 Gremlin shows me where all the lousy AMC cars ended up. The kids are wide-eyed though, and give the thumbs-up and a wave.

The Iraqi dinar is really deflated—3,000-plus dinars per US dollar. Only a few years ago it was a thousand percent better. The streets are dirty, vendors selling cigs, electronics, rugs and pop. Very few women, and those seen wear the traditional long black robe with hoods—no doubt another reason everyone's always angry over here. The famous Palace Hotel is lovely with its garden complete with Bradleys and Abrams surrounding it. But the show will go on, and I sense an air of optimism in most of the area—the chance for a new beginning. As I reflected with a cigar and the sunset back on the palace balcony, I realized that the Iraqis were damn near the end of their decades of hell under Saddam's fist.

JOURNAL, 25 APRIL 2003

After the ANZAC remembrance ceremony, I went with Doc, the Duke, and Denny to another Health Ministry meeting. This time we had no MP support, just the four of us and a young captain from Alabama who had never been out of Alabama. We drove with one M16 and four 9 mm pistols in a soft-top, soft-side HUMMV. We first swung by ORHA and picked up Steve Browning and military historian Professor Gordon Rudd. The meeting would also include Jay Garner—the ORHA head and de facto interim Iraqi president. We ran through downtown Baghdad traffic, coming into a complete jam where we had to run against traffic to get out. Next we got caught on a side street that appeared none too friendly.

Once we crossed the Tigris, we hit a major jam around a traffic circle. Doc hopped out and started wading into the crowd. Denny and I joined him, pushing and pulling and blocking our way through the mess. We ran directly across the circle and forced our way through traffic, hiking around half a mile or so through the masses of old cars and people until we sprang free at last very near the ministry. I drove for the final run to the ministry so the Duke, Denny, and Browning could hop out to meet up with Garner and the ministers. Doc and I joined the meeting, took some photos, and watched Garner, the Duke, and Browning officially stand up the new Ministry of Health.

First Meeting of ORHA and Ministry of Health at MOH Headquarters, Baghdad, April 2003 (ORHA Administrator LTG (Ret.) Jay Garner, center; Senior Advisor Steve Browning, center right)

The security was okay then but not before we arrived, however. The fires were still burning from the night before when the bad guys had tried to torch the place. I took photos of the group and added a few comments to move the ball forward on how to tackle ongoing contracts—particularly bad ones entered into for bad-quality goods and medicines, or for political patronage only. The ministry contracting rules and regulations committee was tasked to tackle the identification of "bad" contracts. The conference was very successful despite security concerns. The bloody-red-painted mural of Saddam in the room seemed to catch the ambiance quite well. Private pharmacists and vendor representatives pulled us aside to make a strong point—that the ministers were all high-level Ba'aths and were corrupt. Even so, we had to get the healthcare systems and country up and running and only then worry about vetting the bad guys and incompetents out. That would come in time, not yet, we told them.

I met with Chris and went over several detainee and mortal-remains issues. We left the ministry and saw a great graffiti sign saying "We love the USA" and "We love Bush" painted on walls down the street. A mob of young Iraqis approached us as we admired the signs, and we watched them guardedly. Fortunately, they turned out to be the group that painted these signs courageously in this rough neighborhood and wanted us to know it and to know that's how they and most Iraqis felt. That was certainly good to hear.

Doc Fisher standing in front of downtown Baghdad wall painted with "God Bless the USA" and "USA + UK Please Stay" near the Ministry of Health. This simple graffiti painted by impressive young Iraqis gave us hope and inspiration for the Iraqi people. (April 2003)

We left the ministry and immediately ran into another traffic jam—caused by, of course, the lack of any police or traffic signals. Doc and I again waded into the traffic, poking and prodding along, smiling, waving and holding our hands across our hearts to indicate our thanks. We received mixed reception—universally good from the youth and noncommittal from the adults. We ran through a better business district and then back to ORHA. A good day for the beginning of a country. We contemplated our full day over cigars, an MRE, and a great sunset.

JOURNAL, 26 APRIL 2003

I hitched a ride to ORHA early this morning to meet up with Col. Mike Murphy, the legal counsel for ORHA. Murphy is a cool and huge Air Force JAG, who played tight end for Darryl Royal and Fred Ackers at Texas. We hit it off immediately. He and his contracting folks were heading out to distribute the second emergency payment in this country, to the utility workers at the Baghdad South Power Plant. However, we had no MP support. They had stood us up, for some reason.

So we headed off with a three-vehicle convoy of a couple of JAGs, Gordon Rudd, and a finance officer. Not much firepower to secure a payroll run. The plan was to pay $20 as an advance emergency payment to all civil-service workers in Iraq to get the economy moving by putting people back to work and holding them over until we could get salaries started again.

The power plant was south of town just beside a river and under an interstate of sorts. Traffic was light as we traveled the interstate past some godforsaken land. We hit the exit ramp and stopped dead in gridlocked traffic at an intersection where the ramps converged from all directions. I mean gridlocked. Not one vehicle was moving, nor could it. The gridlock was crazy: a new Mercedes sitting beside a 1976 Pinto sitting beside a donkey pulling a cart. Once again I waded into traffic, surprising the tag-along enlisted soldiers securing us.

Another COL joined me and we again pushed and pulled traffic around to get something moving. Several Iraqis joined the effort and we finally got things moving. Frankly, we were sitting ducks out there, so to do nothing was not an option. The rest of our convoy were locked and loaded, ready for trouble. Murphy suggested that we hide the cash box in plain sight if the crowd rushes us! After an hour or so, we finally cleared the intersection and made it to the power plant.

The plant looked similar to other plants, except the security was slightly better—two platoons of MPs and engineers and two Chaparral missile batteries. The chief engineer was a cute, elderly man with an infectious smile. He was the "trusted" person selected to pass out the cash, but he had four or five women who really ran the records and payroll and made the payments work. We had some very syrupy sweet tea to celebrate with the chief and his staff.

Except for a near-miss while following a donkey-cart driver who didn't seem to know turn signals, our trip back to ORHA was relatively uneventful. I ran into Bill Lance, a retired JAG COL who was now the DOJ representative to ORHA tasked with helping the Iraqis get the justice system up and running. We discussed his game plan and accomplishments to date as well as a meeting the next day with prominent bar association members. Yes, we'd attend. COL Gordon arrived at the island palace today, and we enjoyed a pleasant sunset meal of MREs as I filled him in on what was transpiring, smoked some cigars with him, and contemplated life. Al, my new friend—a Kuwaiti colonel, jet pilot and translator—joined us again for a sunset dinner, complete with sporadic small-arms fire accompaniment.

IRAQ, CHRONICLE #10

28 APRIL 2003

I've seen a lot of historic moments so far in this war, but today was the most bizarre and something I never imagined I'd see. While passing out the first emergency payments to the civil service workers at the Baghdad South Power Plant, I witnessed an avocado-colored refrigerator being installed at the plant kitchen! But they're extinct, right? No! The fridge joined the AMC Gremlins and K-Cars in the retro-'70s look now apparently fashionable here in Iraq. I'm on the lookout for a shag carpet, one that flies!

An emergency payment of $20 is provided to every Iraqi civil servant to return to work and to tide them over until a salary system can be instituted. This amounts to a large pile of small denominations—funded largely by cash found behind false walls of Saddam's palaces and by oil money. The highlight of this premier payment event was the cute, elderly Iraqi chief engineer passing out the money who pointed to a $5 bill and asked, "Who is this man?" When the 1LT finance officer replied that the man was Abraham Lincoln, the man's eyes got big and he exclaimed, "He is the man who sits in the big chair!" He does, indeed—in every way.

First emergency payments (20 US dollars per government employee) to Iraqi power plant workers, South Baghdad Power Plant, April 2003

They are starting to catch on here, but not everyone. Security is still a big problem. I have been traveling with some doctors and ORHA ambassador Browning to the Ministry of Health, which is to be the first ministry to be stood up. On Saturday, Doc Fisher and I had to play traffic cop in the gridlocked downtown Baghdad for over an hour to and from this meeting. We walked in front of our two convoy vehicles, directing traffic and wading into the traffic to break a path. It certainly helps when you flash them a smile—perhaps the glint of metal from your pistol helps as well—and you can make your own path against traffic and across traffic circles instead of around them, but it's best to do so in sight of our good friends Abrams and Bradley.

Unfortunately, the environment is not yet permissive. The bad guys are apparently onto our team, and the ministry says some sort of fatwa is out on us in an attempt to disrupt the proceedings. This is unnerving, considering that they attempted to burn down the ministry on Friday night and ambushed several of our 30th MED BDE doctor friends on Sunday as we waited for them to arrive—shooting at and seriously wounding them in an ambush at the same location where we played traffic cop the day before. So much for security. Jay Garner, the ORHA big cheese, was with us on Saturday and probably attracted a bit too much attention for my taste and for my sense of survival.

But you must push through gridlock when you're in a convoy. Yesterday while delivering the payroll—remarkably without MP escort—I had to again play traffic cop while we ground to a halt on an exit ramp. You have to maneuver buses, trucks, 1970-model cars and even donkey carts through the entanglements. I've never had to slap a donkey's ass to move on through the crowd before. Join the Army, learn a new trade! At least they had security right once we arrived at the power plant. They had a Chaparral missile battery and platoons of MPs and engineers there. Better than Pinkertons. Outside the power plant it is still Indian country, with sporadic shots and ambushes possible at any moment.

An Iraqi woman giving us a thumbs-up for either a job well done or a hearty screw you.

Today I was part of the first official meeting of the ORHA representative and some selected Iraqi lawyers to discuss the justice system in Iraq. The task was fairly simple: Take a corrupt system, reform it to eliminate political crimes and compromised judges, ensure due process and equality of gender, race and religion where it has never existed before, find good judges, administrators, and clerks, modernize the old Napoleonic-Code system, rebuild/repair the court facilities, and do all of that under fire. No problem.

Lawyers are traditionally a lousy audience, liking to speak more than listen. Lawyers who don't speak your language are even worse. We did our best, and I hope we started the process to a better system. One of the Iraqi judges commented that he and his fellow judges had followed GEN Franks and LTG McKiernan's proclamation and returned to work, arriving at 9:30 a.m. Not having any cases before them, they left court and went home by 2:00 p.m. Hearing this, I whispered to COL Gordon beside me, "I see that the judges have figured out our system already. Now we are making some progress. Now for training the lawyers. . . "

27 APR 03 (D+39)

- **TF Tarawa hires 100 police officers; curfew in Al Kut to stabilize civil unrest**
- **Central Iraq meeting in Baghdad (IIA)**

JOURNAL, 27–29 APRIL 2003

COL Gordon and I hitched a ride from the C9 and his MP crowd to ORHA, met with Mike Murphy, and walked to the first official meeting of ORHA and the Iraqi bar representatives. The meeting was chiefly talk—Lance's speech lasted over an hour and could have been two or three minutes: "We're here, we're the interim authority, we're trying to open and assess the courts, repair them, secure records and a good location, and get things back into gear, knocking out all the bad laws." An hour later Lance was still talking about the "proud centuries-long tradition of Iraqi law not built on sand but in the hearts and minds of the Iraqi people." COL Gordon took copious notes to keep awake. I almost gagged at the lengthy philosophy lecture, but we persevered. Again, as with the Health Ministry, the key concern was getting some police back in the streets to generate the business for the court and for some semblance of security.

After we had returned from the power plant yesterday, Doc was explaining to another MD that there had been an ambush on Dr. Frame and several others from the 422 CA who were assisting us with the Health Ministry stand-up. They failed to show for the morning meeting at the ministry, so everyone got concerned. They later heard that Dr. Frame's lightly-armed two-vehicle convoy had been attacked, seriously injuring four of them in the shooting. This attack occurred exactly where Doc and I had waded into the crowd the day before. The MP support had apparently failed to show up. The next day at a somber ministry meeting, Doc, the Duke and Denny received word that a fatwa had been placed on the ministry by men wanting to disrupt their fine efforts.

On Tuesday 29 April, COL Gordon and I hooked up with COL Marc Warren, V Corps SJA and several of his JAGs—combined, we were known as the JRATs (Judicial Reconstruction Assistance Team)—to find a workable courtroom and a willing judge and clerks. We started at the CMOC (Civilian Military Operations Center), a busy place where the CA teams were hiring Iraqis as interpreters, trying to hire police, and getting people jobs. There, we picked up our translator, a delightful women named Fatima, and headed out to southwest Baghdad to find and assess a couple of courts we had heard were still somewhat intact.

Away we went with some serious force into the streets, guided by Fatima in her flowing white skirt that appears bound to get dirty as hell. We worked our way through the dusty streets of Bayaa attracting stares and attention, finally pulling up at a decrepit old building with a cheap plastic sign of some scales of justice interwoven with Arabic markings. The front entrance was padlocked and everything else was bricked up. A clerk of sorts living nearby saw us, introduced himself, and told the story of how he'd bricked up the court (a criminal felony court) and tried to secure the records. He knew where the judge lived and invited us back the next day to visit.

In just a few minutes, the street was full of wide-eyed children, their hands held out. I gave the cutest youngster the dreaded Charms candy from one of my MREs. He gave me a thumbs-up and hung around me for more. We decided that this court, while a good size, was in the wrong place—impossible to secure and too tough for even a bail bondsman. We maneuvered through the side streets in search of a larger courthouse and a more secure, or more easily secured, facility.

On the way, we passed patrols of the 101st ABN (AA) troops, then found another courthouse with more promise. A local lawyer met us from his office beside the courthouse, and we soon had another large crowd. We also met with the courthouse keeper, who explained that he had been able to secure the records and helped us meet the judge. After half an hour of discussing the court and learning that it was a misdemeanor criminal and family court with little damage, we decided this was the best court to open first. We set up a meeting for the next day at 1000, then left.

Several kids advised us in sign language and facial gestures that three live grenades were strung around a tree across the street from the courthouse. We marked the grid and moved on back to ORHA. Another interesting day. Upon arriving back at ORHA, I met with Bill Lance, who had arranged a meeting for Thursday morning with the ministers of justice. We were now working efficiently together, and all of us, including the two ORHA representatives—Judge Campbell, also MG Campbell, and another DOJ representative, Clint Williamson—would join up the following day.

Email to Diane, 1 MAY 03: *Good day today with the justices at the ministry building. Our security folks took fire but no one hit while we were in the meeting having tea and discussing the courts and records situation with Jay Garner and the justices. We went across the Tigris again and into the masses to find the title registry building to get a grid so our friends at 3ID can get over and secure it . . .* [Note: The Title Registry Building was torched and burned to the ground the next day.]

5.

PHASE IV: STABILIZE
OPERATIONS IN IRAQ
ORHA TO CPA

The Judicial Reconstruction Assistant Team (JRATs) of V Corps/ Combined Joint Task Force 7 (CJTF-7) pose on the parade grounds in Baghdad April 2003. The arms/hands holding swords, depicting those of Saddam (along with giant nets and speed bumps containing captured Iranian helmets from the Iran–Iraq War), festoon the entrance and exits of the grounds. This was a heck of a good crew. (COL Marc Warren on the 50 cal.; LTC Jeff Nance, upper left; CPT Ryan Dowdy, middle; CPT Travis Hall, middle right; Warner, lower right) [Photo courtesy of CPT Ryan Dowdy]

1 MAY 03 (D+43)

- **CJTF-7 established**
- **POTUS announces end of major combat operations while aboard USS Abraham Lincoln**

BAGHDAD, CHRONICLE #11
2 MAY 2003

I came to Baghdad looking for a $1 haircut and I found it. With a hundred percent tip and a number of needy soldiers in line to get clipped in a makeshift barbershop of French dining-room chairs and gold-framed mirrors at the Civil Military Operations Center (CMOC), several young Iraqi lads were making in an hour what most Iraqis make in a month. We didn't complain, however. A buck's a deal no matter where. Of course, most of the Joes were getting a free, yet risky, cut from their buddy with some battery-operated clippers back at camp. Some things do not change in the Army from war to war. The old four-lane, high-and-tight haircut is a good one.

Another great tradition is the British use of Gurkhas from Nepal to serve as guards. Over a hundred stand watch at the ex-Republican Guard Palace that houses the Office of Reconstruction and Humanitarian Assistance (ORHA). They are tireless, fearless apolitical warriors who have watched over the British Empire and its armies for over a century and a half. They give you a ready grin as you enter, allowing you to ponder what appendage they might instantly sever with the long, curved kukri knife they carry as backup to their Tommy gun.

All things considered, though, my favorite Army tradition is the nightly burning of the crap. This timeless ritual falls on the poor young enlisted soldier whose turn has come on some unfathomably warped roster or whose misstep has gained the attention of some first sergeant. The poor sap has to pull the quarter barrel from underneath the port-o-let, douse it with mogas, ignite the festering stew and stand back, occasionally stirring the pot, so to speak. At night along the lake ringing the palace, the flaming barrels are spectacular. Especially when you forget that your clothes are hanging to dry a few feet upwind. Mmmm, if we only had a bag of marshmallows and a stick!

We are working hard to stand up the justice system here. This week we convoyed into southern Baghdad in search of a suitable courthouse in which to consolidate court records, and a proper place we can open for business. We had heard that the courthouses in the Bayaa section of Baghdad were usable, then found the felony district court in a marginally secure neighborhood. A roving patrol of the 101st Airborne Division meandered by us as we assessed this side street facility, now bricked up by the court custodian in order to preserve the records. Soon, we moved on to find a larger courthouse that could better serve our purpose. Of course, there were no working utilities in the building, or for that matter anywhere in Baghdad.

A local lawyer agreed to summon the judges, court personnel, and local lawyers to meet with us. There, in a dark "courtroom" typically used for family and misdemeanor court cases, we met with over thirty lawyers in the light of three small candles and spoke about how to get the court operational. We Army lawyers, a US DOJ representative, and a US judge held a session unlike any other that I've attended. Weird but effective, it became a combination of séance and speakeasy. The translator trying to see and keep up with the lead local judge, a female court reporter writing in long-symbol, not short-symbol Arabic while trying to see and write by candlelight, the thirty lawyers grappling for a seat and a say in fewer than thirty chairs, a mob of interested Iraqis mulling around outside with all sorts of purported business for the court, and us speaking of due process, equal protection (theirs and ours!), and the Iraqi common law.

It was a mess, but a fine mess! Everyone left happy with a promise of justice on the near horizon. A small boy ran up to me and mirrored how I felt by asking "What is my name?" We were off to a grand start! A man with one leg approached asking if he had a claim since Saddam "took" his leg. I may have disappointed him by noting that his claim might not have much of a leg to stand on!

Later in the week—Thursday is the start of the Arab weekend with their Friday being the same as our Sunday—we met for the first time officially with the Justice Ministry in the burned-out Justice Ministry building. Jay Garner opened the meeting and away we went. The chief judge of their highest appellate court (Court of Cassation) was the Iraqi spokesman. We discussed security and how their building was at the top of the list for armed guards from the Abrams and Bradley tank division of Pinkertons! As we discussed this key point and our confidence in a proper security arrangement, a barrage of fire hit just outside the ministry, and our convoy security commander quickly moved our vehicles out of harm's way. Thereafter, the judges' confidence in our ability to ensure court security waned quickly.

We refocused our efforts and went on with the business of law, particularly what law to use. The judges looked surprised when we advised them that the Geneva and Hague Conventions mandated that the occupying power adopt as much of the law of the occupied state as was consistent with international law and human rights and that, save a few of Saddam and his regime's special laws—they were special indeed, 'specially if you agreed with Saddam—they could proceed with the vast majority of their civil law from 1952, and their penal code from 1969, and the common law developed from those laws. With a few sporting prohibitions against gender, race, and religious discrimination, a pinch of due process here and equal protection there, and deleting the interesting provisions making a wife a slave, we would have a good starting point for the Lady of Justice to hang her balances. Though simplified, this is essentially how law was to be reinstated in Iraq.

We did have to secure the Estate Registry Building, housing every property deed and title record since the British Occupation in 1918. Can you imagine the chaos of having to adjudicate every privately-owned piece of property in Iraq? There wasn't much debate as we rushed out the door with one of the judges to find this vital building. As we approached the registry building, we saw that it was presided over by a large mosaic of Saddam holding a sword and the scales of justice. We thought we saw a trickle of blood on the sword. I noted that he had the same grin as the Gurkhas.

To round out a full week, Defense Secretary Donald Rumsfeld visited us here in the palace this week. He squinted and grinned his way around in his cavalier style. His hard exterior did noticeably soften, if that's possible, as he heard the stories of twelve Marine and Army heroes assembled before him. Their deeds were simply breathtaking and inspirational. These brave young men seem to tower over everything, including the SECDEF, the commanders, and the fifty-foot-tall black-marble pillars of the palace. In my eyes, nothing could be bigger than these young warriors.

US Secretary of Defense Donald Rumsfeld visits CFLCC-Forward Headquarters in Baghdad, May 2003. He is accompanied by his senior military assistant, LTG John Craddock, and CFLCC commanding general LTG David McKiernan.

Email to Diane, 3 MAY 03: *It's pretty hot here but great at night. I may try to get a shower tonight. It's only cold water, but it's been almost two weeks, I'm probably pretty ripe . . . Full day today with meetings at the local courthouse, at the ministry with another firefight*

outside, and visited an alternate site for the ministry. Couple meetings at ORHA. I am working on getting fifty-nine Iraqi POWs back from Iran on Monday. They have been in captivity for twenty-two years. Can you imagine? We'll see them on Monday.

Email to Mark Warner, 5 MAY 03: *Just returned from seeing fifty-nine Iraqi POWs returning from Iran. Yes, Iran. They were captive there for twenty-two years since the first Iran–Iraq War. I was the action officer. Great quote attributed to the CG, 1st Marine DIV (a real warrior type—MajGen Mattis) to the Marines here yesterday: "When you guys get home and face an antiwar protester, look him in the eyes and shake his hand. Then wink at his girlfriend, because she knows she's dating a pussy." Sage advice. More good quotes to follow from Rumsfeld's visit and my meeting with Margaret Tutweiler. Also, shot at without result on Saturday . . . Plenty of action here.*

Email to Diane, 5 MAY 03: *A good day for many, I suppose. Although it makes you think what would happen if I were to be captured for twenty-two years. Can you imagine? I won't spend much time thinking about it. It's too tragic for these folks. Another thing to thank your stars about. Speaking of which, the moon and sky are spectacular here. We talked at length tonight. Hope you heard how much I love you. I do indeed.*

BAGHDAD, CHRONICLE #12
5 MAY 2003

Today, I witnessed and was part of something unique in history. The Coalition as the de facto "occupying power" received fifty-nine Iraqi POWs back from Iran after twenty-two years of captivity. They were captured in the first Iran–Iraq War and have rotted in prison camps since then. I was fortunate to be the action officer and International Committee of the Red Cross (ICRC) liaison for

CFLCC for this project. This afternoon a jet chartered by the ICRC from Kurdistan operated by Phoenix Aviation—gee, I wonder which three-letter intelligence agency owned that?—delivered these men here to Baghdad International Airport.

I am not aware of any other time when an occupying power has repatriated POWs from another war. These soldiers, generally senior Iraqi officers at the time of their capture, ranged from forty-two to sixty-seven years old. They had refused all medical treatment for the past twenty-two years as part of their coping ritual and were Saddam fanatics. It was tense when they walked down the steps of the ramp and faced a mass of US vehicles and soldiers who had been allies at the time of their capture but now were enemies and the conquering force of their hero.

In order to cushion their adjustment, we had an Iraqi physician who was also a brigadier general in their army in uniform be the first to meet them. These old men frankly looked better than expected and were moved to tears as they touched their home ground. I thought their tears were genuine joy at arriving home from their decades of hell, but possibly were mixed with tears of sadness at their country's plight in their absence, our presence here, or their reaction to the full salute of all US soldiers present as they departed the plane and left by bus. I know for a fact that they were touched by our salutes.

I had drafted a short POW repatriation document accepting the return and repatriation of these POWs by the Coalition Provisional Authority that was signed by ICRC representatives that had received a similar document from Tehran and, of course, by the Coalition representative, my ambassador-friend Steve Browning.[10] The power of the Coalition was demonstrated at the signing when the ORHA representative signing for the Coalition broke the chair he was sitting on with his bare hands as he attempted to pull the chair back.

---

10   I sadly note that I lost the ambassador's cool desert hat in a "bailment gone bad" that day. It took me months to locate and import a decent substitute floppy hat for him.

Amazingly, these men had not seen a woman in over twenty-two years of captivity. Some non-PC officer beside me suggested that we toss one of the female JAG captains standing near us into one of the buses as a goodwill gesture. I quashed the idea as I realized we only had one defibrillator available for the lot of these older men . . . and that any of our female JAGs was tougher than all of them combined!

I sobered up when I thought, too, about the reward these men receive for being held captive for all these years: a shaving kit, a change of clothes, and a trip home to parents who have died, to wives who have remarried and had kids, and to sons, daughters and grandchildren who never knew them, and to a third of their life lost. I then understood their tears. And with that, our noble salute to them seemed quite inadequate.

ICRC Plane returning fifty-nine Iraqi prisoners of war held in Iran for over twenty-two years to Baghdad in May 2003. I served as project officer for CFLCC/CJTF-7 for the long-awaited but sad return to their homes in Iraq.

We were able to dodge a few bullets again today at the Justice Ministry meeting. Despite this, we're starting to get things on track here. A modest, 2,500-man Iraqi police force hit the streets today, and I hope it will soon bring some business to the courts. We are trying to open a criminal court on both sides of the Tigris later this week and are working on an alternate site for the ministry and the Court of Cassation, the highest court. Of course, Saddam's Special Court is now abolished. His special laws have met the same fate.

Everything is a bit tangled here. For example, the court police are part of the Interior Ministry and not the Justice Ministry. Aside from the small problem of having no court police, no police on the street, and, of course, no city jail, we are doing famously. If only we could get the power back on! We celebrated Law Day on May 1 with our professional brothers here in unique fashion—a tea, some gunfire for musical ambience, and candlelight. Even so, I've attended worse celebrations.

When Rumsfeld was here, he asked several young Marines from the First Marine Division why *they* were here. After several answered "Saddam this" or "9/11" or "WMD that," one of the Marines responded, "Because my gunny told me to get on the damn truck!" Gump! Hearing such inspiration, I finally mustered up the courage to have one of the palace guard Gurkhas show me his curved kukri long-knife. I realized my mistake after gazing at the cool blade and recalled that someone had once advised me that the Gurkha tradition is that one cannot re-sleeve his knife unless it has blood on it! He must've known he had to either cut himself or someone else. As I was the only one around, I moved quickly away down the palace hall, anticipating a yelp from the next person to pass by.

Email to Diane, 6 MAY 03: *Somewhat quiet day here although I was at the Ministry of Health early taking a look at some of their contracts and then at ORHA to watch them offload for safekeeping three truckloads of liquor and wine from Uday's palace. Mike Murphy, the ORHA SJA, noted that we'd have to verify that the liquor was really contraband and there was only one way to do that. Anything for God and Country.*

We are doing something even more unusual. Uday had a lion and all sorts of other wild animals at his palace. The lion is apparently mean and looks at you funny. And there are all sorts of funny-looking bones in the cage with him. Some are probably those of gazelles, etc., but others sure look like human bones. We plan to send in a forensic team to examine them. What a great guy Uday must have been. Let's hope he's dead.

BAGHDAD, CHRONICLE #13
10 MAY 2003

Spring is in the air in Baghdad. The flowers are blossoming, the heat is rising, and the refuse is fermenting. On Thursday we opened two courts in the Adhamiyah and Bayaa sectors of Baghdad, and with the opening, so came the weddings long held in abeyance for the war—hardly the time for a bit of cake rubbed in your face when you're dodging bombs and bullets. I dropped downstairs from the villainy of the criminal courts on the second floor of the courthouse at the invitation of one of the judges to have chai, the very sweet tea, and to observe a few weddings.

Ten couples waltzed into the judge's chambers with papers and birth certificates, and away we went. They were dressed in their finest garb, from traditional Western white to Bedouin-black burkas. They exchanged vows in the presence of the judge and their parents and a few friends, recited the first passage from the Koran, and ducked to avoid the candy and flowers tossed into the air by the jubilant mother of the bride. The mother of the groom contributes to the festivities by ululating, a bizarre, blood-curdling chortle that brings down the courthouse and makes all Coalition soldiers within a two-block radius dive for cover.

The judge is also interesting. He grew up in a small town near the Syrian border, studied British law here, was a JAG in Saddam's army in the wars against Iran, and later was appointed a judge. He and several other judges were herded up a couple of years ago without explanation and were confined to a 2 x 2-meter cell for seven months. To us that would be pure hell; to Saddam it was just "seasoning" the judges.

Speaking of seasoning, Saddam's son Uday has three very mean lions at his palace that look at you as if you were an appetizer. My Civil Affairs veterinarian-friend,who was born in Iraq treated these lions when he first arrived in Baghdad. His stories are remarkable. Apparently the lions were entertainment to Uday. He would throw his lions human prey, generally folks that had displeased him in some way, but sometimes a random person just for kicks. My friend said upon good authority that Uday's treating physician met that fate recently when Uday's leg wasn't healing properly. He agreed that, indeed, some of the bones in the cage were suspicious.

Curiosity was killing me, of course. As luck would have it, I ran into the armed forces forensic team here in Baghdad. They are working on war crimes and forensic evidence gathering. They had a day off and jumped at the chance to see the lions and the bones scattered around the cage. Apparently, there are videotapes and other evidence of the warped ritual that will surface if and when Uday does. Stay tuned. Film at eleven!

Spring also brings out the bad guys. They're getting particularly nasty in their tactics. They were especially active this week. One nice gent simply walked up to one of our soldiers in a crowd, pulled a gun, and killed him. Others have busily been emplacing mines on the main roads and setting up ambushes. My favorite was yesterday when they pulled in front of one of our convoys and tried to slow it down as they entered a kill zone. Unfortunately for them, they chose the wrong column to attempt an ambush upon. LTC Glenn Ayers's Special Forces Psychological Operations team—we rode with them from Bragg to Doha in February—were onto the ambush, and thus shot and killed the driver, who caromed off the road and into the waiting men in black.

Some danger is inadvertent, though. A young girl walked up to a group of soldiers with some UXO (unexploded ordnance) in her hand and kaboom. If the bad guys don't get you, the tan-colored, cardboard-textured eggs with picante sauce they have come up with for breakfast here will. Combine that with an ice-cold field shower and the lovely malaria pills we're forced to take and the streets don't seem too bad. Spring is indeed here. I hope we make it to the summer.

We did have a good day at the courts on Thursday. We opened the first two courts in Iraq and ran fifteen of the Iraqis arrested for the worst crimes—murder, rape, and robbery—though the investigation courts for further disposition and investigation. These hapless prisoners have been kept in the police academy jail. Despite our monitoring, the Iraqi guards don't seem to have our humane treatment ideals yet in mind. The prisoners have been given a can of kidney beans every day, while the guards keep the MREs we have given them for the prisoners. The can of beans may, in fact, be more humane than an MRE, however. The only problem was that they had no can opener, just the can.

We have now taken over the jail slice until we can retrain these guards. It may take a while. These prisoners are marched into the courthouse into the lockup, awaiting a hearing in chambers with the judge, the court investigator, and the prosecutor. If there's a chance, the prisoner may have a defense lawyer present as well. He is brought before the judge and tells his story. The investigator writes it down and adds comments by the judge as to pretrial confinement and court venue and trial date, usually seven or so days later for less serious crimes. This procedure is not too dissimilar to our arraignment process sans Fifth-Amendment rights. So the prisoners emotionally spill their guts and tell their story, followed by the same bizarre, blood-curling chortle as that coming from the mother of the groom downstairs.

Email to Diane, 10 MAY 03: *Had a busy day starting with a briefing before LTG McKiernan and four other generals on the issue of what to do with a guy named Mohammed Mohsen al-Zubaidi, a returned exile associated with the opposition Iraqi National Congress, who had been creating committees to run the city and claimed to have US backing. He was arrested on the bizarre charge of "exercising authority which was not his." He claimed he was the mayor of Baghdad and tried to take a bunch of money out of the bank to run the town.*

That scam lasted about one day before we arrested him. He's been in lockup for ten days cooling his jets. We're trying to decide what to do with him. I drafted some statements and an agreement for him to cooperate with the Coalition and be released subject to certain terms. We went to the prison camp to see him and saw a bunch of folks playing cards near where they are keeping former Iraqi deputy prime minister and foreign minister Tariq Aziz. I'll go back tomorrow with MG Webster as well to work on the issue. It's pretty interesting.

11 MAY 03: Coalition Provisional Authority led by L. Paul Bremer takes over authority in Iraq from ORHA and LTG (Ret.) Jay Garner

Email to Diane, 14 MAY 03: *Just got back from an adventure. We received twenty Iraqi enemy prisoners of war, really bad guys, from the Navy hospital ship* Comfort *that were flown into Baghdad. We off-loaded them at the airport and then took them in ambulances to the Saddam Medical City General Hospital downtown. I ended up having to do almost everything, from carrying the litters to accounting for the patients/prisoners and preparing the transfer forms on the fly. Successful, though.*

BAGHDAD, CHRONICLE #14
15 MAY 2003

Dates are in, candy is out! The things we do as an occupying power are diverse. First, the dates need spraying. Yes, I've made that same comment more than once at a fraternity party. However, in this instance, the date palms of Iraq produce the most valuable agricultural crop in the country. If you've been to any Arab country, you know that the date market is a bustling center of gravity for many cities. Dates, after oil, are Iraq's principal export and the lifeblood of thousands of rural farmers. The annual spraying of the date palm orchards must be underway by 20 May or a "date disaster" looms.

Although I'm sure we have plenty of old Agent Orange, the Army inventory of fenvalerate is understandably nonexistent. Thankfully for all date lovers, the Kuwaitis stepped up to the plate through a grant-in-kind, and, damn the war, the dates will be sprayed. Candy lovers are less lucky. We've had to issue an order making it a punishable offense—first-degree Boston-Baked- Beanery?—if any convoy is caught tossing candy or MREs out of moving vehicles to kids who line the main highway looking for handouts. It's probably a good thing. If you've ever been hit by a 45-mph pack of Charms, you'll agree. Also, the kids tend to dart across the road to get the candy or frantically run away in horror from the MREs, only to confront a trailing HUMMV or Bradley. The children tend to lose in that confrontation.

The gas lines are yet another issue here. Folks wait up to eight hours or more for gas. No wonder our operational environment is not quite "permissive" here. Can you imagine what would happen in a town the size of Los Angeles if you shut down their power and made them wait in an eight-hour gas line. Talk about hostile! You'd think that in a country with all this oil and all these Army vehicles that we'd be able to come up with a quick fix. Of course, nothing is easy or quick here. Only a couple of benzene (MOGAS) refineries are producing, and, of course, the Army runs on diesel. We definitely need mo' gas! Except, of course, in our combined effects shelter module back at camp where the Aviation guys sitting next to me are having a difficult time digesting their MREs. There, we need less gas! Please!

You may have read about an exiled Iraqi named Zubaidi who proclaimed himself the mayor of Baghdad and tried to do a few things like withdrawing a couple hundred million from the bank and holding up the power facilities on behalf of the city that didn't sit too well with the Coalition. He did get to meet some of our MPs from Texas up close and personal and got to sit for a week or so in a hot tent thinking about how much he'd rather work constructively with the Coalition than against it. Amazing how this simple, wordless approach works. I had the good fortune of documenting our ensuing "meeting of the minds" with Mr. Zubaidi and preparing a few things for him to sign to assist his memory should he lose his mind again. We hope that Mr. Zubaidi has seen the light and will help us construct a better Iraq. He was a good day's work.

Yesterday I helped in another interesting affair. We received twenty Iraqi prisoner-of- war (EPWs) patients from the USS *Comfort*. The *Comfort* is a 1,000-bed Navy hospital floating during this war in the Arabian Sea. As the Kuwaitis, with memories of the horrors of occupation by the Iraqis still fresh thirteen years later, refused to let any Iraqis walk or be carried onto their soil, the *Comfort* received many of the first casualties of the war. This is fine and good, of course, until the *Comfort* wants to set sail for home.

These EPWs were pretty badly injured—50-caliber bullets and assorted bombs do that—and needed to go somewhere for long-term recovery following their surgeries. So in they came to us for transfer to an Iraqi hospital. Problem is that most of them are bad guys . . . Fedayeen death-squad guys with all the tattoos. Mean-looking dudes—well, perhaps not as mean as Uday's lions, but plenty mean. You'd think they'd have some security guards on them. No, that would make too much sense. Instead, I was simply handed a manifest indicating that half of the patients should be held for criminal or intelligence reasons. Right.

My pistol at the ready, we off-loaded them in their sad condition and mean looks into six ambulances, and off we went to the soon-to-be-renamed Saddam Medical City General Teaching Hospital from the recently-renamed Saddam International Airport sans security. Of course, I demurred from telling the medics and Doc Fisher that we were delivering this dangerous lot; besides, I figured I could probably outrun the EPW thug with two amputated legs at the very least. We dropped them off to a very surprised Iraqi orthopedist who explained that these were not nice guys, pointing to their tattoos. I had them sign for twenty patients, recommended that they hide the wheelchairs and lock down the gurneys, pointed our convoy back to camp, and immediately put this smelly you-know-what right into the lap of a similarly surprised and very pissed provost marshal colonel. I retreated rapidly as stuff hit the fan. Couldn't help but imagine, though, twenty patients making a break for it, each in different directions, wheelchairs and all.

Email to Diane, 14 MAY 03: *Looks like a slow day here but most do until someone drops a turd in the punch bowl and expects me to pull it out. But that's what we JAGs do . . . Couldn't sleep last night so sat out and talked with you under the full moon.*

Email to Dave Clement, 15 MAY 03: *We met for a couple of hours with the equivalent of the Iraqi Bar Association on Tuesday and plan to meet again with them next Tuesday. Our sense is that the Union of Lawyers, their bar association, is generally comprised of private practitioners and not judges or ministers, so is generally critical of the regime appointees and the Justice Ministry in general. Areas where I think the ABA could be useful is in alternative dispute resolution/arbitration—particularly in property reconciliation and disputes in the north and south of Iraq—judicial standards, judicial qualification review, certain areas of professional responsibility, and possibly even in practice concepts such as specialization, which does not exist, public defender, legal aid, or even firm practice, which also does not exist here—only individual practitioners.*

Email to Owen Lewis and Denise Manning (CPA OGC), 17 May 03: *I believe Clint* [Williamson] *sent the first* [Iraqi Penal Code] *draft, prior to CFLCC's chop, to Washington, so Owen is dead-on on the draft. . . . I also think we should be thinking of including a phrase now or separately later that the 1952 Civil Code and precedent therefrom as well as existing common law of Iraq shall remain in force. Then we have covered a bunch of issues on the civil side, which is underway in several courts and certainly in continuing civil suits, in one fell swoop. I agree with Owen that we should put together the FRAGO and directive and just tell Washington, based on all input to date and urgent need/requirement under Geneva/Hague, this will be issued at such-and-such a day unless you object. Something like that would force the issue. (Of course, we'll use Denise's name so we don't get in trouble! . . . just kidding, Denise.)*

Email to Erin Malcolm, 19 MAY 03: *Some of the boxes arrived here after an interesting journey. We took Baghdad with less effort than it takes to get the mail here. [T]he kiddie Curads and the smiley-face slippers were a hit with the general, although they were a size too small. The sergeant major is wearing them. He looks like a duck. Another batch of boxes, including Jo Reynolds' awesome banana bread, made it somehow to a 180-degree Conex at LSB Dogwood south of here. [The heat] turned Jo's banana bread into something unlike either bananas or bread. Our forensic team is on it as we speak. [T]he gigantic peanut butter M & M grenade that welded into shape in the Conex and the giant boomerang tootsie rolls were both a hit.*

Email to Mark Warner, 16 MAY 03: *I had an Air Force JAG major drop in yesterday to tell us she was going to be the claims officer for Iraq—Single Service Claims and USAF stupidly didn't want to give it to the Army—that would make too much sense. She and the rest of her wing are stationed out in tents at Baghdad International Airport— right in the middle of the sand and heat. My only thoughts when showing her around the palace was that for the first and only time in history, the Army had better digs than the Air Force. I smile every time I think about it.*

BAGHDAD, CHRONICLE #15
21 MAY 2003

Yesterday I attended the first official meeting since the war of the Iraqi Union of Lawyers, founded in the 1930s and the equivalent of our American Bar Association. It was a classic. Democracy rang loud, as did the 500 lawyers who basically ran the president of the bar, Uday's private counsel, off the stage and out the door about twenty minutes into the meeting after a forced show of hands as to who wanted him pitched. The shouting, pointing, banner-carrying, and pitching-out became a bit unruly and the situation became pretty tense as the crowd surged toward the podium. I almost had to give oxygen to our MP security detail and several of the other JAGs attending.

After the ex-president—accompanied by some of his Ba'athist cronies, the now-former bar council—was voted out, pushed, and shoved down the aisle, he muttered curses and promised revenge as he caromed through the crowd and out onto the street. Rough justice, I suppose, and fun to watch. It reminded me of the intro scene from the old show *Branded*. After the president was tossed and things quieted down, MG Don Campbell, upon our wise input, decided to call for a vote authorizing an election on Saturday for an interim governing committee of five to lead the bar until a permanent president and board could be elected in June.

Then ensued a remarkable couple of hours of questions and short speeches by twenty or so of the Iraqi lawyers. The speeches varied from quotes from Voltaire and Jefferson to a cute old man whom even the rest of the bar smiled at in sad acknowledgment that he was well past his prime and clearly one brick shy of a load. Most were thankful for the Americans, some wary that we were invaders, calling on us to confirm that we were liberators and that we'd be out in due course, whereas others just wanted us to pay them some money for their lost fees as a result of the war and the closed courts. Many also were afraid that the man they had tossed and his Ba'athist friends would return and burn the building and all the bar records, down before the next election. We were later treated to a heaping helping of good old-fashioned democracy and the power of the vote. Our national party conventions had nothing on this one. These men are fast learners, and it was a blast to hear 'em.

Meeting with Iraqi criminal defense lawyers at Lawyers' Union, Baghdad, June 2003. These leaders of the Iraq's Lawyers' Union were a true inspiration.

At the same time, across the Tigris, villainy was in play. The valuable property records kept intact since the British Occupation in 1918 were set on fire at the Deed Registry Building. Despite assurances of security and the best efforts of the Iraqi fireman, we lost most of the deeds and property-title documents. It was sad. We viewed the smoldering remnants on the sixth floor through tearful eyes later that day. Our mood picked up as we learned that most of the records had been microfilmed and that the films had been salvaged and secured. I can't imagine a more fiendish move than to burn these records, intent on utter chaos in order to hide the confiscation of property by the regime thugs. One step forward, two steps back.

On a higher note, while I was at the Ministry of Health earlier this week to discuss plans to identify the remains at a mass gravesite near the airport, an older doctor with moist eyes approached Col Williams and me and, as the Duke later recorded it, told us:

"Colonel, I want to express how I feel in my heart, and if you can, I ask that you pass my words on to your leaders and commanders and to the Marines and soldiers who suffered and are suffering for my country. I want all of you to know that the great majority of Iraqis applaud your coming, your success in battle, and your efforts to be kind, decent people now. We suffered for many years and no one would help us—not even our Arab brothers. Only America had the strength, not only in military power, but in vision, in character, in moral authority, in love for its fellow man to come to our aid.

"I know it is hard for the soldiers now—they have no air-conditioning in their vehicles, they must live on our streets to protect us, they are away from their own people. I want you to know that we know the sacrifices they make for us. I pray to Allah that they will sacrifice no more; too many have sacrificed greatly already. I also want to apologize for some of our young people who are not mature enough to understand what you have done and what you have given us. We have not known freedom for a long time, so it will take time to truly appreciate what a glorious gift you have given us.

"Many of us blame the sanctions for all our problems. It was not the sanctions that created what you see today—it was the regime that existed everywhere, to include this building. The regime that cheated the people out of what was by God's law rightfully theirs. When I talk to my family and friends, I tell them what is going on now, the shortages and the suffering, is like a surgery for cancer. Saddam was a cancer, you know. When you operate on someone for a cancerous tumor, you must cut through the muscle and sometimes the bone to get the entire tumor out. After the tumor is taken out, your muscles and bones hurt greatly and give you much pain while you heal. After a couple of days, you start to see a change—you are doing better, you feel better. That is how it is now for Iraq. The Americans came and took out the black cancer and now we must work through the pain of recovery, but eventually we will enjoy a full life, free of pain and no fear of another cancer. I want to thank you from the bottom of my heart."

With a touch of his right hand to his heart and "Inshallah" passing his lips, he was gone. The smoke from the smoldering deeds wasn't the only thing bringing tears to my eyes this week.

The Department of Justice has sent over several United States federal judges (Louisiana, New Jersey, and Sixth Circuit), prosecutors, and public defenders who will do judicial assessments across the country. MG Campbell asked me to brief them on the situation and work with them to accomplish their mission. They will break into four teams and travel to significant governate courts from Mosul to Basrah. They are in for a hard row but are game enough. They made a god-awful hot, dusty, and harrowing sixteen-hour trip with many detours from Kuwait to Baghdad. How they must have looked when they arrived! Federal judges under the heat, how's that for a change? I hope I've given them a chance. In the event I appear before them sometime down the road, I hope they return the favor! It should be quite an adventure.

Churchill said, "Nothing in life is so exhilarating as being shot at without result." I was somewhat less than exhilarated this week when our vehicle took thirty or so rounds as we passed under a bridge heading downtown. At first I thought we had a loose tarp flapping against the HUMMV but soon realized we were being fired on as the rest of the folks in the convoy started shouting and scanning for something to fire on. It was indeed a good wake-up call, a better one than the coffee I tossed in the lap of the soldier next to me as I chambered and targeted my pistol. He was exhilarated, at least. Speaking of coffee, Diane sent me scampering and scrounging when she sent me a real curve ball—a bag of Port City Java, unground! No task too large, I accomplished the seemingly impossible when I conned an Aviation chopper chief to find me a coffee-bean grinder in a war zone. He owed me a favor for some legal advice I gave him after he got a "Dear John" letter. Amazingly, he successfully liberated one for me. Now if I could figure out where to plug it in!

Email to Diane, 23 MAY 03: *After our morning meeting, we were dropping by the bar meeting for one of our guys to follow up on a woman who was looking for her husband whom she had not heard from . . . like thousands of others, and a woman came up who claimed she and her little girl were shot at by their landlord. We called in an MP squad and went to her house to see what was up. There was a shell casing outside her house, and neighbors said they had seen the owner's son shoot a gun to intimidate these folks into moving out. . . . Bottom line, we searched the landlord's house next door, found a clip with bullets, no gun, but gave word to the son that he'd be hauled in if something happened to these people. We'll see. Shows we need to get the civil courts running or we'll have more to do in the criminal courts.*

Email from NBC NewsChannel national correspondent Steve Handelsman to Jim Dorsett, May 22, 2003: *Your partner Kirk Warner's wonderful note 'Baghdad Kronicles #15' was forwarded to*

me on a quintuple bounce. I was riveted . . . And will you ask if I
may forward his note (and any others) to two sources of mine on the
National Security Council?

KURD, CHRONICLE #16
27 MAY 2003

I've decided that I'd look smashing in pantaloons, a bright waist scarf and a turban. The Kurds sure do. Part of the beauty of facilitating the Department of State Judicial Assessment Team is that some of these judges are well past their physical prime and need a little coddling, and a chaperone to Erbil in the Autonomous Zone north of the Green Line—the Kurdish zone. Of course, this mission included site visits to Mosul, Kirkuk and Tikrit for good measure. However good the mission, nothing in this country is ever easy. We headed out in our four-vehicle convoy, including two Nissan SUVs with one spare tire between them. Of course, a couple of miles into the route we had a catastrophic flat. Now, I'm a veteran tire-changer, but a novice at combat tire-changing. Naturally, the tire blew in the worse section of Baghdad—catastrophic risk to match our flat. Have you ever tried to grapple with one of those idiotic, newfangled tire jacks, the one that fits in the palm of your hand? If you're lucky enough to have a PhD in engineering from MIT and can find all of the parts, then you may have a slim chance of getting it to work. After a brief tire summit, we figured out how the damn jack worked.

It is amazing how a breakdown in a bad part of the city in a war zone, like a fine wine, can concentrate the mind. We rapidly changed the tire while the rest of the soldiers formed a defensive perimeter. After successfully manhandling the tire change—breaking a few records and a few knuckles—we threw the remaining parts of the tire jack and a freshly broken tire wrench back into the vehicles and headed back to ORHA to steal . . . or . . . cannibalize a couple new spares for the trip. Imagine our surprise when the driver of another Nissan SUV caught us liberating his spare tire. We explained the situation and calmed him down—a 9 mm Beretta can be an effective negotiator.

Off we went!

Northern Iraq is both heaven and hell. The Autonomous Zone near Erbil is full of rolling, golden wheat fields, snow-capped mountains, shepherds herding sheep, goats, and ducks, smiling people in pantaloons and happy children riding unhappy donkeys. We felt right at home as we proudly shepherded our aging judges north—remarkably, themselves looking and walking like ducks.

We took a side trip up a mountain on the way to Mosul to St. Matthew's Church built in 361 by St. Matthew himself, the founder of Christianity in Iraq. He overdid himself, apparently, and is buried there. Several Iraqi Christians were resting there, too, as they sought refuge from the wrath of Shiites to the south. It was a slice of heaven up there.

Judicial Assessment Team advisors at St. Matthew's Church in mountains northeast of Mosul, May 2003. (Warner, seated center; Col. Mike Murphy (USAF), ORHA chief legal advisor, seated lower right). St. Matthew is credited with bringing Christianity to Iraq. He is buried in the church. [Important health note: Pass on the coffee offered by the padre next time around.]

We saw hell then on the trip back to Baghdad. We ran a course through the Kirkuk oil fields where the 173rd Airborne fought valiantly to secure the fields before the Iraqis could torch the wells. Carcasses of hundreds of Iraqi tanks, artillery, and trucks littered the landscape. Oil trenches still burned in our path, causing us to time our half-mile dash through the black smoke as the wind shifted momentarily. The terrain made the surface of the moon seem hospitable. A massive section of bridge spanning the Tigris north of Tikrit had collapsed from bombing, breaking the ten giant oil pipelines laid underneath the span—the business end of each pipeline still spewing fire like a dragon. It was *Apocalypse Now*.

Meanwhile justice restoration inched forward. We launched the judicial assessment teams this weekend throughout Iraq for a two-week mission. Courts are opening in many areas of Iraq despite efforts by many of the bad guys ("dead-enders") to thwart the effort. De-Ba'athification interviews and screening will likely claim the top three layers of the twenty-three remaining ministries, the Ministries of Defense and Intelligence taking a forced nosedive, including most of the judges on the Court of Cassation—the Iraqi Supreme Court. The Iraqi Bar continued its democratic journey and elected a five-member interim governing council, one candidate chanting "UCMJ, UCMJ" (Uniform Code of Military Justice) to me as he walked off the platform—one of the kookiest moments of a kooky day.

Being an American lawyer, I devised a creative way to pay private lawyers their own emergency payment. We created an Access to Justice Program—a sort of legal aid deal—that paid any Iraqi lawyer who signed on 250 US dollars in exchange for 125 hours of indigent legal assistance such as helping to find lost relatives, settle property disputes, and the like. Nothing like $2 an hour to brighten a lawyer's day! [Note to file: Don't share this with my clients.] I got stuck briefing Jay Garner and MG Webster on Justice Ministry developments this week. A bunch of ambassadors from ORHA, a two-star, two one-stars . . . and I briefed on the status of each ministry. After some intense grilling, I escaped dirtied but unfazed in my quest to march justice onward!

The scams are priceless. The Iraqis will be good capitalists. The garbage and heavy-debris removal folks are the best. They get paid by the tonnage of debris removed per city zone. Some enterprising chaps were caught removing the heavy debris from one zone and just dumping it in another, then picking it up again in the other zone and getting paid for each move. One vehicle carcass was reported to have toured most of the city's fifty-five zones last week. A Trash Summit was called. MG Strock, chief of Task Force Fajr, reported, "If you invent a process, they'll invent a scam." My favorite was that with the gas shortage, gas is a premium and can be sold on the roadside black market for an even greater premium. One enterprising young man was having trouble pushing his car the last few feet to the pump and several soldiers helped him out. They quickly noted that the vehicle was unusually light and asked the owner to open the hood. Sure enough, no engine! These guys are good, really good.

Some guys are really bad, however. Memorial Day was not a good day for the good guys. We lost more soldiers yesterday than at any time since the end of the major hostilities—an RPG attack in the north, a command-detonated bomb cutting a HUMMV in two a couple of blocks from here. A new tactic was thankfully foiled yesterday when a young girl walked up to a checkpoint and handed the soldiers a loaf of bread with a note thanking them for being there. The bread was full of razor blades. Perhaps they were confused. Thought someone wanted razor bread instead of raisin bread. Perhaps not.

28 MAY 03 email:

Communique (Unclassified) to Mrs. Warner's Fourth-Grade Class, Bradford Elementary.

I have just received your great cards and notes. The mail takes a while and went through Kuwait and by truck up the main supply route through southern Iraq to Baghdad. It was the same route taken by the Third Infantry Division in its attack on Baghdad. I thank you for your kind thoughts and comments and the great artwork. We are hot here. Your cards are cool, however. It was 110 degrees yesterday and is supposed to get to 130 degrees in June. It is also still very dangerous now here in Iraq and we have to be very careful and heavily armed. [Stop]

We are making progress here thanks to your help and your encouragement. You are all patriots and my fellow soldiers thank you. [Stop]

Your cards are posted in our Combined Effects Headquarters Command Trailer and brighten our day. We salute you. [Stop]

Rocky is a good dog. Be sure to tell Mrs. Warner that she will be missed since she is retiring. You are hereby ordered to give her a hug and thank her for her service. [Stop]

Respectfully, LTC Kirk Warner, CFLCC SJA (FWD) US Third Army—Baghdad

Email from Erin Malcolm, 29 MAY 03: *"FW: CNN.com Iraqi Missile targeted Coalition HQ during war." Are you in one of those gas masks?*

Email to Erin Malcolm, 29 MAY 03: *I was the one behind those guys looking for a large binder clip so I wouldn't pee my pants!*

This place often reminds me of one large *M*A*S*H* episode—although as noted below we've had a gold-bar heist attempt worthy of *Kelly's Heroes* as well. Some Einstein decided to cancel Movie Night after the first few movies in the palace because it was a distraction!

Pure genius. It doesn't take long for soldiers to get down to basics at any camp. The sound of a game of horseshoes can be heard on the only turf around. The unexploded ordnance around makes it really fun. I think that's where they got the "Close only counts in horseshoes and hand grenades" line. The Aussies have taken up roost across the lake from the palace and commute in a motorboat—they do love watersports. They're the only warriors who dared to be seen together on a paddleboat they liberated. Radar!

A universal truth is that young kids are cute everywhere, except perhaps the grocery store. In Baghdad they are really cute with their dark eyes and dark hair and big smiles as they warm your heart with a "Hey, mister" and a thumbs-up. It hard to resist giving them a piece of candy, a smile, then taking a photo, so I don't resist. No matter how hot and tired you are, no matter how dangerous it seems, the kids help you feel human.

The cards from the kids back home do the same trick. They do say the craziest things. A recent set asked, "Is the airport you blew up and took over rebuilt yet?" [Yes, Johnny, and since we blew it up, we got to rename it!] "Is it hard to stay awake since it is different hours over there?" [Yes, and we use such idiotic time-zone words as Zulu, Charley, Delta, and Lima, so everyone is constantly confused AND tired.] "Is Rocky a good dog? I bet he misses you." [Yes, and I him, and we both are starting to drool.] The firm, led by my intrepid assistant, Erin, has forwarded an entire Toys-R-Us inventory for the Iraqi kids here. There may actually be enough for each child in Baghdad. With the help of our wonderful interpreter, Fatima, and some Special Forces guys with a soft heart (I found a couple after a lengthy search), I plan to get these toys to an orphanage in the area. I can't wait to say "Hey, kiddo" and give them a thumbs-up.

The justice system continues to mature. Our judicial assessment teams are reporting that many courts in the north and south are open and starting to function. In one tough city to the west, Al Ramadi, the court personnel decided to toss the senior judge out for being a senior Ba'athist, but mainly for being mean and corrupt. I tried to whisper the names of a few mean judges I've run across to them for further action, but they had a full plate of democracy to chew on here.

Our biggest problem now is property disputes. Not a few here and a few there, but literally thousands here and thousands there. It's a mess. It is what you'd expect, though, when you've been confiscating property and Arabizing the country for twenty or more years. We are trying to get creative, but the process and progress is slow, and one solution may work in the north, but not in the south. Add to the mix that the civil courts are unique here. The filing fees are prohibitively expensive, perhaps to pad the judge's purse, and the average Akmed can't afford to bring a suit since the recovery is often less than the filing fee. Talk about tort reform! Did I mention that no one said it would be easy?

Speaking of easy, you'd think getting squatters out of a prison would be simple enough. It's not. Especially when there are 135 families living in one of the facilities northeast of Baghdad that we desperately need to repair and use as a prison. The British came up with a novel solution in the south by using a few smoke grenades and a couple of tanks and some money given for the squatters to find another place to live. After the initial shock, everyone is happy. I prefer the simple British approach; it's certainly effective.

We're trying to get the guns off the street. We implemented a weapons-control policy that started Sunday. After many go-arounds, the folks in Washington ended up allowing Iraqis to keep their AK-47s at home and business, and only the police and those issued temporary weapons cards can have them on the streets. The citizens have a two-week amnesty period to turn in any unneeded AK-47s or larger weapon systems that they may have . . . like an artillery piece, crew-served weapon, or tank. They are to be given plastic bags—originally ordered thinking that AK-47s would be banned—to put their artillery piece or tank in. I'm not expecting a rush to the collection point. Ten bucks says we don't get five guns.

We're always dealing with requests for war trophies. The sensible theater policy is no weapons, unless your local post museum is behind your request. But we had a unique one last week. The boys over in the 82nd found 999 gold bars (I'm not asking about the 1000th bar) and thought that they should be able to keep ten or so as war trophies. They actually made the request that kept staggering up the chain one step, followed by "Is this a joke?" and then up one more. Needless to say, it was a nonstarter. They are creative, though. Some soldiers were insistent that they needed to keep a T62 tank since it could be used as a farm tractor at home. Right.

On the sixth day of November 1915—the day after the Brits declared war on the Ottoman Empire and Turkey—they marched from the Arabian Sea to conquer Basrah. An ambitious British commanding general sent Maj. Gen. Townshend north to take Baghdad. Townshend's troops met and were repelled by the Turks twenty-five miles south of Baghdad. They retreated and took a stand at a town called Al Kut. After a mighty five-month siege, they surrendered to the Turks in April 1916. In the process and in the death march to Baghdad that followed, the British suffered 23,000 casualties. Three years after the war and the eventual occupation of Mesopotamia (Iraq), the British found themselves quashing a revolt of the Iraqi people, mainly among the various tribes seeking power, that resulted in over 450 more British deaths. Sir Arnold Wilson told the British Parliament, "What we are up against is anarchy plus fanaticism. There is little or no nationalism here." The British soldiers, 5,000 or so strong, are buried here in Baghdad, ironically across the street from the Turkish Embassy. May they rest in peace. Lessons of history are often hard-learned.

Email to Ray Hales, 5 JUN 03: *The only wine in Baghdad is from 3rd ID when told they would be staying longer than they expected. I forgot to mention General Order No. 1, in effect since we got to Kuwait*

... namely no alcohol. War is hell. Found an [electric converter] *plug; good thing—the coffee beans were turning to espresso before I could get a chance to grind them. It's a little hot over here.*

BAGHDAD, CHRONICLE #18
6 JUNE 2003

The wheels of justice have literally braked some courts to a complete stop in Iraq. Thus, getting the courts moving has involved many twists and turns. In Al Ramadi, for example, the process server used to announce the court docket, notify witnesses, and serve papers by traveling around town on his motorcycle. Since the court was closed during the war, he had to sell his motorcycle to get by, and now we have a court crisis! Sounds silly, but until we get Mohammed new wheels, justice will remain parked at the courthouse steps.

Another court in Al Hosseinia has not opened because of thugs on motorcycles threatening the populace so that they cannot secure the courthouse and open it for use. We went to this courthouse and were met by a reception party of the town cleric and his entourage. It was a city that the Army somehow forgot. Townspeople had barely seen US troops since, or for that matter during, the war. Al Hosseinia was close enough to Baghdad that it wasn't on anyone's radar screen. It is a mess. We marked the grid of the courthouse to get some security. The people in the city can't come out at night because a bunch of gun-toting punks run around shooting up everything, and apparently everybody as well. We were treated as rescuers. Our hosts insisted on taking us on a tour of the city. We toured the shell that was the police station and met the entire force, four guys with two AK-47s and two Toyota trucks—all eight on their last legs. This was going to be quite a project.

We moved to the city center where a daily arms market was thriving. We showed up, spread out, tried to keep our guns in the sun so that our guns reflected their metal, making us look more threatening than we actually were—I thought about using my flashlight to add to the deception. Presumably sensing that we were some motivated JAGs, they quickly disappeared into the crowded city market. It was our own version of shock and awe! However, the thugs may have just been shocked that we were actually there, so they were huddling in the middle of the market, laughing hysterically at "awe" of us. Instead of facing the gun dealers, we soon faced a full-scale assault by a platoon of kids. We barely survived. We marked the grid for a future sting operation and the kids for some future loving. One little girl threatened my heart by whispering in my ear that she loved me. I have that effect on women of all ages. Especially when I bribe them with candy and chocolate.

The child platoon enthusiastically showed some of our guys an ammo dump and some unexploded RPGs buried beside their soccer field, making the sidelines much more exciting in a game that frankly needs more excitement. We marked the grid to pass on to the Explosive Ordinance Disposal guys, then next were shown the city hall that the Mujahideen had taken over. These sick twists were apparently shooting out into the streets at night. We marked the grid for our security guys to come and set things straight. Then, we realized that the whole city needed to be marked for something.

We also met earlier in the day with some criminal defense lawyers. Everyone was talking at one time, everyone listening at one time, all talking with their hands, all animated, and all delighted to have a say. It looked like a Richard Simmons aerobics session. My favorite lawyer here is a towering Kurd who looks like Uncle Fester and talks like Lurch. He is a kick. Seems he and his fellow defense lawyers have plenty to howl about. Unless a relative or the accused hires them from the holding dock, the defense counsels are generally appointed by the court late in the game for 1,000 dinars—less than a buck—per case. At that rate Cochran couldn't buy a glove to fit. They don't get to see their client generally until trial, generally don't participate until after their "confession" is obtained—mainly by crook—and then get to face paper evidence and testimony, get to cross-examine their own client, who is the only live witness most of the time, and, of course, generally lose. Houston, we have a problem. The wheel of justice is flat and needs changing.

Baghdad and Tikrit are as full of Saddam as he was of himself. In his hometown of Tikrit, he has a compound with at least five giant palaces, each larger than the marble palace we have made our home for now. It is at once magnificent and over-the-top nauseating. Seeing the nation's wealth spent on the pleasures of one man while millions starve outside the palace gates is maddening. He is all the evidence of mass destruction that I need to convince me that our cause was just. Saddam is depicted on the wall of every building, in every park, in every building entrance, and on every marquee. He has a bunch of looks—all goofy and egotistical. He appears in Hindu garb (Nehru Saddam) on four corners of a mosque, traditional Arab garb (Arafat Saddam) with half a face left on one side of a giant kiosk near the palace, Inspector Clouseau garb (Alpine Saddam) without a mustache or a face on the other, COL Sanders white-suit garb (Chickensh*t Saddam) without a head at an intersection, judge's garb holding the scales of justice (Wapner Saddam) outside the courthouses, and, my favorite, "man-in-business-suit-shooting-gun-in-air" garb (Joseph Banks Saddam) outside one of the Oil-for-Food warehouses. Of course, it's all garb . . . age. An ongoing contest is to come up with what to do with the four giant Saddam heads in chariot-driver helmets (Caesar Saddam) around the Presidential Palace. First place seems to be to place giant beagle-pusses (nose and glasses) on each one; second place is to use them as the clown's face at a new Putt-Putt course; replacing them with busts of Bush, Blair, Rumsfeld, and Franks received honorable mention. Yes, the cities are full of Saddam, and a bunch of other things that start with S.

*Settled into Saddam's throne located in the Al Faw Palace in Baghdad
(June 2003). I wondered whether the Arabic phrases and symbols
surrounding the chair would give me overwhelming power . . . or a
sexually transmitted disease!*

Email to Diane, 11 JUN 03: *Went with Perry to high-value detainee
location to commence screening for status under Geneva Convention
Article 5. Involved good tour of facilities and of the investigative files
of these blacklist detainees. Late night meeting to brief MG Webster
on mass grave investigation status. Not your typical day at the office,
unless your office is here in Baghdad now. Crazy.*

BAGHDAD, CHRONICLE #19
12 JUNE 2003

The legendary black hole of Iraq is a prison called Abu Ghraib, just west of Baghdad. Temporarily renaming it Camp Vigilant doesn't do it justice. The problem with reinstating justice is that you need prisons. Here, there's an international humanitarian organization for just about everything: vaccines, medical supplies, mine removal, hospitals, and all sorts of other feel-good things. But no one, I mean no one, wants to fund prisons. So we have a problem. Depending upon which side of the bars you were on, Saddam's fall 2002 decree releasing all prisoners from all the prisons has created a nightmare here. This "fresh start" left us holding the bag when it came to recidivists. Now, I am convinced that these convicts will eventually return to their previous home cells, but in the meantime they are causing havoc. Their previous homes are also in havoc, and we are hard-pressed to get prisons up and running to acceptable standards by tomorrow.

So, we have to be creative. First, we had to move the prisons to the Justice Ministry from the Interior Ministry. Next, we had to set up all sorts of temporary accommodations for our new involuntary guests. Of course, the prisoner census mounts as the judicial system cranks up to handle them. The old saying "40 lbs of you-know-what in a 25-lb bag" comes to mind. Finally, you have to find or build usable prisons. We toured the prisons this week in an attempt to round out the judicial system. How fun! It turned into quite an adventure.

We first had to talk Ambassador Bremer out of turning Abu Ghraib into a museum. We needed the cells more than Iraq needs the tourism, for now. So Disneyland has no competition worries from us anytime soon. They don't call it the "dark hole" for nothing. Saddam had been inviting hostile guests down there for years. They checked in and Saddam checked them out. It wasn't quite Hotel California, though.

On a side note, the Army leadership made 3rd Infantry Division take down their Hotel California sign at their hangar camp at the airport—what spoilsports! But the execution building at Abu Ghraib was in the best working order of any facility here, having received the most attention and the most guests during the regime's run. They had a quaint little ritual of a little juice for breakfast before you hang. Nothing like a few hundred volts to add gravy to your death grits.

I passed on the juice but took a turn at checking the trapdoor lever. It still works well. Unfortunately, it's about the only thing that does in the prison. To add to the fun, Saddam marked his presence even there. His portrait was painted everywhere—the kitchen, the "dining" hall, the hallway walls. Looters, probably former political inmates, had taken the tour before we got there and had plucked Saddam's eyes out in each painting. I'll admit that Bremer's museum idea does have some merit.

After figuring out that Abu Ghraib was salvageable once we find the fix-it funds from some Prisons-R-Us organization, we proceeded northeast of Baghdad to a promising facility called Khan Bani Saad prison that was to hold over 20,000 inmates. This prison was in its final stages of construction when our little war broke out. Of course, squatters moved in and we had to figure out how to get them out. While the prison experts were figuring, the squatters were voting with their hammers. In the week since the experts had last seen the prison, the squatters—encouraged by some future Home Depot managers—had torn down the place brick by brick, rebar by rebar, and concrete block by concrete block. A mile-long fifteen-foot wall was in piles along with the bricks from the buildings and the stone tile from the floors. They had completely stripped the place. The smiling deconstructors proudly showed us their handiwork, and the kids posed for the camera holding the hammers they had used to accomplish this remarkable group pilferage—a real family affair. It was as impressive as the looks on the prison experts' faces—they would have the fun of explaining this to the boss. Try tearing your house down piece by piece, then bragging about it. What fun! Things can get a little crazy sometimes over here. You learn to laugh a lot, otherwise you have to cry even more.

I love a parade. It's particularly fun when you can sit in Saddam's air-conditioned parade-reviewing chair, act like Saddam by making that silly wave to the passing troops, hoist a gun in the air, get a column of Bradleys to pass in review—sort of—and act like an idiot. Getting a picture of you doing something that much fun, priceless! In a more meaningful parade, we returned to Al Hosseinia on our way back from the prison tour to try to show a little presence in town. Again, we broke up a lively arms sale and scattered both buyers and sellers into the market. This time we went deeper into the market, having the added persuasion of two mounted 50-cal. guns on our escort vehicles.

Let the parade begin! Rifle-in-air pose in Saddam's outside "air-conditioned" viewing platform at the parade grounds inside the Green Zone in Baghdad. (April 2003).

Another parade we're getting involved in is sorting through some of the "high-value detainees" to determine whether they are civilian internees or prisoners of war. A little treaty called the Geneva Convention keeps cropping up, though. So annoying. The JAGs of V Corps are tasked with assuring compliance. One of our team members, Perry Wadsworth, is heading this unique screening and, as necessary, status tribunal effort. The rest of the 12th JAG members are on the tribunal officer list, and we're here to help.

The random tasks that fill our day are remarkable, too. Today's list included dealing with the guys on the playing cards, following a lengthy meeting on mass graves; some questions on the Tuwaitha nuclear "yellow-cake" site inspections; and a comment or two on the new weapons control and the incitement-to-public-violence orders, all occasioned by a few moments of exhilaration in town here and a smile and hug from a four-year-old cutie there. Repeat this, adding all sorts of sick twists and turns, and multiply that times the number of lawyers on our team and elsewhere around here who are having similarly strange days. Another day at the office. "Honey, I'm home! How's the new trapdoor working? Let me try it out, but I'll take some juice first—and have you seen that lever?"

Testing the nefarious dual-hanging feature of the execution chambers, Abu Ghraib Prison, Abu Ghraib, Iraq (June 2003). Why settle for just one execution at a time? Iraqis would visit Abu Ghraib trying to locate their relatives' remains thought to be buried somewhere in or near "the Darkest Hole in Iraq."

6.

PHASE V: ENABLE CIVIL AUTHORITY
COMBINED JOINT TASK FORCE-7

14 JUN 03: V Corps transitions into CJTF-7 and replaces CFLCC as lead military command in Iraq

CJTF-7 Mission Statement:
CJTF-7 conducts offensive operations to defeat remaining noncompliant forces and neutralize destabilizing influences in the Area of Operations (AO) to create a secure environment in direct support of the Coalition Provisional Authority (CPA). Concurrently, conducts stability operations which support the establishment of government and economic development to set the conditions for a transfer of operations to designated follow-on military or civilian authorities.

Email to Diane, 14 JUN 03: *Kind of a fun day today. Started out with a couple of legal issues, then attended the change of command ceremony for V Corp with my buddy Mark Martins, 1st Armored Division SJA. General McKiernan gave an awesome speech as did General Wallace, the outgoing commander. The divisions held their battle flags with campaign streamers. The 101st for Bastogne, 3ID with the Marne, 1AD and 4ID with Mexican War streamers, and, not to be outdone, the 3rd ACR had a battle streamer for Little Big Horn. I'd be a bit humble about that last one! Went to the confinement facility and did screenings on the high-value detainees and returned just in time to celebrate the 228th birthday of the Army by having some cake with LTG McKiernan. Who could ask for more?*

*With LTG McKiernan, COMCFLCC, celebrating the US Army's birthday
at CFLCC HQS (FWD), Al Faw Palace, Baghdad, June 2003.*

Email to Erin Malcolm, 16 JUN 03: *I've been ordered to new
digs . . . another palace. How ho-hum. I am now down at ORHA in
the Presidential Palace with CJTF-7, which has now converted from
CFLCC to V Corps. I now have to hump up to the roof to smoke a cigar
beside one of the twenty-foot-high Saddam heads that hang out on
the four corners there. I plan to put my cigar out in his face, although
I may have to rappel down to do it . . . it'll be worth it, though.*

Email to Diane, 16 JUN 03: *The courthouse where Jake was
photographed was at Al Hosseinia where we broke up the arms
market. We're standing up a new court here and we've been working
on the concept and the cases. After a meeting this morning, we went
into a forty-five-minute meeting with Ambassador Bremer to discuss
it. The guy has a great political nose and touch. I think he'll make this
country happen. . .*

Email to Diane, 17 JUN 03: *I went with Clint Williamson and
AMB Bremer to open the Judicial College and announce the creation
of the Central Criminal Court system. Met with DOD GC Jim Haynes
there, took him by the lake palace, and then ran him out to BIAP.*

BAGHDAD, CHRONICLE #20
18 JUNE 2003

"There will be no fun until morale improves!" In a final blow to fun, the Army, in response to a soldier's drowning, has now prohibited swimming anywhere that is not a recreational pool. The logic is that troops tend to get hot and tired when doing patrolling or filling sandbags when it's only 122 or so degrees, like it was here yesterday, and when you're that hot you shouldn't swim because you don't realize you're so hot and tired. Hummm, cooling off makes no sense to me, either. Of course, I'm sure the twenty-year-old soldier who just kicked Saddam's butt wouldn't have jumped in if that order had been in place. Frankly, I never even prescribed to the old "Don't swim for an hour after eating" myth. I tend to eat in the pool to avoid the fuss.

The last nefarious order issued by CFLCC, minutes before it handed military responsibility for Iraq and me over to V Corps, was to extend General Order No. 1 and its no-alcohol policy to Iraq. Technically, we figured out after a couple-thousand inquiries, Iraq wasn't on the list of countries covered by the order. Some idiot let the cat out of the bag before the troops realized this little loophole—we called it the "looped-hole." I'll admit that the Army is much better behaved when it doesn't drink, but these young men deserve to hoist at least one victory cup to wash down their MRE's John Wayne bar.[11]

Hence, in an effort to improve morale and to deflect criticism of their fun-quashing regime, the Army is bringing the USO to us here in Baghdad tomorrow afternoon, and it is bringing with it a rich and great tradition of entertaining the troops—this time without the great Bob Hope. Sadly, Bob—who amazingly leads the annual ghoul pool contest every New Year's Eve—is probably soon on his way to the Big USO in the Sky, so he is no longer the headliner. As

---

11   Any candy in Vietnam era C-rations was usually referred to as a John Wayne bar. Usually they were dark chocolate bars which were very hard and very dry. Legend was they were made to constipate you.

a result, there is an element of surprise in who will be the featured entertainment for this war's USO extravaganza.

In a marketing tour de force, they gear up the rumor mill on the headliner. They really know the tricks in getting everyone fired up, shamelessly dropping names like the Dallas Cowboy cheerleaders, Shania Twain, and other budding Betty Grables to start the thousands of high-testosterone troops salivating. Then, they drop the bomb after prepping the battlefield: Wayne Newton. Like any of the troops under forty knows who Wayne Newton is. On the other hand, he puts on a great show and reportedly got General Franks to get up on stage last time around and tell Saddam to "Kiss my ass!" Now that's entertainment! Besides, since I can't go swimming, watch a movie, or toast a worthy sergeant, I will continue to paint my "Wayne's World, Wayne's World! *Danke schön* rules!" sign for tomorrow's show.

We have done one thing unique this week. We established an entirely new court system in less than five days—the Central Criminal Court of Iraq. We secretly call it the "MOAC" (Mother of All Courts). This one came upon a request from the top . . . POTUS [president of the United States]. The concept is simple: Take the top judges from around the country, make sure they aren't fishing buddies with Saddam, select some prosecutors of note, and throw them together in a self-contained, independent, circuit-riding court system comprised of an investigative court, a trial court, and an appellate court. Then run the felonies of national import through them as soon as possible to kick off justice in a big way.

To show that we mean business on the human-rights front, we did throw in a few nice ditties for the court to follow: a real right to silence, a right not to be tortured to confess, and a right to a real defense counsel early in the case. No worries, though. The cases to be tried before the MOAC are to be particularly nasty crimes, such as violence on a scale that transcends provincial boundaries; inter-ethnic and factional violence; terrorist activities; governmental corruption; and perhaps committing a few atrocities here and there.

We are seeking candidate cases to refer to the new court, and business appears brisk. If you have one in your neighborhood, drop me a note!

Five of us met on Monday with Ambassador Bremer to fine-tune the order creating the MOAC. He announced it the next day at the opening of the Judicial College—one of the first government buildings that we have rebuilt here. We knew we were in for a treat when the ribbon and the power were cut at the same time. As temperatures absent air-conditioning climbed in the new law library to a balmy 120 degrees or so, Bremer, in his pressed suit, calmly announced the new court and a few other gems (the Judicial Review Board—the first meaningful judges review) to a moderate crowd of reporters and Iraqi lawyers in attendance.

Unfortunately, most of the crowd—striving to survive the sauna—were so roundly entertained by the ambassador's profusely sweating translator that they may have missed the magnitude of this historic moment. The translator had the equal misfortune of first having to work through the lengthy introduction by the chief judge of the Iraqi Court of Cassation, their Supreme Court, and the scorching heat—particularly a problem since he had a bad wardrobe lapse that morning in selecting a blue shirt and wool suit to wear in the blast-furnace heat. I imagined that the reporters were thinking of swimming (cuz they could) and that the translator was thinking about buying some luggage to move out of the heat (cuz he now could). I, on the other hand, was thinking that although Wayne is a cool dude, our little band of lawyers that put this new system together in less than five days was the coolest. Suddenly, the heat didn't seem all that bad.

Special envoy and CPA administrator J. Paul Bremer announces the creation of the new Central Criminal Court of Iraq (CCCI) at the Justice School in Baghdad (June 2003). The CCCI and its select judges would cross jurisdictions in Iraqi to try cases of national security importance, including eventually the trial of Saddam Hussein.

Email to Diane, 20 JUN 03: *After lunch, I met Robert De Niro and got my photograph with him and Gary Sinise. Talked with GEN Tommy Franks as well.*

JUNE 23, 2003, *CHRISTIAN SCIENCE MONITOR*

In Iraq, a battle for credibility

US military officials investigating the case [Hamza detention-abuse claims] *at the* Monitor's *request firmly reject those allegations. "We found absolutely nothing to substantiate that claim," says US Army Lt. Col. Kirk Warner, the deputy staff judge advocate for coalition forces in Iraq. "Those folks were not abused," says Warner. "[They] are taken to a pretty sizable detention facility. It's not like they are taken to a back room somewhere."*

Email to Diane, 25 JUN 03: *Another day that seemed to fly by with meetings, capped by a two-hour meeting with Amnesty International. As expected, they were three no-personality know-it-alls with nothing else left to do in life except make us feel that we were abusing everyone else. Actually, they weren't too bad, and we talked them through what we were doing with justice, prisons, and the prisoners. We'll see. Now on to the ICRC.*

BAGHDAD, CHRONICLE # 21
26 JUNE 2003

An entry from a US Air Force Manual states, "It is generally inadvisable to eject directly over the area you just bombed." One wonders whether that includes Baghdad. We've had a rough week or so here with UK and US troops running into ambushes, mines, and sick twists with a gun or grenade. When the deaths of these brave troops are reported to us in the Joint Operations Center (JOC) for the Combined Joint Task Force here at the Presidential Palace, it makes us wonder why it happened to them, not to us.

For we travel down that same road, wade into the same crowd, and ride in the same vehicles. These are last-ditch attempts by dead-enders to shake us up, and they do. We are pretty stubborn, though, so we ignore the reminders of home from my man Wayne Newton and his playmates from the USO, and suddenly get more inner fortitude and resolve. The kids patrolling and watching the streets also become more fierce and wary, and then the normal folks tend to suffer a bit because we're more thorough in every way as we get on with keeping order. I'm not taking any chances, however. I've been grabbing the chaplain's phone behind our JOC station on the first ring just in case it's the big guy calling. I'm also planning to sneak back and check out who's on the padre's speed dial when I get a chance. Even here at the palace we've lost power and water this week due to sabotage. They must've had me under surveillance since they timed it just as I lathered up in the shower.

Speaking of surveillance, a fragmentary order issued yesterday directed some poor medical unit to surveil sand flies across Iraq. I can just imagine these guys sitting at some stakeout tracking a sand fly and calling in a report that the suspect had just sneaked out for lunch on a pile of camel dung. Apparently there's some nasty parasite that is transmitted to you causing leishmaniasis when that same suspect bites you. Thankfully they had the good form to let us know that it can potentially kill you. Shows what I know. I thought leishmaniasis could only occur while you're walking your dog.

Another important preventive medicine tip is don't drink the local water, particularly if it's in some strong coffee offered by the cute little priest at the ancient St. Matthew's Church in the mountains north of Mosul. Man, oh man, it's a real out-of-bowel experience. I now know how that stupid race-walking Olympic event started. I suspect sabotage. After my daily IV-saline infusion, I've doubled my malaria pills just in case our mosquito surveillance team fails in their duty.

Detention is a four-letter word. We are having an awful time in Baghdad keeping up with the criminal detainees. Imagine a city the size of Chicago and no brig. Logistics are a mess, as is dealing with the mounting number of criminals. We can thank Saddam for many of our woes. His release and pardon of close to 120,000 felons from prisons last October accounts for one in four of our detainees. For good measure, the regime and its former prison guests looted and destroyed every prison and prison record in the country. Guess who was busy leading the looting festival from the moment the boys from the 3rd Infantry Division pounded into the center of Baghdad until we could get some more guys here to restore order?

We deal and meet with all comers on detainees. This week we met with the International Committee of the Red Cross, real professionals; the press, who are hit-and-miss professionals—they hit you with an accusation and then often seem to miss your response in their stories; the amateur Iraqis who perceive everything through a dark prism; and even the non-professional Amnesty International who are a well-meaning but peculiar bunch. (I sensed they had just finished performing the eye-of-newt and toe-of-frog cauldron scene in *Macbeth*.)

No one is ever satisfied when it comes to detainees. Even our own commanders get riled. The Marines were hell-bent on finding out what idiot mistakenly released some scoundrel they called the "Grandfather of the Ba'ath Party," whose release apparently led to protests outside their gates. Turns out the same "scoundrel" was released by a 1st Armored Division brigade commander because he was eighty years old and in poor health and because they kept getting many protests because he had been detained! Okay, folks, make up your minds; either protest his detention or his release, but not both!

The next time we occupy a foreign country, I recommend that we pick an English-speaking one. Translating is a bear, particularly from Arabic, with its many interpretations for the same word. Last week we published the Official Gazette for the first time in several years, the equivalent of our federal register. Thankfully we detected Saddam's Eagle symbol on the front cover and removed it. We didn't quite catch the nifty border symbols around the eagle, however. Oops! Hundreds of Saddam's personal octagon marks were printed in the green border on the cover of the first issue announcing the first of the Coalition Provisional Authority orders. We turned the same color of green when we realized the mistake.

On another effort, we sent out a transcribed hearing notice to the more important detainees that mistranslated "status in doubt" to "status in suspicion," causing quite a stir. As a result, Perry Wadsworth, our team's detainee-status tsar, took over the translating and was able to convert the following:

English: LTC Warner has a status that is in doubt. He is acclaimed as a man of intestinal fortitude. Check for prisoner of war criteria. Arabic Translation: LTC Warner is a suspicious man. He claims to have intestinal blockage. Check this critter in prison.

Yes, next time let's occupy Bermuda.

Email to Diane, 26 JUN 03: *I just finished up a tough day. Man, everything happened. We had two guys and a vehicle come up missing while guarding one of the palaces in the north and we've been trying to track them down. Keep them in your prayers because it doesn't look good. I had to call CENTCOM directly in Tampa to provide some insight on this one. Also, busy with several projects that are kicking up. Detainees are on the plate for now. Met the Commish today. Bernie Kerik, who was the NYC police commissioner on 9/11. He's tackling the police-force stand-up here. We are also standing up the new Iraqi Army. Seems somewhat odd when we are still fighting the old Iraqi Army.*

Email to Diane, 28 JUN 03: *What a day . . . and it's only 5 o'clock. Started out riding with LTG Sanchez on his command Black Hawk choppers out to Abu Ghraib prison. Cool ride and great to see the city from that height. Then on our way to Khan Bani Saad we rerouted to a roadside north of Baghdad upon notice that one of our patrols located two bodies covered in straw beside the road. We landed on the side of the road and inspected the bodies . . . American soldiers who had been kidnapped/killed a couple of days ago while they were on an observation post at a rocket demil. plant. We'd been looking for them since. I was the only one with a camera and thus had to take a few shots since CID had not arrived yet. It was sad.*

Yesterday, I had to sign for over 500 teeth pulled as evidence from 299 bodies at a mass grave down near Al Hillah. Guess I will keep them in my file drawer instead of in the vegetable tray in the GC's fridge after there were some objections and no little squeamishness.

Finally, met with the Red Cross for two hours today and took a pounding on detention issues. Will start some status tribunals on the high-value detainees this week. At least we're doing a bunch of unique things here.

BABYLON, CHRONICLE #22
30 JUNE 2003

I'm up to my teeth in teeth. In one of my most bizarre experiences to date in this war, I had to sign for 556 teeth from 299 skulls (I know this sounds like the start of a good West Virginia joke, but I won't go there; besides, we wouldn't have that many teeth then, would we?) that were extracted, so to speak, for DNA sampling from the mass grave at Musayib from the 1991 Shia uprising. The kicker is that someone marked the evidence custody sheet "refrigerate." Imagine my surprise when the lawyers in the Coalition Provisional Authority general counsel's office objected to my storing my new charge in their fridge's vegetable tray. Under my pillow will have to do. Besides, I may get rich if the tooth fairy finds me and pays up.

Owen and I made a trip down to Babylon to meet with the First Marine Expeditionary Force (I MEF) SJA today. Only the cool I MEF commander (LtGen Conway) would have the audacity to choose Saddam's palace overlooking the ruins of Babylon along a branch of the Euphrates for his headquarters. After all, he had the audacity to kick every Iraqi butt between the Euphrates and the Tigris all the way to Baghdad and then take Tikrit, all in less than a month. Babylon, of course, was one of the great ancient cities, long the largest city in the world at an impressive 2,500 acres. The walls are largely in ruin, the Ishtar Gate with its brightly colored glazed brick and lions and dragons long removed to Berlin by German archeologists at the beginning of the last century, the legendary Tower of Babel gone and the wondrous hanging gardens no longer hanging in there. Still, it's as cool as Conway.

Saddam in his vanity has tried to reconstruct the city of Babylon by adding his own marked bricks to what is left of history. He has built another tremendous castle to his ego on top of a giant mound and has made two other giant mounds reportedly to build palaces for his sons. I MEF is using one as a helipad. The Lion of Babylon, which was too heavy for the Germans to move, proudly anchors the site as well as appears to be dropping anchor on the woman underneath him. I lay down where Alexander the Great had lain down—unfortunately for him, for the last time in 323 BC—in the palace which had surrendered to him seven years earlier. He caught some fever and died at thirty-one there, although his *résumé* was fairly impressive for a young man. We drank of the waters of Babylon—actually a chug of the bottled water we brought with us—and left. I couldn't help but wonder why no one seems to leave this place after conquering it.

Bowing to the Lion of Babylon with reconstructed walls of the most famous city from ancient Mesopotamia, whose ruins lie in modern-day Iraq sixty miles southwest of Baghdad, June 2003. The statue is considered a national symbol of Iraq. Saddam was attempting the full reconstruction of the ancient ruins, with one of his castles towering over the project. Alexander the Great died there in 323 BC.

This week we had many losses. We'd been going all out trying to locate two of our missing soldiers who disappeared from their security post on the perimeter of a demil. site earlier this week. Despite a massive search and investigation, they were never found. The mood here was solemn as more and more details developed and more days went by. Then while accompanying the Combined Joint Task Force commanding general (LTG Sanchez) inspecting Abu Ghraib prison, a patrol located the bodies of these poor men barely covered with straw beside the road. We were in the command Black Hawk choppers en route to another prison site when the call came in and we diverted to the scene northwest of Baghdad.

There are few things in life sadder than this. Young, brave men in a faraway place doing great things for you and me, then making the ultimate sacrifice . . . it hit close to home. After making sure CID was en route, the scene secured, and the shaken patrol calmed, we left the remains and parts of our souls behind. On the quiet flight home, we reflected and resolved. Alexander the Great, as impressive as he was, had nothing on these boys.

Email to Diane, 3 JUL 03: *Hosted a three-hour prison-and-detainee summit here with reps from all over. It went pretty well and made the commander's briefing tonight. We're having a good time with the playing cards on the high-value detainees. Owen and I are doing a tribunal tomorrow with some of these guys. We're considering asking them to autograph our playing cards before we rule. Don't know which ones yet. Will travel out to the facility in a cool Aussie armored personnel carrier as our Aussie and British lawyer friends will tag along on the 4th of July. Funny, the Brits don't think much of our July 4th celebration for some reason. . .*

Email to Diane, 4 JUL 03: *We did three tribunals yesterday with the high-value detainees, one pretty high up the playing card deck. Interesting fellows, actually, but too bad they participated in slaughtering thousands of folks. Aside from that, all went well.*

BAGHDAD, CHRONICLE #23
5 JULY 2003

Maybe it's just me, but there's something odd about packing heat to a Fourth of July party around the palace pool. No odder, I suppose, than seeing a bunch of Marines cannonball off a five-meter platform in full gear while a medivac chopper breezes by to the rhythm of James Brown at Saddam's Presidential Palace. The old burger and potato-salad picnic may appear dull if this keeps up. On the plus side, I was able to carry on my traditional twelve-pack-of-silver-bullets-in-the-sand routine—this time with real bullets, not Coors. They did have a gun policy at the entrance door: if you didn't have one, they gave you one.

One of the beauties of being in a joint command is that you get to celebrate Independence Day with the Brits. They aren't quite into it, for some reason, but they are good sports. This morning at our 0700 tactical operations update, we were greeted with a cheery "Happy Birthday, Yanks!" from British Maj Gen Freddie Viggers in the Joint Operations Center and a crowd-pleasing follow-on "Can't find any bloody tea around here, either" comment. The 5K fun run and catchy T-shirt ("I Ran Iraq") was another hit, along with the 150,000 steaks that made their way around the horn (probably where they came from) onto the plates of soldiers here on order of the commanding general.

Topped it off by presiding over three Geneva Convention Article 5 tribunals on our playing-card chums, traveling there in a cool ASLAV (Aussie Light Armor Vehicle), tossing in a few timely explosions courtesy of EOD when you least expect it and the fear of a few enemy mortar rounds when you don't expect it at all, and you have a star-spangled whopper of a celebration. It's one I won't soon forget. Pass me my gun, please.

One of the greatest military celebrations is the change of command ceremony. The Army Band plays some of the all-time greats, although not many in the crowd really know what a caisson is, let alone how it keeps rolling along. The outgoing commander thanks his troops and his own crew at home for making him look good, and the incoming commander tells the troops that they will repeat all the sweat and tears that will make him look good. The tradition is inspirational. The usually stoic commanders are moved to tears and proclaim things like "We'll meet again on the high ground" and introduce a Marine comrade as "my good shipmate" as if we're at sea here. Guidon-bearers from subordinate commands like the impressive 1st Armored and the 101st Airborne Divisions struggle to hoist their impressive unit flags fully festooned with battle streamers from every campaign from Veracruz to Desert Storm. Among the great battles adorning the posts, one particular streamer of the 3rd Armored Cavalry Regiment caught my eye. Call me a spoilsport, but I'm not sure I'd be spouting off about "Little Big Horn." I suspect that they got it from the 2nd Armored Cavalry Regiment.

The Article 5 tribunals we're doing on the high-value detainees are, on reflection, a bit odd. I can't think of any other time in history when any army has had to do these formal status hearings on high-level government and military officials. We review their intelligence files and then we examine the detainee to make determinations as to whether he is entitled to prisoner-of-war status under the Geneva Conventions. Aside from the fact that some of these folks participated in killing thousands of Kurds, Kuwaitis, and Shias, plotted assassinations of presidents and oil ministers, and said "Yes" way too many times to the big boss with the thick mustache, they are as interesting as you'd expect for a bevy of former ministers, ambassadors, and officials in the highest levels of the regime. Aside from that, Mrs. Lincoln, how was the play?

A couple of nuggets from this week's events here are worthy of honorable or not-so-honorable mention. Romance is in the air

. . . along with the smell of gunpowder, sweat, and smoke. Several of our soldiers have already married Iraqi girls! Nothing like the power of running a security checkpoint, festoons of concertina wire, an extra clip, a salt stain on your flak vest, and a big gun to impress the local honeys. Jake, despite his poor hearing, thought he heard some sort of cat crying out in pain in one of the small buildings on Victory Camp at the lake palace. He investigated but found nary a wounded cat, but instead he found a lovely couple having enthusiastic sex. Someone besides Jake was hitting the buzzer prematurely.

In other news, a local sheikh, captured after a failed ambush attempt on an American convoy, was taken by troops to his mosque where he sheepishly told his followers that "I am not so good at ambush." In Basrah, the Brits busted into a house to the surprise of five naughty occupants, a couple of whom stood up and yelled, "We're just criminals, we're not part of any organization."

The few dead-enders here are still causing a bit of trouble every day but are getting creative. Kids are handing our troops cigarettes with propellant sticks in them (Surgeon General Warning to follow) and sodas that explode (Talk about over-carbonation!). A white kite is being used to signal the presence of Coalition troops in the north— more environmentally sound, I suppose, than the traditional burning of a tire. Finally, the Marines have discovered a new and exciting response to an ambush—they attack! Unlike the sheikh, the Marines "are very good at ambush." Thank God for that . . . We may get to celebrate the next holiday.

Geneva Convention Article 5 tribunal panel at Camp Cropper, Baghdad, for status tribunal on Dr. Saadi, high-value detainee, July 2003. (Front row left to right: MAJ Wadsworth, Warner and MAJ Lewis) Members of the 12th JAG served on most of the Article 5 status tribunal panels held on captured regime leaders depicted on the famous most-wanted playing cards identifying them.

Email to Alex Warner, 5 JUL 03: *The place last night looked like China Beach without any women. We did have a fireworks show at about 11:00. We took a bunch of fire from the Tigris banks in back of our palace and some of our guys laid into them pretty heavily. No big deal. Hell, I barely knew it took place we're so used to EOD blowing up a stash of unexploded ammo. Here's an interesting thing: There was a helluva fight back in April when 3ID forced their way into this place and killed a bunch of Iraqis. Most of the dead lay out there a few days, so we finally buried them across the street. We forgot about it and put in our parking lot on the site. So we've been parking on fifty-one of these bastards for a couple of months over in the corner of the lot.*

Now, we have to dig them up and turn their remains over to the Red Cross. Other stories are just as unbelievable. Tonight we raided a house of a drunk Iraqi who kept lobbing improvised explosive devices *over the wire into our Civil Military Center. This guy was using the little Tabasco bottles that come in our MREs for the shrapnel. Of course, they're plastic! It probably pisses our guys off seeing the waste of Tabasco, so they wanted to off the f**ker. The I MEF CDR is credited with a great comment before the war. He was asked by POW internment guys how many EPWs (enemy POWs) he expected to capture on the way to Baghdad. He said, "Two, and I already have their names." I MEF didn't take too many prisoners, but they left a lot of dead Iraqis in their path.*

An amazing twenty-nine boxes of toys and kids' clothes and other good stuff, minus the plastic yellow ducky I slipped out for myself, arrived from my firm this week. I was *persona non grata* with our postal unit here until they learned that I was taking my newly-delivered stash to a Baghdad orphanage. Now everyone loves Uncle Kirk. Another universal truth is that toys create smiles, and kids' smiles are the best of all. Countries on the rebound after thirty years of Saddam, sanctions and war are no exception. It should be a blast. Ambassador Bremer is planning to join in the fun. He's not getting my duck, however!

Ambassador Jerry Bremer is the Coalition Provisional Authority (CPA), the de facto government of Iraq until we can pass the mantle back to the Iraqis. He's the man—looks decades less than his sixty-one years, has killer hair, and even eats with us peons. His real power secret is his general counsel's office, co-located with our Combined Joint Task Force SJA Office. The five lawyers, including one of our team, MAJ Owen Lewis, are doing some first-rate work. They instantaneously pump out orders and proclamations for AMB Bremer that surface from the various ministries or from within. The proposed orders are generally routed to Canberra, London,

Washington, Bremer, and our office for comment and scrubbing before they become law.

A new Iraqi army, first billed as the National Iraqi Corps (NIC) until someone pointed out that "nic" is a dirty word in Arabic, with an entirely new code of military discipline was created in about three days. I tried to sneak in as the first Judge Advocate of the Army, but they caught it in the final draft! A penal code that Messrs. Miranda and Gideon would be proud of, and a borders and customs order took several weeks, while the independence of the Central Bank took a record fifty-five minutes, cradle to debut.

In de-Ba'athifying an Iraq that needed a bath, they've prepared orders canceling holidays like the Ba'ath Party birthday and daylight savings, called "Saddam time" in the south. They've also helped us create the self-contained federal court system (CCCI), and even banned tinted windows in autos. It's fun to watch and participate in. I'm thinking of slipping in a few orders that I'd like to see: the Iraqis deserve a Groundhog Day once Saddam is found buried beneath the business end of a JDAM strike; a de-sand-at-your-party order, banning those nasty horizontal sandstorms; an order restricting daylight temperatures like those at the surface of the sun to a couple of blistering minutes instead of twenty hours a day; and a minister of information tribute night monthly on Comedy Central.

A couple dits from the Brits this week made me smile. Because I was getting a bit ripe, I was ordered to Bahrain for a couple of days of Ba'athification and, unfortunately, an after-action report conference on the war with senior JAGs from Washington and CENTCOM. My initial thought was that the gents from Washington needed reminding that we were still engaged in a bunch of action up here in Baghdad, so an "after-action" report was not as ripe as I was.

As usual, the Brits were the real entertainment. One British colonel made the astute observation that once the rules of engagement had changed to prevent our troops from toppling and smashing Saddam's monuments and statues, the "Brits done some very bad driving around Basrah" thereafter. The Brits always seem to add some spice to most occasions. While we were prepping LTG Sanchez for a press briefing earlier in the week, the commanding general teasingly suggested that we should call the dead-end rabble that were still attacking our convoys "shitheads." Our British Public Affairs officer immediately retorted that he supposed "shitheads," sadly, didn't have enough "Rs" in it for his or the press's taste.

Otherwise, it was your typical week. We dealt with a Turkish crisis when we arrested a bunch of Turks creating a stir among the Kurds (a real Tu-rd affair); managed a mounting number of detainees; dealt with the International Red Cross; treated some tuberculosis here and there among the detainees; and made sure we don't release a really bad guy by mistake while preparing cases for referral to the new Central Criminal Court of Iraq that opens next week.

I also flew back from Bahrain on an Aussie C-130 hop that took us on a real roller-coaster ride on our lengthy tactical approach. Everyone save me was instructed to put on their flak vest and helmet about fifty miles out. Of course, the fact that I'd left my tactical gear in Baghdad pleased me no end. I sat back, thought about snaking the sleeping combat wombat's flak vest and helmet, and noted that we had a way to go before we opened the airport to commercial traffic next week. On the plus side, I was comforted, however, that our new contract for security at the Baghdad airport was let to a company named "Custer Battles." Great. They did so well at Little Bighorn.

Email from Jim Stephens, 11 JUL 03: *Like the ripples on a pond, your Chronicles have spread from friend to friend all across the nation. We are Jim and Johanna Stephens [Tucson, AZ] who via a friend of some friend or family of yours, has included us in the weekly report from Baghdad—we find them all delightful, insightful, and free from bias that assails us from all media—TV and print. The very sad ending for those two young soldiers in Chronicle #22 was*

sensationalized by the TV news when your telling of it was all that was or should have been printed. Your obvious love and appreciation for the American GI is so very refreshing, an ongoing treat in all your Chronicles that truly lifts us up. You are painting some wonderful first-hand pictures of history; the daily frustrations along with a deeeeelightful sense of humor, firmly rooted in being an American, just tickles us no end.

Email to Diane, 14 JUL 03: *Although I never know what day it is since we have no weekends, today was a busy one. Went with LTG Sanchez on the Black Hawks to see the MEK compound where they have been held following their surrender in late April. They are about 5,000 Iranians who are part of a kind of cult. They backed the Iranians taking our embassy hostage in 1979 but then grew disenchanted with Khomeini and his regime. Encouraged and supported by Iranians exiled in Paris, they now fight against the Iranian regime. The commanders are women and they are an odd lot. We really don't know what to do with them. Returned for a meeting of the Special Prosecution Task Force trying to get cases ready for the new Central Criminal Court of Iraq.*

Email to Diane, 15 JUL 03: *Hectic day again. Had to finish a memo for Bremer this morning and then brief him this afternoon. I plan to go to Mosul again tomorrow with Judge Campbell to look at courts and prisons in the 101st ABN area. Last time I was there we barely got downtown into the old section, so this visit should be worthwhile.*

Email to Diane, 17 JUL 03: *Went to Mosul on choppers. Great ride, great views. Went to courts and prisons up there with 101st ABN guys. Saw some old friends including Paul Wilson there. Had a meeting with MG Petraeus the CG and took a photo of the battle stick with Bastogne streamer in honor of* Band of Brothers. *They had only one chopper to return, so I hooked a ride with DASD Linton Wells and choppered to D-Rear at Mosul Airport and hopped on his C-130 to BIAP. Long, long dusty day. The C-130 pulled some pretty impressive Gs on the spiral approach.*

BAGHDAD, CHRONICLE #25
18 JULY 2003

Sadly, on April 4 at the height of the war, Mr. Abud S. Mau'ed claims that his house was "bumped," causing "serious hurts" for Mr. Abud and killing his wife, his "sixteen" sons, and 100 sheep as well as doing "huge material destruction in his house." So says the poorly transcribed complaint filed in the Court of First Instance in Ramadi against the "Minister of American Defense and the Commander of the Allied Powers in Iraq." That's a hell of a bump, presumably by a pretty sizable "bomb." Although the translation is quite funny and I can't help but think of the great Carnac line on Johnny Carson—A: "Sissss booooom baaaaah. . . " Q: "Describe the sound you hear when a sheep blows up!"—the factual situation is sad indeed. As Carnac rejoined, "May the swami of Baghdad squat on your fez!!"[12]

On the plus side, the newly unshackled Iraqi lawyers are feeling their oats and quickly adopting Western ways. I have stopped giving them my hot black coffee just in case they learn our caffeine addiction too quickly as well. Several of these lawsuits have trickled into the system and will no doubt be quashed by the courts faster than the Mau'ed house and sheep, based on a variety of sovereign and other immunities and the laws of war. I'm sure we'll help Mr. Mau'ed out soon despite his lawsuit being tossed because that's the way we are . . . and that is good. No one ever said war was pretty or perfect. We sure tried not to hit anyone who wasn't aiming at us, but I'm sure

---

12   Thankfully rare, these war collateral damage claims typically get dismissed from the courts pursuant to law or a status of forces agreement (SOFA), but many non-war claims are handled by a claims office established by JAG officers or are handled by commanders if they have solatia (good will) monies and authority.

a few like Mr. Mau'ed and his house were caught in the crossfire. In the fog of war, we just don't know whether his house could have housed an artillery battery. But for a moment a defense litigator like me got a chance once again to craft a few unique dispositive motions, a demurrer, and a few novel affirmative defenses based on some interesting root causation concepts. I'm baaaaack!

When the story of this war is told, one of the most bizarre stories is that of the People's Mujahedin of Iraq or the Mujahedin-e Khalq (MEK). Formed in the 1970s as an underground Iranian political movement aimed at overthrowing the Shah, they quickly realized their mistake and have been taking on Khomeini and his crew ever since. They were driven into exile in France and later began operating in Iraq with the patronage of Saddam. The MEK, almost 5,000 strong, operates tanks, APCs, artillery, and an impressive show of other armaments. They also happen to be the only army in the world with a women-only officer corps in command.

Many members have advanced degrees from the US, UK and France. No one save the commanders has rank, and soldiers must be single or divorced. Men and women live separately at compounds and do not mix, except in battle. Most have had relatives killed, tortured, or detained in Iran. Their twenty-square-mile cantonment area, Camp Ashraf, is located sixty-five miles northeast of Baghdad, close to the Iranian border. Although they are the enemy of our enemy, which in diplomatic terms generally makes them our friend, the rub is that they're on the State Department's terrorist list and were thus declared hostile under our rules of engagement. "It's complicated."

In mid-April as our tanks were poised on their perimeter and they were looking down our ready gun tubes, they declared they had no beefs with us and sought to negotiate an understanding. Well, we and the 4th ID JAGs scratched our heads and drafted all sorts of agreements, instructions, and understandings that sort of worked around them having to admit that they had capitulated and surrendered. I had the honor of explaining what all the options were, what they meant, and what they finally agreed to with LTG McKiernan and MG Webster.

They [the MEK] probably were as confused as I was, but had the good sense not to let on, sort of. Eventually, however, they submitted to our control to avoid being steamrolled by our armor. They were smart and professional and did the right thing, in sort of giving up. After all, as Nathan Bedford Forrest noted, "A good run beats a bad stand." They circled their tanks in universal submission and properly capitulated, although they wouldn't quite agree to call it that. The circle was so perfect and so large that you could make it out from space.

The MEK Persians are an odd lot, indeed, and no one really knows what to do with them now that we sort of caught them. They are problematic, neither fish nor totally fowl. They seem to be self-sufficient even though we sort of guard them to keep them from getting to their weapons, but we also let them make trips sort of off their compounds. It's a whole lot of "sort of" going on. This sort of pissed off our commanding general and those in Washington, though, so I flew with LTG Sanchez up there on his Black Hawks this week to get the ground truth. We sort of did, touring the place under their watchful eye as they followed us in white trucks around the place, knowing what we were doing before we did.

They had an ammo bunker complex of eighty-four large bunkers that covered at least four square miles of the compound. The bunkers were full of artillery shells, AK-47s, M16s, RPGs, Smith & Wesson pistols and just about every other type of weapon and ammunition known to man, or in this case woman. It was impressive. These gals were well funded. Daily they work on their tanks and equipment that have been consolidated under our control. They cried when they had to give up their tanks and other toys to us. We got the grand tour but never really saw more than a handful of these hellcats. It was eerie. We left with a better understanding, a way ahead, and a whole lot of sort of. I wonder what old Nathan would have thought. My guess is that he'd still be running!

Inspection with LTG Ricardo Sanchez, CG CJTF-7, of the Mujahedin-e Khalq ("MEK") complex. The MEK compound was located ten miles from the Iranian border northeast of Baqubah, Iraq, June 2003. The MEK forces were completely commanded by women. Although on our terrorist list, the MEK opposed the Iranian regime across the border so were an enigma for the Coalition. Many ammo bunkers filled with US artillery shells captured by Saddam during the Kuwait invasion in 1990 were found inside the MEK compound.

★ ★ ★ ★

Email to Diane, 18 JUL 03: *Went on choppers early with Ambassador Bremer and UN special representative de Mello to Abu Ghraib prison and the detention facilities. Fielded a few questions for both during the visit. Got back just in time for a Ministry of Justice meeting, then out to Victory Camp for a 1600 VTC with Pentagon lawyers . . . and then a 2200 conference call to DOD general counsel's office . . . [T]he paper I prepared on Sunday was sent to the Pentagon and they are using it to brief Rumsfeld. Pretty cool.*

Email to Diane, 19 JUL 03: *I still can't imagine how the married men made it during WWII with just a letter every once in a while over a two-to-four year period. Amazing. Another crazy-busy day. A meeting with British major general Vickers about shutting down a newspaper here that has been inciting violence against the Coalition and those who cooperate with the Coalition. Then I had three meetings in a row with LTG Sanchez about MEK processing, oil smuggling, and KMEK (the MEK radio station) and how to handle it. Then ran to ICRC for a couple-hour meeting across the river and back to tackle a few more projects. I'm tired.*

7.

CONTROLLING THE *ZONE OF ACTION*

22 JUL 03: Qusay and Uday Hussein are killed after a three-hour firefight with US forces in the northern Iraqi city of Mosul

BASRAH, CHRONICLE #26
23 JULY 2003

I've seen many great fireworks displays but none as exhilarating as the one last night here in Baghdad. When news of Uday and Qusay's deaths was out, so too was the celebratory gunfire. The boys from Special Operations and the always-dependable 101st Air Assault Division did great work in timely prosecuting these sick twists with extreme prejudice. Four of our boys were wounded in the action. I had just gotten back from Basrah in time to review the press statement to be made by LTG Sanchez when the Iraqi celebration commenced. The sky was full of red tracer fire and the staccato of automatic weapons.

Our weapons-control policy was not working as planned. But several of us went to the roof of the palace to watch the show. After an initial report that one of our guys had been hit by celebratory fire, we recalled one of the guiding principles of physics: what goes up must come down. We swiftly retreated, grabbed our Kevlar helmets, and returned to the rooftop for the finale. We looked a bit silly, but until they invent a Kevlar umbrella for the rain of steel, we had to make do. After all we've been through, an epitaph of "died watching fireworks" didn't seem worthy. Someone thought to sound the alarm to wake up anyone still sleeping, as if anyone could sleep through the barrage, when the bullets started penetrating our aluminum-clad trailers out back of the palace. They always warn that fireworks can be dangerous, but this was ridiculous. Nothing that night, though, compared to the dangers the four boys wounded in the assault upon Uday and Qusay had encountered. Trading four good pawns for two evil bishops may seem like a deal, unless you're the pawns. The pawns are the kings in my game.

The Turks are an interesting ingredient in the potentially lethal brew in northern Iraq, specifically in the autonomous Kurdish zone. The situation requires a scorecard to keep the players straight. Some of the Turks are here legitimately as the Turkomans and as part of the Peace Minding Force (PMF). The PMF has been here since 1996 when they became the buffer between the two major Kurdish factions— the PUK (Patriotic Union of Kurdistan) and the KDP (Kurdistan Democratic Party). The PUK and the KDP have since gotten together and were our allies in throwing out Saddam and his regime, so the PMF was no longer needed and sort of transformed into an armed proxy for Turkish influence within the Turkoman community. I hesitate to mention the PKK (Kurdistan Workers' Party), Turkish Kurds living in northern Iraq, for fear of confusion. The PMF is still here technically watching the PUK and KDP while keeping an eye on the PKK so that nothing happens PDQ on the QT. Got that?

Our Special Operations troops dropped in on twenty-plus unsuspecting Turkish Special Forces folks and their weapons cache a couple of weeks ago in a neighborhood in northern Iraq, creating some international fuss. The raid was unique to my knowledge, resulting in bagging sixty-two AK-47 rifles, ten M-4 rifles, three M-60 machine guns, an RPG with fifty rounds, eight 9 mm pistols, twenty thousand 7.62 rounds, one land mine, one M203 grenade launcher, one blue bikini (so says the inventory), and a British clown! Frankly, bagging a clown seems good sport. Seems a British chap named Michael Todd, who listed his occupation as a clown, had just arrived in Kirkuk searching for his lost daughter conceived with an Iraqi girlfriend. As luck would have it, Todd was dropped off from a taxi just as the raid began, and so was caught in the net. He was bagged when he couldn't outrun the troopers, or anyone else for that matter, in his floppy shoes!

Despite a small chuckle over the feckless clown, there was a big fuss raised by the Turks, but has since somewhat been smoothed out. Nevertheless, we spent some long hours here trying to come up with a game plan. After the good efforts of a high-level joint fact-finding board, I'm happy to report that Mr. Todd was given back his horn and was last seen in his big floppy shoes and rubber-ball nose heading north in search of his daughter and some better luck.

It's shutdown week here in Iraq. We're trying to shut down a heap of oil smuggling in the south. The illegal hemorrhaging of oil is costing us millions and it must be stopped. I suggested that we call it Operation Clampett—as in Jed, the bubbling crude, and a great pun, to boot—but it was shouted . . . er . . . groaned down by the operation guys. We also have to shut down a newspaper that was declaring open season after Allah expressed his will to kill those cooperating with the Coalition. When they threatened to publish a list of names, enough was enough. I was secretly hoping that the mission would also re-bag the clown, whom we sorely missed, and thus was mildly disappointed when all we got was a few computers, some diskettes, and a night watchman without floppy shoes. Our closure notice slipped nicely under the front door as it lay flat on the ground.

Amnesty International is revived and stirring again with another barrage of "concerns" they brought to us that some Iraqi looters and murderers aren't given enough cigarettes, are having to sleep in a tent in the sand and heat, and are having to eat MREs (as are 135,000 US soldiers here). We countered that, unlike our soldiers, the prisoners have some opportunity for release on bail! Ambassador Sawyer at my urging aptly pointed out to the Amnesty delegation led by—I kid you not—Curt Goering, that instead of carping at us every chance they get, they need to explain where they have been for the past thirty years here during Saddam's sick regime.

They didn't have a good answer to that, so the carping became somewhat less carpy. We kindly referred Mr. Goering and his *Sturmtruppen* to the ambassador's deputy chief of staff, Mike Hess. I imagine that they had some great human-rights stories to swap! In the meantime, our troops will go on eating MREs, sleeping in tents in the sand and heat, and getting no lovin' from Amnesty International. That, too, is Allah's will.

Email to Sean Delaney, 21 JUL 03: *If this place just had beer . . . it would still suck. Your package arrived and Owen and I are wearing Thee Doll House tees (tease). It's my only non-Army clothing apparel, so I look particularly dapper in it trudging off to the cat-hole latrine and watching the sun set over the palace. I know it was a bold effort for you and James to obtain them, but war is hell.*

Email to Diane, 21 JUL 03: *We're working on an oil-smuggling problem and I hope we'll come up with something to stop the hemorrhaging. Will go early tomorrow to Basrah with MG Campbell to look at prisons/courts and I need to separately meet with the Brits on a case we are working up for the Central Criminal Court.*

Email to Diane, 22 JUL 03: *Long day starting at 0500 for day trip to Basrah. Not much of a city—flat, dusty and everything sand-colored. Not much character. Went to the temporary House of Justice and met with judges, toured the city and burned-out courthouse, then went to one of the prisons before flying back. In on the final press speech draft for LTG Sanchez after I returned. He will use it to announce Uday/Qusay killings. Great news. We went up on the roof to watch and hear the gunfire into the air all over the city, wisely wearing our helmets since some of the bullets were coming down in our compound, one hurting a soldier. Since they could pierce our tin trailers, everyone was called inside for a while just to be safe. Even so, it was pretty cool hearing the celebratory fire everywhere over the city.*

Email to Diane, 24 JUL 03: *Not much else here except 120 Iraqis were admitted to hospitals yesterday early morning with gunshot wounds from the aforesaid celebratory fire.*

Email to Diane, 24 JUL 03: *Great day today with some meetings in the morning about whether to release the photos of Uday and Qusay and what to do with their bodies. We took all of the twenty-seven or so boxes of toys and clothes and several hundred beanie babies to an orphanage today as well. It was great. The kids ranged from toddlers to teens. They were cute and the place was great. They put out a big spread for us.*

BAGHDAD, CHRONICLE #27
27 JULY 2003

One measure of a man is how he treats dogs and children, particularly children. Therefore, the thugs cowardly engaging our troops by abusing the children of Iraq are beneath contempt. They are not men at all. In my book, they are the real weapons of mass destruction that we are searching for. Nothing is more despicable than forcing children into the deadly game of war. We have had a series of incidents involving children throughout the war. Saddam's Fedayeen routinely used children as human shields and hid behind them knowing we, unlike them, wouldn't target the children. Some held children hostage, forcing their fathers to strap on bombs and try to take out checkpoints. Others sent young kids up to soldiers in crowds with live grenades and improvised explosive devices.

Yesterday, they specifically targeted our troops as they guarded a children's hospital. We lost three and they injured four, including loss of a leg, when these young soldiers were attacked by hand grenades from a roof above them in Baqubah. When you hear news like this come over the speaker at the JOC, you get pissed and you want to scream. I trust the public here will turn on these pusillanimous twists. That would be the true measure of the people of Iraq.

Children were front and center all week here. One woman and her children came forward and pinned a tail on some of the Iraqi police leaders who in the mid-1990s killed her husband and tortured and tormented her and others here in Baghdad. The tales were remarkable, yet typical of Saddam's corrupt, brutal regime. A couple of our guys down in the Ministry of Justice went to the police academy and grabbed the suspects at gunpoint. It was a bit comical since neither of the justice guys were particularly fierce and came from Mayberry Central Casting.

In fact, as one held the police chief at gunpoint, the other stage-whispered to him that he may want to consider chambering a round! Hell, those two were lucky he had his one bullet with him. We have been meeting about the case and are pushing the investigation along. I get this sinking feeling that we are just nicking the tip of the iceberg. We're starting to see some of the Iraqis come forward with their stories. The killing of Uday and Qusay clearly have some Iraqis breathing better, some less, as 120 Iraqis were hospitalized with gunshot wounds from the celebratory fire the night the brothers' deaths were announced. What a party! It was a real bang.

The best party of all was our long-awaited trip to the children's orphanage this week. We descended with our thirty-plus boxes of toys, clothes, sundries, and my ducky from the firm, over 250 beanie babies from the thousands received by the commanding general's driver, and one box of MREs courtesy of you all that was inadvertently carried in from the HUMMV by mistake. We debated whether to pull the MREs back, but the helpers at the orphanage were so nice, fascinated as they were with the MREs—although frankly, the only surprise inside each one would be if they found any taste there.

Al Najat Orphanage, in the Adamiyah section of Baghdad, is the home of forty or so orphans from all over the Baghdad area. Some are placed with foster parents, some sadly remain. None are adopted, as adoption is illegal here, as in most Arab countries. The children ranged from toddlers to teens. They were cute, they were well mannered, they were kids dealt a bad hand in a bad country, but they were suddenly given a trump card when they were placed at Al Najat. The toys, and reluctantly my ducky, were passed out—I swear I saw a couple beanie babies walk on their own to a couple of cuties in the corner—and the smiles began on the kids and on us. The women working there put on a huge traditional spread for us. When we had picked our way down the table, the kids swarmed the feast. Smiles turned to more smiles—making one smile-filled day in a frown-filled country. I suspect that when all is said and done, the most important mission we have here is to make this a smile-filled country.

Delivering hundreds of toys and Beanie Babies in exchange for hundreds of smiles at the Al Najat Orphanage in the Adamiyah section of Baghdad. (July 2003) These kids cornered the market on cute and cornered our hearts.

Email to Diane, 1 AUG 03: *As usual I chaired two long meetings over four hours today on Special (Sensitive) Prosecution Task Force and prisons and then was involved in the Ministry of Justice meeting. A slower afternoon but several quick projects and a couple of wild events. One is too good not to share. Seems the forensic pathologists who did the autopsy on Uday and Qusay decided that one of the identifying methods would be to confirm the correct manufacturer's number on the plate in Uday's leg (where he was shot during an assassination attempt several years ago). I think these guys really wanted to have a keepsake for the forensic museum back in the States, but they claimed that they didn't have an Allen wrench to remove the plate to see the manufacturer's number, so they removed the plate by simply cutting the bone above and below the plate and taking the ten-inch bone back to the States with them. Oops.*

Someone found out, so we had to negotiate to get the bone back here for eventual burial. They had been planning on using a plastic replica and replacing that back into the leg as necessary. Bad idea. Someone way up the ladder made them see the light, so they had to fly back here with the bone to replace it. They did negotiate to keep the plate. I would simply have court-martialed the a-holes. Anyway, Uday is back together with his leg. What a deal. Stuff like that happens almost daily here.

In fact, several former inmates at the Abu Ghraib prison came back after the war to try to locate their hands that had been chopped off and buried there on the prison site.

Email to Diane, 3 AUG 03: *Interesting twist yesterday going to the ICRC. At a big traffic circle downtown when you cross the Tigris River, this guy runs out in an attempt to stop us to tell us something, like he saw Saddam or something, but who knows? I was driving the SUV in between two MP HUMMVs. He ran right in front of me, causing* *me to stop or run him down. The first HUMMV was already moving forward, and the rear one swung around instantaneously and cut the guy off. The gunner in the turret yelled at the guy while pointing his weapon a couple feet from him to "Get the f**k back" about ten times until the guy peeled back from in front of our vehicle. Heck, I was grabbing my gun and going to roll down the window to talk to him, but I guess not. So we have no idea what he planned to tell us . . . or do to us. That is life here. Anyway, no other real excitement than that.*

BAG DAD NEXT, CHRONICLE #28
4 AUGUST 2003

Talk about a hazard! Thanks to a 6-iron that made its way here from my office, I played some combat golf yesterday. The first and only tee-box on the "course" was some sandy spot along the Tigris River behind the Presidential Palace. My swing path was a little constrained by my flak vest, canteen, pistol, and holster, and my Kevlar helmet prevented me from fully addressing the ball, giving a new meaning to "bunker shot." But all in all, taking a few shots to clear the Tigris toward the Palestine Hotel felt great and provided some comic relief to the kids in the guard tower with their .50 caliber also fortunately pointing downrange. Although they were laughing at my perfect swing path, I noticed that they adjusted their IBA (Interceptor Body Armor) in case I shanked one their way. The reporters in the Palestine Hotel, like the guard tower guys, had nothing to worry about, however.

I'll admit that with my sweet swing, malaria tablets making me hallucinate, they may have been fearful of another tank round shot into their upper deck. In truth, I barely carried the reeds before my balls found a familiar resting place—water—at the bottom of the river. I've also confirmed that no downed aviators were hiding in the reeds, for surely they would have surrendered after my third shot! I have now proudly added the Tigris River to my long and distinguished lost-ball RIP résumé. On the other hand, I did not want to draw any return salvos from the thugs across the river that kept us up with steel-ball volleys during a few of their probes the night before. After a restless night, it felt good to return some fire in their direction, and I hope "Titleist" means something nasty in Arabic.

We have been wrestling with the bodies of Uday and Qusay since they were transported down here to Baghdad last week. Appropriately, they continue to cause havoc even in their deaths. I've mentioned the celebratory fire by which we took one US casualty from above, and now we had to figure out what we needed to do with the brothers' remains. Sounds pretty simple. But with most of Iraq and all of the reporters wanting confirmation of their deaths, and most of the country wanting also to drag their bodies through the streets Mussolini-style, it was definitely not simple. The easiest part was identifying these bastards. Witnesses, dental and leg radiographs, orthopedic plates, and circumstances made that easy. They definitely did not suffer from iron deficiency, especially after catching the task force and the 101st ABN's un-celebratory steady fire.

A parade of representatives from the new Governing Council, including a former college classmate and a bevy of reporters, made their way to see the corpses and assure themselves that these were the real Husseins. Once we applied some needed makeup—we've ordered a gallon of Grecian Formula in anticipation of bagging the big guy—the real trick was then what to do with the remains. I suggested we simply invite good old dad to swing by and pick them up. That, or give Uday's lion a familiar taste of home!

But waiting out the old man or feeding the kitty wasn't acceptable under the Geneva Conventions, so we worked with the ICRC, who really didn't want them, and then the Governing Council, who really, really didn't want them, and then the Iraqi Red Crescent, associated with the former regime, who finally agreed to accept them, take them off our hands, and get them to the family.

So off the brothers and one of their sons, who was also killed in the shootout, went early Saturday morning, fittingly packed in ice vaults, on a US Chinook chopper to Tikrit and the old family stomping grounds that our guys had also stomped about four months ago. Although there was some momentary confusion when one of the ice vaults being used as a drink cooler next to the vaults was inadvertently dropped off instead of the grandson, the vaults with the bodies were eventually dropped off to the Red Crescent at the rendezvous landing area near Tikrit, making their way to some of the family. Sadly, the Red Crescent "hearses" were too small for the large vaults, causing quite a stir. You can imagine the rest. I suspect that someone from our side kept track of who signed the guest book, just in case. We hope this funeral was just a rehearsal for the real show sometime soon. We'll keep the Grecian Formula ready just in case.

Email to Diane, 4 AUG 03: *Meetings on oil smuggling, Danish consulates, and such. Funny, Scott Castle (CPA GC) was on a conference call with some folks at the American Bar Association and I impressed him by walking up to the conversation and jumping in on the speakerphone with a "Hey, Bob" (Horowitz, whom I've been emailing with) and "Hey, A. P." (Carlton—ABA president from Raleigh, whom I have personally known for years). Small world.*

Email to Diane, 6 AUG 03: *Went to Baqubah, a city an hour-plus northeast of here. Went with Judge Campbell to the courts there and spoke with the judges and lawyers. (Flora Darpino, 4 ID SJA, met us there and escorted us around.) Also, met with several guys out at the 2nd Brigade Combat Team, 4th ID camp. It's at an old airport. They take mortars every other night or so, and one of the legal NCOs was hit by shrapnel a week or two ago. I talked with him a while and saw the JAG computer screen with a hole in it from the shrapnel. Talk about a lucky shot or a near-miss, whichever! Working on some really good issues/crises tonight and have full plate of Article 5 tribunals of the HVDs tomorrow.*

Email to Diane, 8 AUG 03: *Busy day yesterday planning an operation and doing a couple of Article 5 tribunals. The last one was sad because we had bagged the wrong guy. He had the same name as a bigwig and was just a long-retired sergeant who was driving a taxi cab during the war. We knew we had the wrong man pretty shortly after he told us he only went to primary school, yet he was supposed to be the director, legal branch of the Special Security Organization. All comical, but sad, too. Busy today and will go to Basrah and Umm Qasr tonight for a special operation.*

Email to Diane, 9 AUG 03: *Flew down through Kuwait to Basrah. Stayed with our British hosts and worked up a game plan for the boarding and investigation of the* Navstar *tanker at Umm Qasr that is going down today. We'll talk to the crew this afternoon/evening. The A/C is off at the Basrah Airport where the Brits are located and the heat is brutal. I suspect that Umm Qasr will be around 135 degrees this afternoon when we arrive. We stink. Dan Shearouse wrote that he had met with the Clerk of the US Supreme Court (former TAJAG William Suter) who was getting my chronicles and was sharing them with Chief Justice Rehnquist. Pretty wild.*

BAQUBAH, CHRONICLE #29
12 AUGUST 2003

Unless you happen to be a JAG who flies F-14 Tomcats on television, judge advocates get little attention and most of the work. However, some are real heroes. A JAG captain with the 101st ABN was one of the most grievously wounded casualties of the infamous grenade attack by a member of the division on the third night of the war. Lucky for the young captain, he was actually sleeping in his flak vest. Two others weren't so lucky.

The SJA of the 1st Marine Division was shot three times while investigating the shooting of two journalists who, giving them the benefit of the doubt, were unknowingly in a column of Fedayeen in Basrah targeted early in the war. He wouldn't have been investigating the incident while the bullets were flying if not for the hue and cry of the media demanding an immediate investigation while the battle still raged. I hope they're satisfied.

JAGs from the 1st Armored Division performed an heroic rescue operation this past week in Baghdad. They were in the area of an RPG and small arms attack on a MP patrol. Instead of ducking for cover and running out of harm's way, these heroes—young captains and enlisted soldiers—charged ahead towards the attack, laid down suppressive fire, and extracted several wounded MPs by litter, saving their lives. Sadly, one of the MPs later lost both legs but was alive thanks to some brave JAGs. Ambulance chasers? The ambulances here are chasing the JAGs.

During a trip to Baqubah, about an hour and a half northeast of Baghdad, I met with another hero. SGT Davis, 27D (paralegal), with the 2nd Brigade Combat Team ("Warhorse") of the 4th Infantry Division that lives in a godforsaken patch of six inches of powdery sand that was once an airport. Although the 4th ID is the Army's high-tech division of Abrams tanks and Bradley Fighting Vehicles, the area assigned to Warhorse was as low-tech and inhospitable as there is, but a few mortars every other night adds some glitz.

The Warhorse Tactical Operations Center (TOC) was recently hit by mortars, and the brave JAG cell took the brunt of the action. This young sergeant and his laptop computer were hit hard by shrapnel. Both are still ticking, but barely. Davis was the last member of the TOC to try to jump into the rear of one of the armored personnel carriers that line the TOC. As he pivoted to make sure everyone was under cover, he was hit just below his knee. Despite serious injury, he has toughed it out with little relief despite the Army's offer of more specialized treatment, even a return home. Davis refuses either course and immediately returned to duty because he refused to leave Warhorse.

Both he and his logic are worthy. SGT Davis will simply not leave his duty or his fellow soldiers under fire as long as he can do his job. In the hellhole and mortar magnet that Warhorse has to live, those two factors are what sustain him and the rest of Warhorse. Some things are timeless. The hard-charging young heroes from the infantry and armor columns have nothing on this kid. Amazingly, despite a growing hole the size of a Kennedy half-dollar dead center in the screen, caused by the mortar that hit him, the brigade JAG laptop computer still serves Davis well, squeaking and moaning only a bit, like he does. Although the screen only partly works, Davis refuses to turn it in for a new one. Both continue to do their duty. You don't need to fly an F-14 Tomcat or be a point man to earn my respect. I may even be nicer to my computer from now on.

Who said there was "No time for sergeants"? We recently gave enough time to an old sergeant to figure out that he was doing time by involuntarily impersonating a "high-value detainee." We're continuing to do the required Geneva Convention Article 5 tribunals on the big fish from the former regime. Although the file for one Basim al-Tikriti reported that he was the former director of the Secret Security Organization, the man who appeared before us didn't seem to quite fit that mold. It soon became apparent that we had the wrong man. Basim "the Unlucky" kept pointing to his right sleeve and stating that he was just a sergeant, a typist medically retired back in 1991. His primary school education hardly matched the education level of our Basim either. In fact, the prisoner was a taxi driver. If it wasn't so sad, it would have been hysterical. The stories he can tell his family will be priceless: "There I was, hanging out with Tariq Aziz, Chemical Ali, the whole deck of cards, the former ministers of this and directors of that . . . and me, Basim, the taxi driver!" Hell, none of the rest of the guys had seen anything less than a limo for years. I doubt that they even knew how to drive a car on their own! I wondered if he got to room with the British clown caught as he was dropped off by a taxi during the Turkish raid. I bet they'd have a million funny taxi stories to share!

He was animated, to say the least. Because his name matched one of the high-value targets, he was grabbed mistakenly by our hunters. At one point early in the very, very short tribunal session, Basim mounted a spirited response to some question, after which the interpreter pointed out that he was swearing profusely. I guess I would be, too. I hope he is now home with his taxi and family. I picture him picking up our British clown with floppy shoes and rubber nose, who was last seen trying to hail a cab. If I were Basim, though, I'd keep on driving. That clown is nothing but trouble.

My favorite inane line often heard in North Carolina used to be "Hot enough for you?" No more. The heat is so intense in Iraq that even the dogs have asked for days here other than August. And the Iraqis themselves have sensibly altered their routine by timing their demonstrations to morning and evening to avoid the mid-day blast furnace. Demonstrating is hard work, you know. Particularly when you don't even know what you're protesting. They protest at random here.

To sample some serious heat and to bag a big boat, a couple of us in the Special Prosecution Task Force have been down in Umm Qasr and Basrah the past few days. It was a bear. 130 degrees in the shade if you can find any. I counted thirteen trees between the Umm Qasr Port and Basrah. The locals find shade by standing down-sun from each other. The taller Iraqis always have a host of shade worshippers hanging about in their shadows. For us, the flak vests and Kevlar helmets add to the fun. Several soldiers have even been able to scratch out "wash me" in the salt stains that have formed on their uniforms. It's quite an art form.

If you can take a shower, you find that the water from the hot spigot is much colder than the water from the cold. And, while you're attempting to dry off, you sweat so much that you have to take another shower. You could spend the whole day cycling back and forth a few steps from the shower. The port-a-lets heat up, too, and are cozy. For the full effect, try defecating in the sauna. It has cut my reading by half. The seats there are also a few degrees shy of the temperature on the face of the sun. I always wanted a tattoo but this is ridiculous. I'm the one with the horseshoe brand on his ass, but our herd is increasing in number as I speak.

Email to Diane, 12 AUG 03: *Been incommunicado doing all the interrogations of the* Navstar I *crew with our Russian interpreters, borrowed from the Brits. The tanker finally made it to port yesterday morning with their US Coast Guard escort, so we worked from 0800 to midnight on the ship. We uncovered all sorts of smoking-gun documents and found 3½ times the diesel on board. It is a big ship and soon to be the newest member of the Iraqi merchant marine because the captain and the chief officer are going down. We had a few adventures along the way, but everything eventually worked out fine, just took us a day or two longer than expected. Back to Basrah from Umm Qasr at 0200 and back to Baghdad first thing in the morning. We're pooped but put a serious hurt on the oil smuggling in Iraq.*

AT SEA, CHRONICLE #30
13 AUGUST 2003

I've always wanted to be a pirate. Swashbuckling around with an eye patch, hook hand, peg leg, and a parrot on my shoulder. I even trained by hitting a Jimmy Buffett concert shortly before mobilizing for Iraq. I finally got my chance this week. We've been facing some serious oil-smuggling operations in the southern Iraqi waters that were costing the people money, oil, and electricity. Our Special Prosecution Task Force (SPTF) looks into special crimes of national import to be prosecuted before the new Central Criminal Court, so we were tracking the smuggling developments in search of an opportunity to stop the hemorrhaging.

Coincidently, the HMS *Sutherland* had been tracking an oil

tanker *Navstar I* anchored in the northern Arabian Gulf along the outer road to the port of Umm Qasr, Iraq. Our team recommended that the vessel be seized if it pulled anchor and attempted to run. In the early morning hours of 5 August, the *Sutherland* sent a team of Royal Marines aboard the *Navstar* to review its official books, then held the *Navstar* at anchorage for three days until a team from the USS *Rodney Davis* and the USCGC *Thompson* crew aboard the *Wrangler* re-boarded her on the evening of the 8th.

Iraqi tugs began the slow process of moving her to port. The MV *Navstar I* is a GP3, 138-meter long, 17.5-meter beam oil tanker with, of course, a Panamanian registry and is owned by a shipping company from UAE. It would soon be the pride of the new Iraqi merchant marine. The captain and crew were, of course, Russians from the Crimean coast of the Ukraine.

Our SPTF JAG team of three flew down immediately from Baghdad and were waiting at the port for the docking of the *Navstar I*. It took her a couple of days more than expected to get into dock, though. In the meantime we had our crack team of Iraqi police ready to escort the captain and crew off the ship for further interrogation and processing. They kept showing up at our request every time the ship was supposed to come in. We felt so bad by Sunday night that the tanker hadn't made it in yet, we had them pose for a photo along the ramp to another ship just in case the media needed a good shot. The reaction from the sailors guarding the other ship to our local Iraqi cops running up their ramp carrying AK-47s and dressed proudly in their new uniforms—all about three sizes too small—was priceless.

On the morning of 11 August, our SPTF JAG team of three finally assaulted . . . er . . . boarded *Navstar* with our three Russian translators the moment she hit the dock at Umm Qasr. Fortunately, the British pack something for every situation in their kit bag, including Russian interpreters. Although we planned to board the ship the pirate way, by climbing ropes with blades in our mouths and eye patches worn jauntily, we decided on using the ramp since it was already lowered. The captain, squeezed into his old uniform festooned with ribbons, was an old U-boat commander from the Russian Navy, straight from Central Casting and complete with a ruddy face, a generous paunch, and vodka-slurred speech. We found him in his cabin, the walls lined with Russian pinups. He carried his sixty-seven years poorly, fueled by his despair at a retirement plan that now included a cruise through a sea of Iraqi prisons. The motley crew of twenty-one, counting the ship's cat, Kuzma, fit the mold as well. The scene had all the fixings of a great Clancy Cold-War novel.

We first reviewed the logs and ship's documents. I quickly found the only document of immediate concern. Yes, the ship had a de-ratting exemption from the Tanzania Board of Health! Kuzma looked game and satisfied, so I felt better about this adventure and quietly slipped out the round chambered in my pistol when no one was looking.

I made sure the bridge looked like a bridge and searched for a gangplank in the off chance that we had to exercise some good old-fashioned pirate justice before we set about interrogating the crew. We divided up the crew for interrogation, and I drew the first contestant—one of the two females on board. We knew the crew had two women on board, and the high/low bet on their weight and length of their single eyebrow was 220 and 4.5 inches.

We were pleasantly surprised that the steward I had to interrogate was a twenty-year-old Ukrainian knockout named Olga, who cost me my weight-estimate wager. She apparently had caught the captain's eye in Kursk a few months ago, and he brought her on board for more than her eyes. She had other ideas, and as a result she was being sacked, although not quite as the captain had hoped. My interpreter was an elderly British army gentlemen who kept puffing on his pipe throughout the interrogations. Olga kept leaning over the table to answer my questions and in doing revealed enough cleavage to take a frigate through that channel. Every time she leaned forward, my interpreter's pipe would raise and put out more smoke than a steam locomotive making the ascent up Pike's Peak! Fortunately, I was all business and fully under control as I pressed her to answer my tricky question on her favorite color.

The other interrogations went slightly better. Fortunately, I was in the chief officer's cabin and stumbled onto a log book hidden in plain sight that kept a list of twenty-eight smaller vessels—nice additions to the growing Iraqi merchant marine fleet—that had loaded the diesel fuel we and they knew was illegal onto the tanker over a period of eight days. Along with that, I found a bunch of other smoking-gun documents and receipts. In the process, we uncovered over 3,500 metric tons of oil and two falsified documents prepared at the captain's request that showed only 1,100 metric tons of fuel oil. When I showed to the British navy, they confirmed that these constituted ample fraud for our prosecution. All of the fuel was illegal and created a more-than-slight problem for the captain and crew of the *Navstar*. Fifteen hours later the crew started some serious singing, diming out the captain, the chief officer, and several other big fish, including an Iraqi sailor with a peg leg!

The media eventually arrived late in the day, and we finally got to call our Keystone Coppers on board to march off some of the crew for processing. The faces of the cameramen as they saw Olga wedged in between six gnarly Russian seamen were hilarious. By midnight we had completed processing all of the crew except the cat and the captain, whom we left for the Iraqi investigative judge to entertain in a couple of days. All in all, a good day's work for the people of Iraq and for the newest pirates of the Coalition forces. We had earned our parrot-head ribbons with eye-patch devices this day. Aaaarrrgh, maties!

Special Prosecution Task Force on board NAVSTAR I at Umm Qasr port, Iraq, August 2003. (Warner; Colonel Mike Kelly, Australian Forces; and Captain Brian Cook, USMC). The oil-smuggling tanker NAVSTAR I was escorted to dock at the port of Umm Qasr, Iraq, August 2003.

Email to Gil Steadman et al., 13 AUG 03: *Folks, Perry's email summed it up. It's tougher than it looks. You probably can see the low boy that I caught thin in my picture. The radar picked it up as a heat seeker but couldn't figure out what it was since it was outgoing!*

[Perry's Email:] *We were trying to hit golf balls into the Tigris River with a six-iron out back of CPA. It was about 120 degrees that day. We were hitting over an area on the shore that still had unexploded ordnance on it. . . . I managed a few stiff practice swings. Got into a good stance, had a smooth back swing, a powerful forward motion at about 120 miles per hour, and then duffed it about 100 yards into the lower shoreline. The one time I try to hit it into the water I can't do it. Thankfully I didn't hit a landmine or something. . . . Like any golf-hacker, I have to think of some good excuses which—individually or in combination—might possibly account for my chokingly poor performance. First, it was hot. Sweat was running everywhere and I almost lost the club in the backswing. Second, it was a sand shot. We used a tee, but the thought of sand under the tee would make anybody choke. Third, I had to maintain situational awareness and scan the horizon for potential snipers. Fourth, I subconsciously thought that I might knock out one of the hotel windows on the other side of the river. The hotel was only 500 yards away and you know how good I am with a six-iron. Surely one of these will garner a nod of sympathy. Anyway we laughed, especially at LTC Warner trying to get a full swing while wearing his body armor. What a sight.*

Fore! Testing distance and clearing minefield with my six-iron across the Tigris River behind Presidential Palace, Baghdad, Iraq, July 2003. Nightly incoming mortar and sniper fire inspired my own return fire. They survived the meager barrage. The fish were less lucky.

Email to Diane, 14 AUG 03: *Really wild day today. Started out on smuggling and working up some stuff when I was ordered to go to An Najaf by Marine chopper at 0930. I ran to the helipad and learned the choppers were delayed until 1230. In the meantime I covered several matters, then flew with Mike Kelly, the Aussie colonel, and MG Campbell to An Najaf aboard two Marine Chinooks. We met with the Marine battalion commander and went to meet with a judge about a major case and the arrest of a powerful cleric and thirty-one others in the killing of another big-time cleric in Najaf in April. Bremer wanted us to go down and get the ground truth and talk to the judge. We met with the judge downtown and then choppered back by 1730. I then had to hop in a convoy out to Victory Camp where I used to stay and backbriefed a planning team of five generals including LTG Sanchez and about thirty other officers. That lasted until 2200, and then COL Warren and I met with the V Corps JAGs to plan some stuff and busted back to the palace a couple minutes ago. Whew. Ernie Simons sent me an email saying that he'd analyzed my golf swing and detected a strong "reverse pivot" that could affect my swing path. He recommended that I take three weeks off . . . and then quit the game!*

Email to Diane, 16 AUG 03: *Had to meet with three reporters from* Newsday, *the* Wall Street Journal *and the* London Times *for two hours this morning about juvenile detainees. The* Times *girl was a know-it-all who just wanted to argue against everything we were doing. I thought about it but decided it would have been a problem if I'd pulled my pistol and shot her. The other two reporters were fine. Had a meeting with AMB McManaway about detainees and then an oil-smuggling meeting.*

Email to Diane, 18 AUG 03: *Flew down to Basrah yesterday afternoon for the oil-smuggling task force. We worked into the evening down there and then went to Umm Qasr for some coordination and boarded the* Navstar *again for a moment to check on things. I will return to Baghdad on the 12th Royal Air Force Command jet in the morning for a prison summit tomorrow.*

AUGUST 19, 2003 *NEWSDAY*
Iraqis: US Not Providing Detainee Info For Iraqi kids held by US, a legal morass

Lt. Col. Kirk Warner, a military lawyer known as the deputy staff judge advocate general, acknowledged that the coalition theoretically could hold a 6-year-old deemed a security threat to the coalition forces without the child's having any of the rights that a 17-year-old suspected of murdering a fellow Iraqi would have. "We try to recognize all international laws but we have to balance them with the security of the people of Iraq," he said. "The security of the people of Iraq is the trump card." Of the soldiers interviewed, only Warner spoke with clarity and without contradiction about the way US forces are treating the juveniles. "We're crawling, then walking, then running to try to get this working," Warner said. "We know we haven't done great."

19 AUG 03: Bombing of the United Nations compound in the Canal Hotel killing UN secretary general's special representative Sérgio Vieira de Mello along with twenty other members of his staff.

Email to Diane, 19 AUG 03: *Bad bomb blast at UN hotel headquarters this afternoon. The UN chief envoy de Mello was killed with a bunch of others. Sad. These terrorists are beneath contempt. De Mello was a friend of Bremer. I gave both of them a tour of Abu Ghraib a month or so ago. Really nice guy. What a senseless loss! These thugs are hitting Red Cross employees, UN employees, mortaring their own detainees . . . They have no honor, so I guess it's good we're killing them.*

AUGUST 20, 2003 *WALL STREET JOURNAL* (FRONT PAGE):
Iraq Blast Prods US to Choose: Go It Alone or Give UN Big Role
One of the most ominous possibilities is that the attack [UN Headquarters and death of UN head of mission Sergio Vieira de Mello] *means international terrorism is moving into Iraq. L. Paul Bremer III, the top US administrator in Iraq, has said the US-led coalition has strong evidence of foreign fighters with ties to al Qaeda, including some from Ansar al-Islam, an organization*

once active in Iraq's Kurdish region. A US officer, Lt. Col. Kirk Warner, says that in the past week, soldiers have arrested "at least a dozen people with clear connections to al Qaeda, some of them non-Iraqi Arabs."

Comical email from LTC Don Perritt (former CFLCC DSJA) to Lake Summers, 15 AUG 03: *We constantly see the self-appointed CPA Governor Kirk Warner on the front page of the top periodicals circulating the DC area, but alas, you are conspicuously absent from the pages. There have been numerous comments attributed to "an unnamed government spokesperson" and "key officials in the Coalition" that could only be you. Regardless, we are all proud of you and the members of the 12th LSO! I had the opportunity to break bread with the TJAG himself last week and I tried to repeat as many of the exploits of the 12th LSO that I could recall—to say that he was rendered speechless is an understatement.*

With the VIPs at Abu Ghraib Prison, July 2003 (Bernie Kerik, former NY City police commissioner, CPA senior advisor to the Iraqi Police, center left; CPA administrator Paul Bremer, center; UN special envoy Sergio de Mello, center right). Kerik left Iraq shortly thereafter. Bremer served nobly for that first year as the leader of the Coalition Provisional Authority in Iraq. He was a close friend with de Mello, who died a month later as a result of a VBIED explosion at the UN Mission in Baghdad in August, 2003. The UN pulled out of Baghdad as a result of the bombing.

Email to Diane, 20 AUG 03: *Everyone's pissed about the UN thing. I was somehow quoted on the front page of the* Wall Street Journal, *frankly by mistake. I was being interviewed on juvenile detention issues, and after two hours one of the journalists asked, "Have you captured any al Qaeda?" I answered, "You'd need to check with the MI guys, but I understood that there were a few suspected to have al Qaeda ties." From that they ginned up the quote. Unbelievable what they can come up with. . . . I saw Bremer and talked with him some about de Mello. Sad stuff.*

Email to Diane, 22 AUG 03: *Busy Friday as usual, with meetings all morning on detention and then I had to advise an investigating officer and sat in on interviews concerning the Reuters photographer's shooting last Sunday by one of our troops. Tragic, but caused by the fog of war, in my book.*

BAGHDAD, CHRONICLE #31
23 AUGUST 2003

It's been a sad week for the good guys. Three weeks ago, I toured the Abu Ghraib prison with UN special envoy Sergio Vieira de Mello and Ambassador Bremer and had to field some softball detainee questions from them. Remarkably, the prisoners within the concertina wire holding areas gathered in the corner near the two diplomats and started clapping for them. I don't know what they were clapping about, but to me it meant recognition that they were the future of Iraq. Even the prisoners somehow knew. Both are the sort of men who leave impressions of competence, dignity, and grace everywhere they go. As a result, they are special.

However, de Mello's light was snuffed in the sordid bombing of the United Nations compound here earlier this week. It was a tragic loss. I cannot imagine what drives such evil. I've been stuck as the legal advisor to the Army Mortuary Affairs team tackling the horrific task of identifying, treating, and properly disposing of the remains of well-intended souls here from all over the world. Talk about unsung heroes, both the team and their charges are that.

The sick résumé of the terrorist and former regime leader's thugs is growing. Add the attack upon and killings of innocent Red Cross workers in Al Hillah a couple of weeks ago to the Jordanian embassy bombing, and we've got us a regular old thug-fest going on. Now they're even starting to kill their own. Not that I mind that, but we often get in the way. Take Abu Ghraib . . . please. It is now home to hundreds of Fedayeen and other thugs recently snatched in operations throughout the country. It is also homed in on by their brethren's deadly mortars. Last weekend they lobbed in three mortars, killed six, and wounded over sixty of their own. Now they're onto something—I'll send them the grid coordinates if they continue their accuracy.

The day after the mortar attack, on a highway just beside Abu Ghraib, a Reuters cameraman who was filming the exterior of the prison for a story about the mortars suddenly stopped his unmarked black BMW on the entrance ramp and jumped out, hoisting his large camera to his shoulder as a column of tanks approached. The commander of the tank column tragically mistook the camera for an RPG and, with amazing accuracy, felled the camera and man with only a handful of shots while the tank was rolling.

I'm the legal advisor for CJTF-7 to the officer investigating the incident. Normally, interviewing the Reuters, French FR2, and BBC press who witness some of the event would be a turnabout to relish. This occasion was not. It was tragic all the way around. Of course, the French refused to make it easy, insisting that their journalists speak only in French, even though their English is far better than mine. So we had to filter the interview through a French interpreter in Germany on a bad phone. Toot sweet! As if that helped clarify things.

Remind me why we like the French? Oh yeah, we don't! For a moment, I thought about issuing the French crew the same RPG-looking news cameras. Another tragedy is that the commander who fired the shots is a superb young captain who had bravely commanded the cavalry company for the past eighteen months, and he was at the airport ready to head to his next duty assignment. When his replacement was killed in action, he was recalled to command, return ticket still in hand. Welcome back.

The Central Criminal Court is up and walking now. We've cycled the first few juicy cases into the new court system we created. The first investigative hearings have concluded and the first trial starts this week. It's a beauty. Some young Iraqis thought a Red Crescent truck they stole would easily hold over 500 RPG rounds and slip by the 3rd Armored Cavalry Regiment checkpoint on its merry way to the arms market. Oops, I guess not.

We have a few good ones on deck as well: a corruption case involving the mayor of Najaf; a counterfeiting case involving a close friend of Uday; some nifty kidnapping cases; and the *Navstar* oil-smuggling case. It should be a fun fall for all involved, unless you're the Ukrainian captain and his chief officer, who are lounging in an Iraqi jail in Basrah. As a side note on the *Navstar*, we're having some difficulty lightening the bugger since every pipeline in Iraq only goes one direction . . . out. Oops, again. Anyone with a hose for siphoning, please report to Umm Qasr immediately.

Meanwhile, the British continue to play themselves superbly. The 3rd UK Division in nearby Basrah have a great field kitchen, with half-decent steak and kidney pie and a mean spotted dick. The Brit commanding general has a nice jet run by the 32nd Squadron of the 12th RAF that he will let you ride if you're nice as well. I suspect the truth is that the CG wanted to get me out of there on the fastest means available after I hung out there a few days too many and he may have grown tired of me responding "Quite!" with my lousy British accent in response to everything they said. The Brits do tickle me. In the latest comedy, the British are switching out their major generals assigned to the Combined Task Force, Vick Figgers for Freddie Viggers. Go figure. Quite!

Email to Diane, 23 AUG 03: *My day was a bit slow after an interesting morning interviewing a French journalist in connection with the Reuters cameraman's killing. We were going to the ICRC this afternoon, but they advised us that they were bugging out after receiving some bomb threats. I got stuck instead in a couple of meetings on the mortuary remains from the UN bombing. Never a dull moment, at least. Well, tomorrow may be one since we'll be reviewing prisoner files all day in a JAG fest. I hope we will be able to clean up the backlog and recommend release of some of them; e.g., ninety days in prison for violating curfew is probably enough.*

Email to Diane, 25 AUG 03: *Attended the first trial in the Central Criminal Court. It was interesting and turned out to be two trials. Jake's Bible was used to swear in the US soldiers as witnesses. The three-judge panel convicted the defendants, but gave them light sentences due, apparently, to some confusion. Anyway, it went smoothly.*

BASRAH, CHRONICLE #32
29 AUGUST 2003

"He's lucky to be alive!" So noted a patrol from the 82nd Airborne Division on the arrest report. In order to put our arms around the over 5,000 detainees that the Coalition forces are holding for processing by Iraqi courts, by our military intelligence folks, or, possibly, by our own military commissions, we held a screening party to beat all parties and coincidentally to comply with our Geneva Conventions requirements.

We invited all the JAGs in the area to bring their brooms and magistrates' hats for twelve hours of fun called Operation Clean Sweep. Although I've been invited to better parties, this was one of the most unusual. Thirty-two of us reviewed over 3,000 case files.

Thanks to looters and the former regime, we have the pleasure of hosting most of the country's criminals as they process into a court system too fragile to tackle the task. We had banked on a bunch of security internees who may have information on WMD and atrocities, but we hadn't factored on having to keep thousands of Iraqis who commit crimes against other Iraqis. As General Schwartzkopf said, you can script the perfect play, but you don't count on someone coming out of the audience with a pitchfork chasing the actors all about. The criminal detainees are the pitchfork; we're the haystack.

Speaking of haystacks, one of the internees was captured hiding a Milan missile in a stack of straw. Being larger than a needle, the missile was found without much difficulty. Other cases were more difficult. Among the more memorable from the hundred or so files I reviewed was one Iraqi caught stealing some pipe. I was going to recommend his release until I noticed on the report that he was using a crane. Another gem was from a kidnapping file involving two brothers: "He told me if I gave him two million dinars, he would tell me where my son was." Q: "How did you respond?" A: "I beat him until he told me where my son was." Of course! Why didn't I think of that? The arrest report in one car-jacking case indicated the suspect was caught traveling on foot. He must not have been too good at car-jacking! Another sad case involved a baker who was snagged in a raid. He eventually fessed up to deserting [desserting?] from the Iraqi Army. Aha! Wait a minute, guys, isn't that a good thing?

A sad case of mistaken identity came to the court this week. An American visiting his Iraqi parents and sister here thought it a good idea to drop by CPA (Coalition Provisional Authority) and assist his sister, a Baghdad lawyer, in getting a job with CPA. Some Iraqi identified him as one of the perpetrators of the kidnapping and murder of two of our soldiers back in July. Our guys appropriately detained him for questioning. Four days later at our tented corps holding area, they realized we had the wrong guy. One of our guys drove him home to his parents, hired his sister sight unseen, and thanked him for visiting. I bet he can't wait to get back to work in Detroit to tell them how relaxing his vacation in Iraq was.

The always helpful soldiers from the 82nd ABN noted on one arrest report under "additional helpful information," "Did you know that an ant can lift 100 times his own body weight?" and on another noted that they used "zip ties" to cuff the suspect and added the informative "Did you know 'zip' is Iraqi for 'penis'?" I do now, and thanks, guys. I reviewed a tough-to-prosecute case involving "communication of a threat with a butter knife." Stand back and spread 'em? And so it went.

Our oil-smuggling cases in the south are moving forward with the help of the local police and an investigating judge from the Central Criminal Court who was willing to set up his courtroom, complete with defense counsel, prosecutor, reporter and clerk, in the *Navstar*'s galley. Pass the popcorn and some justice, please. I went down to Basrah and Umm Qasr again to assist on the case and to work on some operations aimed at stopping the oil smuggling in the south. We found out the local police had been perfecting a novel deterrent themselves. The opportunity to try it out came when soldiers from the 3rd UK Division spotted a suspicious pipeline branching off from the main line from Basrah to Al Faw in the Khawr az Zubayr.

Who knows how long smugglers, likely funneling some of the take to corrupt local enforcement officers, had been tapping directly into the main line of crude oil and opening up the spigots at night to load oil directly onto small barges and boats to the tune of a million dollars a night? Direct action was needed. You can make a healthy profit if you don't pay anything for the oil, but the scheme was about to become unhealthy for the perps.

Within minutes of the Brits' arrival, the local police also appeared with an offer to help. Hmm. The Iraqis decided that the best course of action was to set fire to the barges. This brilliant plan dimmed swiftly when the barges suddenly exploded, which oil barges are apt to do, killing some of the smugglers and, unfortunately, some of the

Iraqi police. As a concept it was fine; the execution, however, left much to be desired. Scratch one oil-smuggling operation and a few of Iraq's finest. It should be great sport to catch smugglers when we eventually field an effective riverine force. I suggested that we request the services of McHale's Navy if we want to match the Iraqi performance so far. In fact, Ensign Parker may have already been in charge of their last debacle. I wonder if he ever made admiral?

With Navy captains Mike Dugan and Tim McKee arriving on a Royal Air Force C-130 to Basrah to develop plans for Operation Sweeney Todd to thwart oil-smuggling operations in the Arabian Gulf, August 2003.

On returning from Az Zubayr to Basrah, we tackled the road less traveled and promised not to travel it again. A sandstorm had kicked up, making the already barren terrain look more inhospitable than ever, as if that were possible. We bounced our way along some deserted tank track for enough miles to make any chiropractor smile, and found over a hundred burned-out Iraqi tank carcasses from the largest British tank fight since WWII. In this nowhere, the dead tanks were everywhere. No one had bothered to recover anything along this desolate stretch of road. In the blinding sandstorm and 135 degree heat, we expected Mad Max to appear suddenly on the scene. Amongst the carnage was a rest area with a row of concrete picnic tables. If there had been a scenic overlook, you would easily have seen hell from there.

Email to Diane, 28 AUG 03: *Arrived back in Baghdad after some adventures on Wednesday going to all the ports along the Khawr az Zubayr (the "Shatt"). Went to Umm Qasr to see the crew of the* Navstar *again and explained the court processes starting Saturday on the boat where they have been held. Went to two other ports and then cross-country home through a hundred or so dead Iraqi tanks/ artillery pieces along a dirt road-from-hell around Az Zubayr. A major battle took place there between the Brits and the Iraqis, and the Iraqis didn't fare well.*

Email to Diane, 29 AUG 03: *Long, tough day of meetings and drama in the operations center over the bombing and killing of one of the Hakims down in An Najaf this afternoon. I've been working on the case against one of the Hakims' Shiite rivals, Sadr, down there for weeks. Sadr's enforcers are no doubt to blame for this bomb. All hell will probably break out down there, so we're monitoring the situation. Hakim's uncle was wounded in an attack earlier in the week. His brother is on the Governing Council. It could get interesting.*

BAGHDAD, CHRONICLE #33
30 AUGUST 2003

Steal 512 RPG rounds and a Mercedes truck, paint a red crescent on the side of the truck . . . and you end up in jail. The Red Crescent case was tried in two separate trials as the first cases before the new

Central Criminal Court of Iraq. The three-judge trial panel from all over Iraq tried the case. The three defendants stood, although one wavered later on, during the entire trial before the bench as witnesses cycled up to give testimony that was in turn summarized by the chief judge for the court reporter. The judges do all the witness examination and ask any questions for the defense counsel and prosecutor. Prior sworn statements made during the investigative hearing are reconfirmed and admitted. When the defendants testify, the other defendants are sequestered.

The appointed defense counsel asked one question between them all during the separate trials on both pending counts but did a nice job in their closing argument. The arguments are interesting since the attorneys write them out, sign each page, stamp them, read them to the judges and then submit them to the panel. The rules are simple but hard to follow. No drink, no smoke, no crossed legs. They mean it! One of the soldiers in the audience was pitched for crossing his legs. It was excruciating for the four-hour, seven-witness trial (times two).

One of our team's Bibles served to swear in the soldier witnesses. Everyone in the courtroom stood every time a witness was sworn. The courtroom is cleared while the judges deliberate. Guilt is proclaimed with sentence in a tidy manner. The entire process is repeated for each count against the defendants. It is fairly efficient, openly fair, and the results seemed just. Every document, including the reporting, is stubby-penciled, pinned not stapled, and then tied up by twine. They used to save some twine to hang the defendants . . . and some participants who refused to follow Saddam's rules. Now they can save the twine for more cases.

The next case in the Central Criminal Court should be a counterfeiting case. We have several in the hopper as a cottage industry in counterfeiting is underway while the old dinars are still out there. We're replacing dinars with new ones sans Saddam's puss on the front. The biggest counterfeiting grab to date involved a reported friend of Uday who was printing out dinars like dates (both kinds) around here. The beauty of this latest grab is that the Iraqi chap going down is a fellow Ohio State alumnus who also went to law school there. I know our Buckeye alumni association will be pleased. I can't wait to tell him the good news that OSU's football team won the national championship to temper the bad news that he's won a ticket to the Central Criminal Court and may not be attending the Michigan game this year. First dibs on his tickets!

In other tree-bearing developments, the date season is starting here. As with buckeyes, consumption of these beauties may on occasion be hazardous to your health. First off, dates are starting to drop from the palm trees with some force. I'm evaluating the need to wear my Kevlar helmet just to run to the privy out back of the palace. Second, the date surplus is being tapped into by crafty sorts. The latest craze, and I mean craze, is the "date bomb." Now, I had a few of those in college, but this iteration is downright lethal. The bad guys pack explosives into a cake of dates that explodes with more than flavor. Third, the other "date season" involves fraternization with the Iraqi nationals here and is a not a season well suited to the well-being of our soldiers.

Although all are romantics at heart, we are issuing a general order prohibiting dating, intimate relations, and marriages between our soldiers and Iraqis until the security situation stabilizes here. We did delete the "blanket waiver" provision, as we figured we couldn't keep a straight face while presenting it to the commanding general. You wouldn't think we'd have to remind our troops that sneaking through concertina and our perimeter guards for a conjugal visit is not the best of ideas. But we do have to. Shock, awe, and the mightiest armed force in the world pales in the face of the rites of spring. And I thought we had sprayed the dates sufficiently last May. I hope these aren't bearing fruit yet.

Email to Diane, 2 SEP 03: *Had to give an hour and a half briefing to Bremer today on short notice, but it went well. Chaired a meeting with ICRC for two hours, then an oil-smuggling meeting and a bunch of other stuff. I'm whooped. At some point I'm going to have to pack. We go to the Air Pod tomorrow. Will be nice to touch down in Kuwait.*

BAGHDAD, CHRONICLE #34
8 SEPTEMBER 2003

An Najaf is known as one of the holiest cities in Islam. Shiite guns have recently peppered the city with bullet "holes," making it even "holier." Bullet holes are in almost every wall of every principal mosque, and in the skulls of many of the principal clerics and ayatollahs who have sought power or peace, creating a giant hole in the harmony among the city's Shiites. Last week's bomb blast outside the Grand Mosque of Im Am Ali decapitated the head of SCIRI, the Supreme Council for Islamic Revolution in Iraq, Baqr Al-Hakim, as well as the heads of over a hundred other innocent family households in the area. An attempt on the life of Hakim's uncle —the Grand Ayatollah—earlier in the week made the city seem like Tombstone, a lawless Old West.

Hakim's brother, a member of the Iraqi Governing Council and head of the militant arm of SCIRI called BADR Corps, probably will not take these assaults lying down. The bomb was a VBIED (vehicular-borne improvised explosive device—fancy for "very big IED"). We've been all too familiar with An Najaf since early April 2003 when armed thugs believed to be associated with another rival faction entered another mosque in town and gunned down a popular cleric named A-Khoei just as he was about to give an anti-regime/pro-Coalition speech at a critical point in the war. Sadly that very, very short speech ended with a bang. The Hatfields and McCoys have nothing on the various Shia factions in the South.

There is a new sheriff in town, however.

A-Khoei's execution had been investigated by a brave young judge who also investigated and is now prosecuting the former mayor of Najaf for corruption. We have grabbed the case for trial in the Central Criminal Court because our Special Prosecution Task Force has been following the A-Khoei murder investigation with interest. We were so impressed with this judge that we ended up offering him a position on the new Central Criminal Court. He is the most courageous Iraqi I have met, looking corruption and brutality in the eye, and affirming that justice will prevail. Judge Campbell, the famous Aussie combat wombat Mike Kelly—a legend in the operations law arena—and I were sent down on Marine Chinook choppers on short notice by Bremer to meet this brave judge and to find out what's up with the investigation since the results could further ignite the An Najaf powder keg.

Certainly, the A-Khoei murder investigation is one fraught with peril and intrigue. Many people want other people dead, so the judge certainly could be in the crosshairs. Despite this threat and pressure to conduct the court's proceedings in secret to protect the witnesses, the judge adamantly refuses to keep anything secret, insisting that that was the old Iraq and that in the new Iraq justice must be open and obvious. He tells witnesses that someday you will have to stand in front of the defendants and tell them that they are killers. He personally takes a stand on justice, law, security, and order on behalf of all Iraqis. The rest need to follow suit, or this will be a long journey here for the Coalition—and for the Iraqis.

Speaking of long journeys, the Coalition forces continue to gain troops from all over the globe. My favorite additions are the Norwegians, the Mongols, the Mozambigues and some unknown country sporting the coolest dudes I've seen here. These last guys wear a camouflaged leisure suit with a marching-band-leader hat complete with chin strap and flat black loafers. Remarkably, the uniform also has a short-pant option worn with black socks that takes your breath away. I try to avoid them since they must be pretty damn tough to wear that pansy outfit around here! The Norwegians are all fair-skinned blonds, thus faring badly in the heat. Find an English-speaking Mongol and I'll give you fifty bucks. The Mozambigues are our mine-sweepers and our best friends as a result. If they still have toes, I hope they are long ones. Their unit consists of sixty well-trained minesweeping troops and a full-time podiatrist. Ear plugs and athletic supporter/cup are standard issue. The Brits are doing their best to host ten nations in the southern provinces around Basrah.

Ministry of Justice team on US Marine Chinooks en route to An Najaf to review arrest warrant on cleric al-Sadr with investigating judge, August 2003. (Left to right: MG Don Campbell, senior advisor to the Ministry of Justice; COL Mike Kelly, Australian Forces, Office of General Counsel, CPA; and Col Don Armento, I MEF SJA)

The RAF throws a mean party on Wednesday nights just off the tarmac at the Basrah airport. It is an amazing mix of uniforms, accents, and conversations all melded together by a common task. Last Wednesday, a British Tornado fired up its engines on the tarmac just behind where the DJ had set up, and the back-blast knocked the stage and DJ over. The ensuing chaos was hysterical! The beer was saved, however.

The best part of this fusion of troops is the nightly commanders' updates now that they are engaged in the multi-national divisions (MNDs) in the south and south-central regions, appropriately including Babylon. Frankly, between the static of the communications and the lousy but very genuine accents, we have our own Tower of Babel. Everyone loves the MNDs because they are one of the tickets out for many of our troops and they're a lot of fun. Many smile and have a set response of "Nice to meet you" to almost every question. So the conversations are fabulous.

"Hey, where's the latrine?" A: "Nice to meet you."

"Hey, what time is it?" A: "Nice to meet you."

"Hey, wasn't that an RPG round that flew by our pod?" A: "Nice to meet you, I'm getting the f**k out of here!"

Speaking of which, we received orders to redeploy. We are now heading back to Kuwait for a journey home from this adventure. More to follow. "Nice to have met you, we're getting the f**k out of here!"

When you are really tired and need a pick-me-up, some emails are over-the-top nice and encouraging. For example, email from Patrick Carmichael, 5 SEP 03: *You don't know me but I am one of your fans based in Dhahran, Saudi Arabia. . . . I started receiving the Baghdad Chronicles a couple months back from my in-laws in Michigan. . . . Since receiving my first copy, your fan club has grown exponentially throughout the Eastern Province. I forward copies to our Legal Department, as well as to a host of other internal organizations. If I fail to send a copy within a week, I receive a barrage of email. I also wanted to let you know that you have a growing number of fans in the SEAL Teams. My nephew is in SEAL Team III and he's also in Baghdad. He complains if his Chronicle is not delivered on time. . . . [T]hey provide us a glimpse of life in Iraq that we are unable to obtain from any other news source. Thank you for that!*

★ ★ ★ ★

Email to COL David Brown ("Brownie"), CJTF-7 deputy chief of staff, 4 SEP 04: *Nice twenty-five hours (and four flight cancellations later) for a one-hour flight from Baghdad. Hell, V Corps covered it almost as quick! You can run, Brownie, but you can't hide now that I have your email in my sights. Take care and duck for cover when you can. Take care of the SJA [COL Marc Warren] as well. Both you guys are special. Thanks for everything.*

CJTF-7 SJA COL Marc Warren, MAJ P. J. Perrone, MAJ Owen Lewis and me on the rooftop of Presidential Palace, CPA Headquarters, September 2003. COL Warren was the best of the best among JAGs and all officers.

*Last cigar in Iraq. With MAJ Owen Lewis at BIAP awaiting our C-130
departure from Baghdad, September 2003.*

8.

PHASE OUT!
HOMEWARD AND ONWARD

BAGHDAD, CHRONICLE # 35

20 SEPTEMBER 2003

"A warrior's seasons are marked by clashes and conflicts from which time effaces all superficial recall, leaving only the fields themselves and their names which achieve in the warrior's memory a status ennobled beyond all other modes of commemoration, purchased with the holy coin of blood and paid for with the lives of beloved brothers-in-arms."

—Steven Pressfield, *Gates of Fire* (1998)

As we went wheels up from Baghdad International Airport in a C-5A and spiraled slowly skyward toward home, I could think only of the remarkable Iraqi season just passed and now marked by the battles and warriors of the divisions under Victory Corps and the I Marine Expeditionary Force. The noble effort of soldiers, sailors, airmen, and Marines with legendary divisional and regimental names such as Screaming Eagles, Marne, Iron Horse, Iron, Rifles, Bold Eagle, Warhorse, and All-America have left an indelible mark of liberty, justice, and freedom on Iraq. They represent what is best about America and its ideals. Their unity of resolve, clarity of purpose, and dedication to duty have driven an evil regime from its den, and, despite a pitiful collection of dead-enders remaining inside Iraq and now traveling there from parts unknown, newborn freedom in Iraq is growing quickly, nurtured by good folks resolute in their desire to see the Iraqi people succeed in defining, then living by, their own freedom, responsibility, and opportunity.

The media and others continue a campaign to see failure in Iraq. They cry from afar about phantom weapons of mass destruction. In so doing, they hurt the soldiers' morale with their verbal slings and arrows far more than do the enemy's grenades and improvised explosive devices. In fact, the media miss the point entirely. The weapon of mass destruction was the regime. Now the regime is eliminated. That is the truth for this country and its people. The Greek poet [Archilochus] observes that the fox knows many tricks; the hedgehog one good one. We are the hedgehog, but we're right.

For us, our mission is complete. It was a remarkable victory for a bunch of citizen-soldiers rudely thrust into this arena. We hunkered down, dodged a few missiles, bullets, and ambushes, and pulled our weight and then some. We were fortunate to have been on the playing field and in the game, not on the sidelines or "shoveling shit in Louisiana" (George S. Patton). We now return to our home fields to spread the word of the good work of those who remain and those who have gone before and, I trust, to help prepare those who will follow.

I hope we have done some good. Lord knows we tried. It's been a hell of a ride. As my late friend Eddie Green used to say, "What a deal!" *Inshallah*, y'all.

And that will teach me not to answer my damn cell phone!

9.
REFLECTIONS

"It is much easier to unmake than it is to remake the world by war or any use of force."
—Larry Arnn, *Three Lessons of Statesmanship* (2017)[13]

A nd how! Nation-building is hard. It's a search for an antidote to chaos. As I look back on my remarkable time in Iraq and my fight to get there, it is the hard work, problem-solving ability, and heroics of those who served in Iraq that exemplify what is good about Americans. We have a century's worth of liberation *ethos* under our belts, and, in return, we have asked the liberated for only a small patch of ground in which to bury our dead. In Iraq, we saw active evil and tried to do something about it. American soldiers for the most part did become "hardened" by what they saw, but never gave up their humanity. That is something to be proud of.

However, one of the great truths of the campaign for me is that combat operations alone will not attain that desired end state. From the start, American political objectives in Iraq were bold and ambitious. The military operation was intended to do more than defeat a dictator. It was meant to eliminate Iraq's weapons of mass destruction and implant a moderate, pro-American state in the heart of the Arab world, transforming a region and sending a message— an object lesson for Iran, Syria, and other would-be foes—that America's "global war on terror" was for real.[14] Thus, the campaign to liberate Iraq required more than removing Saddam Hussein and the Ba'athists from power. It required establishing a stable, secure,

---

13 *Imprimis* (Vol. 46, No. 1), December, 2017
14 *COBRA II*, 497.

prosperous, peaceful, and democratic Iraqi nation that is a fully functioning member of the community of nations.

The formal COBRA II military campaign was a phased construct—Preparation, Shaping the Battlefield, Decisive Offensive Operations, and Post-Hostilities—that crossed the entire spectrum of conflict, from combat to peace support to humanitarian and security assistance. Each phase was linked by a rolling transition to stability operations while combat operations were ongoing elsewhere. Phase III Decisive Offensive Operations of the campaign plan seemed complex. But it proved relatively simple compared to the complexities of the Phase IV Post-Hostilities stability and security operations that constituted nation-building in Iraq. This last phase was our most challenging zone of action.

Commentators have consistently pointed to several key mistakes made during the COBRA II and OIF campaigns. These mistakes can generally be summed up as follows: underestimating the enemy by failing to recognize that we were fighting both a conventional and unconventional war against both a centralized army and "a decentralized enemy that was fanatical and not dependent on rigid command and control [and] whose base of operations was dispersed throughout the towns and cities of Iraq"; failing to fully appreciate the disparate ethnic groups and tribes that comprise Iraq; putting too much confidence in technology and speed rather than in the blunt mass needed to "seal the borders, guard the copious arms caches, and dominate the terrain, all of which allowed the province to become a sanctuary for insurgents"; and disbanding the Iraqi Army.[15]

Despite less-than-optimal Phase IV planning, many Iraqis at first were just thankful for the removal of Saddam's regime, or too staggered by the display of Coalition power to push back. As that good doctor once emotionally explained to us, they needed to endure the short-term pain caused by the removal of the "cancer" that was Saddam's regime. But when order and critical services were

---

15   *COBRA*, 497-507.

not immediately restored, American prestige eroded quickly. As the Iraqis were quick to note, "The Americans could put a man on the moon but could not provide electricity."[16]

At the less macro level, we encountered things in Iraq that made no sense to us, the Coalition, in ways and in places that could not possibly occur, and yet they occurred, and regularly. How can a country that created the Hammurabi Code and the cradle of law become so lawless? It wasn't because of our efforts. The great JAGs engaged in this battle worked hard to get Iraq's justice system back up and running. We brought order to chaos. We established a new "federal-style" court system for complex cases of national security import. We enforced the Geneva Conventions and brought humanity and due process to many peoples and systems across Iraq. We instigated an armful of new and creatively established laws. Most importantly, we kept a healthy outlook and a "can-do" spirit to tackle the daunting tasks we faced. We forged new ground, always carrying with us "skepticism and irony, those twin lenses of modern consciousness that help parse military life."[17] Those lenses kept us sane and in good spirits throughout the ordeal. We never lost faith that what we were doing with our might was right.

On Sunday, 14 December 2003, Special Envoy Bremer and LTG Sanchez announced that the 4th Infantry Division had captured Saddam Hussein. He was captured without a fight, denying him the opportunity to honor his claim that he "would be a martyr but never a captive." He emerged haggard and disheveled from a hole in the ground just large enough for him to lie in. In a certain way, we did the same in Iraq. We were grateful to have done so and stake out our own claim to honor and humanity.

---

16   *COBRA*, 506
17   Rick Atkinson, *The Guns at Last Light*, Henry Holt & Company (New York, 2013), 20.

12th JAG DET JAGs waiting to redeploy at the APOD in Kuwait, September 2003. (Left to right: MAJ Jacobsen, MAJ Lewis, MAJ Summers, MAJ Wadsworth and LTC Warner) [MAJ Lenski returned a week earlier for the birth of his son.]

EPILOGUE
THE 12TH JAG IN SUPPORT OF OPERATION IRAQI FREEDOM
(7 FEBRUARY 2003 TO 12 OCTOBER 2003)
AFTER ACTION REPORT

On February 4, 2003, the 12th Legal Support Organization received orders to mobilize a team of six lawyers and two paralegals to report February 7 to Ft. Jackson, SC, and to the Combat Readiness Center (CRC) at Ft. Bragg, NC, on February 10. The team (12th JAG DET) rapidly graduated from CRC and deployed to Kuwait and reported to the Coalition Forces Land Component Command (CFLCC) at Camp Doha on March 3. The team immediately assimilated into CFLCC serving in a variety of demanding wartime positions throughout the theater with CFLCC, V Corps, 3rd MP Group (CID), Coalition Provisional Authority (CPA) and CJTF-7 in Kuwait and Iraq during Operation Iraqi Freedom. Judge advocates of the 12th LSO team were the first to conduct EPW screenings and Art. 5 tribunals at the Theater Joint Internment Facility in Umm Qasr, Iraq, as well as for all of the high-value detainees in Baghdad. The 12th LSO team members successfully integrated with the Office of General Counsel, Coalition Provisional Authority as well as with the Ministries of Health and Justice in the new Iraqi government.

The judge advocates of the 12th JAG were intimately involved in the stand-up of the courts and detention facilities in Baghdad and across Iraq, detainee operations, military justice throughout the theater, and served as charter members of the Special Prosecution Task Force responsible for the first trials before the new Central Criminal Court of Iraq and for oil-smuggling prosecutions in southern Iraq. Team leader, LTC Kirk Warner, also served as deputy SJA, Combined Joint Task Force-7 (Coalition Provisional Authority) in Baghdad.

On September 13, 2003, the 12th LSO team redeployed from the theater of operations and demobilized through Ft. Bragg, North Carolina. During its wartime service, the team tackled myriad thorny issues and challenges throughout the campaign in operational, military justice, law of war, and occupational law arenas. The issues we confronted were as volatile, uncertain, complex, and ambiguous (VUCA) as Iraq itself in the face of the fog of war of major combat and stability operations in Kuwait, Iraq and the zone of action therein. We were fortunate to be at the tip of the legal spear during the launch into Iraq and in the stability operations that followed.

The following is but a brief compendium of some of the key actions conducted/confronted by the 12th during Operations COBRA II and Iraqi Freedom.

1. CFLCC Command Operations Center, Camp Doha and Camp Arifjan, Kuwait

- Senior Judge Advocate and OIC (Night) of the CFLCC Command Operations Center
- Operations Law Attorneys, OSJA, CFLCC

The judge advocates of the 12th JAG served in the CFLCC Current Operations Center at Camp Doha, Kuwait, during the heavy combat operations in March and April as elements of CFLCC assaulted Baghdad. LTC Warner served as the senior judge advocate and OIC (Night) in CFLCC Command Operations Center from the start of war through the fall of Baghdad. MAJ Owen Lewis and MAJ Lake Summers were judge advocate representatives to the Future Operations Cell and continued to work on operations law issues and Phase IV planning. MAJ Perry Wadsworth and MAJ Craig Jacobsen provided operational law input in the Current Operations Center at CFLCC (Rear) at Camp Arifjan, Kuwait.

As assistant staff judge advocate to the CFLCC SJA (COL Dick Gordon and COL Karl Goetzke) and Night OIC, LTC Warner was the primary judge advocate responsible for legal guidance on operational law issues to CFLCC command and supervision of four OSJA personnel during war operations. In addition, Warner and other CFLCC JAGs provided extensive air and artillery target vetting and review nightly during the attack. The team also prepared multiple FRAGOs tasking investigations into friendly-fire and civilian-shooting incidents as well as reporting potential violations of law-of-war incidents. LTC Warner represented the SJA at night battle update assessments (BUAs) and current operations (COPS) staff update briefings. He participated and supported night FUOPS planning, including staffing of future operations involving northern Iraqi attack courses of action, engagement of 4th ID into the fight, FIFF incorporation, and myriad other operations.

The 12th JAG team and CFLCC survived over seventeen enemy missile attacks directed at Camp Doha and over twenty missile alerts. Patriot batteries located just outside the defense perimeters of Camp Doha launched counter-missile fire, successfully engaging many of these inbound missiles but, unfortunately, a couple of Coalition aircraft, too.

Key topic areas included the following:

A. The War Room: "Working the Desk" ranged from tedious to exciting. As the representatives of the SJA office, JAGs were called upon to provide timely and accurate advice on a wide range of operational law matters. Complicated issues that did not fit neatly into one staff section were often referred to the SJA desk. We tackled battle questions far outside the issues expected, including detainee matters, repatriation of refugees, and the establishment of local governments via selecting local officials, as well as filling traditional JAG roles, such as settling and investigating claims, advising on rules of engagement and targeting, and validating rewards programs.

B. Scuds/Missiles and Patriots: The constant in-bound missiles were a real threat to command and control. With the uncertainty of chemical warheads, force-protection posture naturally required masking and putting on JSLIST suits. Complying response waned as troops wore out. Expect some soldiers to have difficulty responding to alerts. Make sure check-in plans are established and that all soldiers understand their responsibility to check in once the all clear is given.

C. Targeting and Rules of Engagement: We were heavily involved in target analysis, particularly time-sensitive targets arising from fresh HUMINT. JAGs need to be proficient in ADOCS and other target-vetting systems. Real-time chatrooms promote target analysts to coordinate vetting and capture events to allow for investigations of friendly fire, misfire, and collateral damage investigations. It is essential that the JAGs understand that the rules of engagement, including targeting decisions, ultimately belong to the commanders. We remain the "honest brokers" for the commanders. We need to be candid, current, and spot-on correct in our assessments. Lives are at stake and consequences significant.

D. Operations Law: Operational law attorneys must be able to read and draft text messages. In an operational environment, units communicate with messages. While the formats are subject to local command variations, the basic elements of messages are the same. It is essential that all JAGs filling operational law functions understand how to draft text messages, including proper formatting and security classification and the steps to get the message through the message center for release once approved.

E. Future Operations (FUOPs)/Operational Planning Group (OPG): Our team's judge advocates serving in FUOPs and OPG made substantial contributions to CFLCC OPLANs and fragmentary orders (FRAGOs). COBRA II OPLANs contain the traditional annexes requiring JA input in rules of engagement, claims, and EPW-handling issues, but the JAG mission set expanded to include other vital stability/Phase IV tasks, including screening of local officials, messages to the people, judges, police, and former Iraqi soldiers, and guidance for the resumption of civil functions. As the OPLANs were put into action, however, FUOPS prepared many FRAGOs directing additional actions supporting the original OPLAN. This included a number of incomplete or confusing orders to provide guidance to commanders. We worked to improve clear communications, thus ensuring their execution that is vital to operational success. We must speak clearly to the commanders so that they can make decisions based on clear guidance. As MajGen Mattis succinctly put it, "We don't need a [expletive] FRAGO, just give us an eight-digit grid and we will go kill the bastards." This is speaking clearly.

F. Akbar and the 101st ABN (AA): The attack by one of our own soldiers on the brigade TOCs of the 101st ABN just as the war started required our guidance to our Public Affairs and command in light of SGT Akbar's Islamic roots. We had other Muslim soldiers, and we needed to fight the enemy yet also prevent retribution based on religion. Fortunately, strong commanders and professional soldiers overcame that potential urge, and the fight went on without incident. At the same time, we had to ensure we collected evidence and ample information to support the subsequent prosecution of SGT Akbar.

G. Ambush and Capture of 507th Maintenance Company and Rescuing PFC Lynch: The lost column of the 507th drew us into significant law-of-war and Geneva Convention issues. Commanders wanted to strike back on perceived law-of-war violations in connection with the treatments of our soldiers while prisoners. We provided guidance to the task force charged with rescue operations for PFC Lynch to include evidence collection and preservation issues while not affecting the rescue itself. MAJ Summers worked closely with CID on these evidence issues and on the investigation into whether war crimes had been committed and whether prosecutions were warranted.

H. Friendly-Fire Investigations (Patriots vs. British Tornados and FA18s): Perhaps no other area more deserves our best than our legal advice and review of friendly-fire investigations. We provided legal support to many friendly-fire and safety investigations of sad events, some preventable, most not. We have the noble task of ensuring that commanders have ample and accurate information to provide to the families of the fallen. These families are already hurting. It is one thing to die by enemy fire and another to die by "friendly fire." Full, clear explanations and full-on compassion are essential. Nothing less should be expected. Our legal reviews and support to the investigations must be complete and leave nothing unchecked.

I. FIF and FIFF (the Iraqi Freedom Fighters): Nothing could have prepared us for this curveball from the State Department. Engaging exiled Iraqis in the fight sounds worthy but is almost completely unworkable. The effort to equip, arm, supervise, monitor and engage these well-intended, revenge-driven fanatics in the middle of our major combat operations, consistent with law of war, is problematic. But optics trumped common sense. LTC Warner became the legal advisor for CLFCC's efforts to get the FIF and FIFF into the fight. Issues ranging from juvenile fighters, the weaponry, command and control, translation, and law of war sprang up at every turn. We did our best, but fortunately the fight outpaced the FIF so they did not meaningfully engage in combat operations.

J. The Fall of Baghdad: Inside the Red Zone was tense. The Thunder Runs by the 3rd ID Abrams tanks and Bradley Fighting Vehicles cracked open Baghdad as the pinchers of the MEF and V Corps overwhelmed the city and its defenders in short order. The sudden collapse of the regime government created a target-rich legal environment for our JAGs. Reminiscent of the problem of what happens after the dog catches the car, commanders now faced a fallen city unchecked by any order or governance. Unique legal issues came to us rapid-fire. Chaos, looting and violence surfaced immediately. Combat troops became policemen. And the fight continued to the north. We became the sounding boards for commanders now tasked to secure the sectors of the city. Civil military affairs became predominantly rule-of-law focused. Like the fighters, the JAGs had to wear many hats during this hard transition from law of war (LOW) to civil rule of law (ROL). Detainee operations and urban ROE became critical. We considered the questions of when soldiers are allowed to use deadly force in post-combat urban environment. Guidance on what to do with looters and thugs stealing and destroying Baghdad and its museums, culture, and people also becomes paramount. In each case, JAGs must drive the correct response given our obligations under LOW and ROL.

K.   Capitulation and Surrender: The law of war includes the right to capitulate and surrender and the recognition of same. Our JAGs provided guidance on this critical component of battle. Training the commanders on what is acceptable conduct on both sides of the equation is essential. The COBRA II planners expected mass capitulations during the powerful thrusts of MEF and V Corps to Baghdad and the potential obstacle of surrendering enemy troops slowing down an attack based upon speed. A simple, systematic method for whole units to surrender was felt necessary. PSYOPs prepared leaflets which we dropped over southern Iraq during the days prior to the war, explaining how enemy troops and units may properly surrender to the expected onslaught during the attack. Only a few units of significant size capitulated. The effort did not go for naught, however, as the same rules allowed the MEK north of Baghdad to "properly surrender" following negotiations with the 4th ID JAGs in their sector, along with input from CFLCC JAs (including LTC Warner) in Baghdad and Kuwait.

M. Violations of the Law of War: As more fully described below, MAJ Summers was assigned to the 3rd CID headquartered in Arifjan to provide legal advice, to investigate and to collect evidence for prosecution of war crimes. Legal interpretation and guidance concerning enemy violations of the LOW were routinely provided to the command from the CFLCC COIC during the march to Baghdad. Perfidy, using human shields, poisoning wells, arming children with bombs, and co-opting schools and mosques for observation towers and shooters are just a sampling of the issues filling our JA in-baskets. This guidance enabled our troops, Public Affairs, CID, and commanders to recognize, thwart and preserve our adherence to the principles of the LOW.

2. Repatriation of American POWs

• Judge Advocate Member of the POW Repatriation Team

LTC Warner was selected to serve as the judge advocate member of the CFLCC repatriation team in repatriation of seven US POWs rescued from enemy captivity. In this unique role, he provided legal assistance to POWs, legal counsel to the repatriation team and effort, legal guidance to the CI, CID and SERE assets conducting interviews for war-crime information during the four days of seclusion, and debriefing of the POWs before their transfer to Germany and their return to the United States.

As a result of this experience, LTC Warner developed the first SOP and a detailed AAR for future use by the repatriation team and the OSJA. The protocol recognized the need to get POWs to a secluded area to conduct debriefings and to allow them time and space to reorient. There are multiple areas where legal advice is essential, including eliciting evidence of war violations, facts surrounding conduct of prisoners while captured—to include cautions against self-incrimination—and regulations on accepting gifts and promises for publishing their stories.

3. EPWs and Status Tribunals, Camp Bucca, Umm Qasr, Iraq

• OICs of EPW and Detainee Operations

• Legal NCOIC of EPW Processing

In early April 2003, MAJ Wadsworth and MAJ Jacobsen moved to the EPW Theater Internment Facility built by the Coalition at Umm Qasr, Iraq. In a Coalition effort under highly austere conditions, they developed a preliminary Article 5 screening process for status determinations of captured Iraqi civilians, prisoners of war and civilian internees, including captured foreign nationals, at Camp Bucca Internment Facility, Umm Qasr, Iraq. The Article 5 screening process was used to determine the status of prisoners, who were captured on a fluid, chaotic battlefield; and to determine whether civilian detainees who were captured continued to be a security threat to Iraq and/or Coalition forces. This was done in conjunction with United Kingdom judge advocates. MAJ Wadsworth and MAJ Jacobsen personally screened or vetted over 600 detainees by conducting comprehensive interviews with each detainee. At the end of the session, they made the decision to classify each detainee as either EPW, civilian internee, innocent civilian, or as a "hold" for further CID or MI vetting.

One of the largest difficulties in this mission was in dealing with a wide range of cultural, educational, and occupational issues. Because of a lack of completed capture tags, captured property, or military intelligence, rarely did any evidence shed light on the status or threat potential of a prisoner. Consequently, the judge advocates were required to elicit necessary information through creative questioning of the prisoners.

MAJ Jacobsen and MAJ Wadsworth were responsible for training line officers, NCOs, interpreters, and other judge advocates in the screening process of prisoners. In performing these unique duties, they worked closely with Coalition partners, including United Kingdom line officers and attorneys. They served as board members of the first formal Article 5 tribunals of Operation Iraqi Freedom.

SFC Beverly Smith moved to Umm Qasr in May 2003 as the legal NCOIC for EPW processing. She developed and maintained a comprehensive database for tracking and processing EPWs. She also supervised six enlisted soldiers in GPW Articles 4 and 5 detainee-screening operations and tribunals. Remarkably, SFC Smith supervised and transcribed over 150 screening hearings and Article 5 status tribunals as well as maintained and prepared screening sheets for detainee status determinations.

4. Theater Military Justice, CFLCC Headquarters, Camp Doha, Kuwait
- Chief of Criminal Law, CFLCC
- NCOIC, Criminal Law, CFLCC

MAJ Phil Lenski served as the chief of criminal law for CFLCC. In this position, he was the chief legal advisor for criminal law to the Coalition Forces Land commander during Iraqi Freedom war operations. He was the lead prosecutor for a jurisdiction with over 150,000 soldiers. MAJ Lenski successfully tried thirteen courts-martial in theater between May and July 2003, to include the first court-martial tried in a combat environment during the operation. He conducted Article 32 investigations and pre-trial proceedings while in a combat environment and despite wearing JSLIST chemical protection gear and proceeding in face of several enemy missile attacks. He revamped the CFLCC criminal law section and supervised, managed and trained four junior officers and two NCOs to ensure effective, efficient criminal law operations, including supervising the first court-martial trials with resulting convictions. He drafted and supervised the preparation of dozens of Article 15 actions and administrative reprimands. As the senior prosecutor in the theater, he coordinated military justice with major subordinate commands' judge advocates to ensure comprehensive coverage of criminal law administration throughout the theater. He also served as the lead trial counsel for the high-profile MP EPW-abuse prosecution and led the Article 32 investigation hearings conducted at Camp Bucca in Umm Qasr, Iraq.

SSG Amanda Eisman served as the NCOIC and senior paralegal who managed the CFLCC criminal law office during Operation Iraqi Freedom war. She coordinated multiple Article 32, UCMJ and court-martial proceedings, including the creation and preparation of courtroom facilities as well as coordinated witness, judge, and panel-member appearances. SSG Eisman established the foundation to conduct the first courts-martial during war operations and Article 32 proceedings during a Scud missile attack. She also arranged and transcribed five Article 32s during the war and arranged and assisted the trial counsel for thirteen courts-martial, including nine general courts-martial and four BCD special courts-martial, which resulted in a 100% conviction rate during the war. Among these successful prosecutions was a difficult EPW-abuse case that required witness testimony taken in Iraq. MAJ Lenski essentially constructed a new CFLCC criminal law section, and supervised and trained the JAs and legal specialists in the section while providing advice to the command. The section meted out justice through formal courts-martial and scores of nonjudicial punishments under Article 15.

SSG Eisman located witnesses and made arrangements for appearance, including emergency contacts with experts for contested cases. She served as senior NCO in theater for criminal law affairs. She also convened six panels and coordinated two general and two special court-martial convening orders. She traveled to the Theater Internment Facility at Camp Bucca, Umm Qasr, Iraq, and to Basra, Iraq, to assist in pre-trial witness preparation and case investigations.

5. War Crimes Investigation Team, Camp Arifjan, Kuwait
•   Chief Legal Advisor, War Crimes Investigation Team, 3rd MP (CID) GP

In late March 2003 MAJ Summers single-handedly established the legal support cell to the US Army's War Crimes Investigation Unit (WCIU), which investigated and prepared cases for prosecution of all war crimes, crimes against humanity, and atrocities committed by the Iraqi regime. He assembled key personnel for the legal support cell who succeeded in getting this unprecedented organization fully mission-capable and operational by serving as chief legal advisor. MAJ Summers drafted a field guide of substantive war-crimes offenses to assist war-crimes case managers and CID agents as they executed the mission and coordinated the efforts of the WCIU. He provided investigative and legal guidance for the WCIU's efforts in high-profile investigations of crimes by the Iraqi "55 most wanted," and specifically for the ambush of the 507th Maintenance Company and the subsequent treatment of POWs, including PFC Jessica Lynch, and deceased soldiers as well.

MAJ Summers led and coordinated the investigation effort in An Nasiriyah, Iraq, with the CID agents that ultimately led to the identification and detention of several potential war-crimes suspects. He prepared a comprehensive presentation concerning these potential war crimes and also materials used to guide the exploitation of mass gravesites in Iraq and to guide counterintelligence missions and debriefings of Iraqi detainees. MAJ Summers provided legal advice in many highly visible and sensitive criminal investigations during the war. The War Crimes Investigation Unit established protocols and procedures for investigations during future wars as well.

6. <u>CFLCC (Forward) and the Early Entry Command Post, Baghdad, Iraq</u>

• CFLCC Staff Judge Advocate, CFLCC (Forward)

One week after the 3rd Infantry Division Brigade Combat Team punched its way into Baghdad, LTC Warner moved with LTG McKiernan to Baghdad as the senior judge advocate, CFLCC Forward, at the early entry command post in Baghdad. The operational and "occupational" issues continued firsthand as the Coalition moved to consolidate victory in Baghdad and continued the fight in the north. LTC Warner became the primary legal advisor to CFLCC in Baghdad and to MG Webster specifically as DCG, CFLCC. Legal support and guidance was provided on a variety of operational, detainee and administrative-law issues, including MEK guidance, looting rules of engagement, Zubaidi/Obaidi release issues, preparation of the Zubaidi release agreement, ITO issues and a myriad of other issues and briefings.

LTC Warner represented CJTF-7 and CFLCC in meetings with ORHA/CPA legal and other ministry teams in implementation of ORHA and CJTF-7 policies and procedures and served as CFLCC-SJA Forward from 21 April to transition of CJTF-7 to V Corps on 15 June. At all times, CFLCC continued to command the major subordinate commands across Iraq and tackled mounting operational issues while serving as the military command accompanying the Office of Reconstruction and Humanitarian Assistance led by LTG (Ret.) Garner. In addition to being the principal CFLCC legal advisor in Iraq, LTC Warner served many roles for CFLCC while at the lake palace, including LNO to the Ministry of Justice, Task Force Fajr, and the Ministry of Health; to the Judicial Reconstruction Assistance Team formed by V Corps SJA office; and to Col. Mike Murphy, USAF, who headed the ORHA Office of General Counsel.

Key issues and topics included the following:

A. Operations in the North: While securing Baghdad, combat operations continued in the north towards Tikrit, Mosul and Kirkuk. These operations were largely run by the CFLCC (FWD) from the EECP at the lake palace (Abu Ghraib North). LTC Warner and Maj Kevin Chenail continued OPLAW, LOW, ROE and targeting advice to the commanders in the continuing fight in the north. Heavy combat operations by MEF and V Corps elements raced to capture the northern cities and secure the Kirkuk oil fields. Coordination with the allied Kurds in the autonomous region in northeast Iraq created issues engaging the EECP JA team. The negotiated surrender of the MEK fighters was a continuing issue.

B. The Surrender of the Women Fighters (MEK): The Mujahiden-e Khalq have fought a covert and overt war against their native Iran. A force of over 4,500 led by a commander corps mainly comprised of women holed up in Iraq under the patronage of Saddam Hussein. There the Iranian women brandished guns and drove tanks as they were bent on overthrowing the Iranian government. Still on the State Department's list of terrorist organizations, the MEK were a hostile force under the Coalition's rules of engagement. Staring down the barrels of the 4th Infantry Division, they commenced negotiations to effect a capitulation. At the moment of truth, theater judge advocates, including LTC Warner, were called by LTG McKiernan and MG Webster for immediate advice and eventually to review the draft "surrender" documents which required the MEK to consolidate all weapons, to submit to interviews, and to be biometrically screened. Neither fish nor fowl, they were merely termed "detainees" until their status could be determined. The issues concerning the MEK are complex and novel. They will likely continue to occupy CJTF-7 and CENTCOM in the future.

C. The Zubaidi Agreements: In late April 2003, United States resident Mohammed Al Zubaidi proclaimed himself mayor of Baghdad and attempted to extract over $200 million from the city coffers held at the Iraqi National Bank. He was one of several political candidates interested in establishing a foothold on the emerging national political scene. His welcome wore thin, so he was arrested and detained by the Coalition forces. After a week of detention, he agreed to terms providing that he constructively cooperate and support the Coalition's efforts in Iraq and exert his energies to civic matters, humanitarian assistance and civil-administration issues or be returned to the United States. As a result of personal negotiations conducted by MG William Webster, DCG, and LTC Warner with Mr. Zubaidi and his consultant Jawdat Obaidi, release agreements and statements prepared by LTC Warner were signed and eventually made public.

D. War Trophies and Captured Treasure: One of the most frequent issues involving the SJA's office was tackling requests from units for war trophies. These requests ranged from gold bars and T-62 tanks in the extreme to bayonets and artillery in the routine. Everyone seemed to have a request and a need. The requests were rarely granted. Millions worth of currency were uncovered. The coffers of the Iraqi Development Fund grew exponentially, as did the resulting commanders' discretionary funds, monitored and administered under the watchful eye of the command staff judge advocates. Novel fiscal policies, including the purchase of trailers, sports bras, and fans, as well as contracts to repave the MSRs crept into the mix. It was a busy time.

E. Mass Graves and Transitional Justice: The quest for justice against the former regime perpetrators became an early hot topic. ORHA established an Office of Transitional Justice (OTJ) that documented mass graves to preserve evidence for eventual prosecution for crimes against humanity and atrocities. We worked closely with the OTJ in coordinating the mass-grave evidentiary collection effort. In a testament to the breadth of the role of the judge advocates, LTC Warner even became for several months the involuntary custodian of over 560 teeth extracted from over 300 skulls for DNA preservation from one mass grave near Al Hillah. Just another bizarre day in the life of a typical judge advocate in the early days of occupation.

F. Iraqi POWs from Iran: In late April 2003, LTC Warner became the action officer appointed by MG Webster to effect the return of Iraqi POWs from Iran. Talk about standing Geneva on its head! Imagine the issues surrounding the return of fifty-nine Iraqi POWs from the early years of the First Iran–Iraq War, 1980-1988. These middle- to upper-level officers were captured while allied with the United States. Then, after twenty-two years of captivity in some hell-hole in Iran, they came home to a country now defeated and occupied by their former ally. LTC Warner worked closely with the International Committee of the Red Cross, supervising and coordinating support for the return movement and repatriation of POWs arriving at BIAP, negotiated their return with ICRC, and prepared an official memorandum accepting return of POWs on behalf of occupying power.

7. Office of Reconstruction and Humanitarian Assistance (ORHA), Baghdad, Iraq

• Action Officer, ORHA and Liaison to ICRC for Returning POWs from Iran–Iraq War

• Legal Advisor, Task Force FAJR

• Ministry of Justice LNO, CFLCC

In addition to the command of all ground forces in Iraq, CFLCC also served as the military force that supported and coordinated the early administration of Iraq through the Office of Reconstruction and Humanitarian Assistance (ORHA) led by LTG (Ret.) Jay Garner. As the senior judge advocate for CFLCC (Forward) in Baghdad,

LTC Warner assumed a variety of direct and liaison legal roles to the ministries formed by ORHA early in the occupation of Iraq. In addition to being liaison to the ORHA chief legal advisor and to the senior advisor to the Ministry of Justice for the stand-up of the Iraqi court system, LTC Warner also served as the legal advisor to Task Force Fajr and to the senior advisor to the Ministry of Health. Key topics and issues confronted included the following:

A.   De-Ba'athification: With the exception of the decision to disband the military forces, the policy of de-Ba'athification is one of the most controversial aspects of the post-war reconstruction. All persons who were members of the Ba'ath Party at certain ranks are precluded from future government service. The policy was intended to remove regime leaders and other bad actors. The decision has been criticized as inflexible and out of touch with the reality that many members of the Ba'ath Party were only members of the party in order to receive more pay or professional advancement. The implementation of the de-de-Ba'athification policy, however, has been uneven. Some ministries quickly "de-Ba'athified." Others requested numerous exceptions. Until November 2003, Ambassador Bremer retained authority to act on de-Ba'athification exceptions. Now, the Governing Council has a leading role.

B.   Abolishing the Regime Secret and Special Courts: One of the early orders of the CPA was to disband the courts used as instruments of oppression. Iraq had a fully developed criminal justice system for "ordinary" crime, but also a system of special courts that acted on matters at the direction of Saddam Hussein. These courts were disbanded while leaving the ordinary criminal and civil courts in place.

C.   Revising the Criminal Justice System :   There   are distinct limitations on the CPA's ability to change Iraqi law under international law. The Iraqi court system was shaped by British and French colonial efforts following World War I. The Iraqi penal code as it existed prior to March 2003 was largely based on the penal code established by the British in the 1940s. Shar'ia concepts have been woven into the code over time as well as other amendments by the former regime, including certain crimes against state security. The CPA undertook to suspend capital punishment, a decision many Iraqis criticize. A few offenses and defenses related to human rights and gender concerns were also eliminated, but generally the penal code remains largely intact.

D. Weapons Policies: The national weapons policy was a hotly-debated topic. Opinions were greatly divided over whether ordinary Iraqis should be permitted to have AK-47s in their homes. Prior to the war, Iraq had a straightforward system limiting weapons ownership. All weapons were licensed and registered by the Ministry of the Interior, and military weapons, including AK-47s, were outlawed. However, Saddam Hussein distributed large numbers of weapons just prior to the war, and many Iraqi soldiers abandoned their units with their weapons during combat operations. In the post-war environment, some commanders viewed AK-47s as the main force-protection threat, arguing AK-47s should be outlawed. Others argued that prior to the reestablishment of the Iraqi police or security forces, Coalition forces were unable to provide overall security. Personal weapons were, therefore, the only means ordinary Iraqis had to protect themselves. The decision to allow Iraqis to keep AK-47s was made at the highest levels of DoD. In future operations, a thorough review of existing weapons laws is necessary for effective stability operations planning.

E. Task Force Fajr: LTC Warner provided legal advice and guidance on contracts and medical legal issues in connection with Ministry of Health stand-up, including special counsel to ORHA senior representative Steve Browning. LTC Warner was the principal action officer appointed by CG, CFLCC, and by ORHA representative Browning to coordinate Iraqi EPW-patient return to Iraqi hospitals from US Navy *Comfort* ship. In that effort, LTC Warner coordinated the return of twenty-one EPW/detainee medical patients, including medical and legal transfer issues for patients arriving at BIAP, and assisted in transfer to Saddam Medical City Hospital in downtown Baghdad.

F.   Ministry of Justice Stand-Up: LTC Warner also assisted in the stand-up of the Ministry of Justice by serving as the CFLCC LNO to the MOJ from April to June 2003. In that role, he met with Iraqi judges and lawyers and worked with the ORHA senior justice advisor on restarting the court system and as part of the V Corps OSJA Judicial Reconstruction Assistance Team (see below). LTC Warner served as the lead justice briefer to ORHA Administrator Garner and CFLCC DCG MG Webster throughout this period. LTC Warner worked closely with judges and courts in the Baghdad area to open courts as well as assisted and supervised the Iraqi Union of Lawyers in leadership elections.

G.   Judicial Assessment Teams (JAT): LTC Warner was requested by MG Campbell, senior advisor to the Ministry of Justice, to be the liaison and controller of the judicial assessment teams comprised of judges, public defenders, prosecutors and court administrators from the United States to evaluate the Iraqi court system. He worked with the JAT members in coordinating military security and logistic support to teams as they ventured across Iraq, including preparing multiple FRAGOs and coordinating meetings with involved Civil Affairs lawyers in their respective regions. LTC Warner also moved with JAT North team to Erbil, Mosul, Kirkuk and Tikrit to coordinate and secure the JAT team assessments in northern Iraq and the Autonomous Zone.

8.   <u>Phase IV Planning and Effects Synchronization, CFLCC, Camp Doha, Kuwait</u>

- Phase IV Legal Effects Planner, CFLCC

MAJ Lewis served as judge advocate to the Effects Synch Board working group and as a current operations attorney. In that role, he participated in the drafting of Phase IV OpPlan legal annexes and provided legal reviews of other annexes. MAJ Lewis developed the effects objectives, stability tasks, and measures of effectiveness for the legal aspects of the rule of law and governance lines of operations in the CFLCC Phase IV campaign plan. He wrote and made significant contributions to "weekly effects" fragmentary orders and fragmentary orders giving guidance with respect to the settlement of property disputes; the national weapons policy, including the development of the soldiers' card and public notices; and Coalition Provisional Authority orders, including guidance in implementing eviction procedures and public-incitement-to-violence limitations. MAJ Lewis also provided advice to the Future Operations Effects working groups regarding rules of engagement, including the engagement of militias and other forces, weapons buy-back and rewards programs, and many other operational law issues. He developed a reporting format to facilitate the collection of information on courts throughout Iraq and produced reports regarding the status of courts for use by CENTCOM and CPA Ministry of Justice. He also prepared transition information in connection with the transition of CJTF-7 authority from CFLCC to V Corps and participated in the "right-seat ride" transition to assist in ensuring a smooth transition of legal issues.

9. The Judicial Reconstruction Assistance Team, V Camp, Baghdad, Iraq

- Chief, Judicial Reconstruction Assistance Team, V Corps/ CJTF-7

In April of 2003, the Judicial Reconstruction Assistance Team (JRAT) was formed with personnel from V Corps, OSJA, with the specific purpose of assessing the structural condition of each courthouse in the Baghdad AO, most of which were severely burned and damaged by looters when the city fell to Coalition forces, and making recommendations as to repairs or, if the courthouse was severely damaged, finding an alternative location. To accomplish this mission, over the course of the next four weeks JRAT members, including LTC Warner, traveled to each courthouse in Baghdad, met with the judges and personnel from each court, and prepared a final report regarding specific recommendations as to a course of action. The JRAT reports were forwarded to representatives from the Ministry of Justice (MOJ), Coalition Provisional Authority (CPA), who then used them as a basis for specific funding requests. While awaiting funding from CPA, it became imperative to provide funds to the courthouses to get them functioning as soon as possible. To this end, JRAT personnel secured $10,000 in commanders' discretionary funds, which were earmarked toward the restoration of four preselected courthouses. As the restoration of the courthouses began, JRAT personnel continued to conduct periodic inspections to assess the restoration progress and maintain contact with the judges and court personnel.

In late May 2003, MAJ Jacobsen moved to Baghdad and was appointed by the V Corps SJA (COL Marc Warren) to be the chief, JRAT. At that time the JRAT's mission changed from assessment to action. In response to a presidential directive, the JRAT was tasked with devising a temporary system to immediately open the Baghdad criminal courts and begin transporting Iraqi detainees to court—those accused of Iraqi-on-Iraqi crimes who were in Coalition custody. To accomplish this mission, the JRAT solicited the assistance of the chief judges from the Rasafa and Khark appellate districts, and selected two courthouses in Baghdad, one in each appellate district, Adamiya and Bayaa criminal courts. To hold those detainees before court appearances, two jails were also selected in each appellate district, Tas Farat and Abu Ghraib. All detainee property and evidence was transferred to designated evidence rooms at each jail. JRAT drafted a FRAGO which instructed MP units from the 400th MP Battalion to transport the detainees to court and provide perimeter security for each courthouse, while the Iraqi court police provide security inside the courthouse and escort the detainees from the holding cell to court. JRAT obtained two buses to be used by the MPs to transport the detainees, and also secured uniforms and weapons for the Iraqi court police. Each week, the military magistrate forwarded 120 criminal files to JRAT that were then translated from English to Arabic by Iraqi translators at CPA. From these files, JRAT created a weekly docket for each court. Once the docket was created, it was forwarded to the NCOIC at each jail, who would use it to bring fifteen detainees to each court, four days a week. In order to facilitate the Coalition's relationship with the Iraqi judges and court personnel, two Iraqi "court liaisons" (Iraqi lawyers) were hired by JRAT, who assisted in keeping track of the court docket and recording the dispositions of each case. The files were brought to the court by the court liaisons and given to the judges and court investigators as a "starting point" to build their own files and investigate the cases. On 24 June 2003, the Bayaa and Adamyia criminal courts opened their doors and began hearing criminal cases. Each court has averaged approximately fifty to sixty cases per week since its opening.

10. Detainee Operations, CJTF-7, Baghdad, Iraq

Several judge advocates of the 12th LSO team were heavily involved in detainee operations throughout Iraq. LTC Warner chaired the weekly prisons-and-detainees meeting at the Coalition Provisional Authority hosted by CJTF-7. This meeting involved representatives of the Ministry of Justice prisons division, SJAs and JAs from the divisions and separate brigades as well as the military police commands throughout Iraq. Coordination of detainee operations was planned and efforts consolidated at the weekly "summit." MAJ Jacobson was integral to detainee operations as the lead judge advocate responsible for coordinating the prosecution and court processing of criminal detainees under Coalition control. MAJ Wadsworth led the effort in dealing with Geneva-status issues relating to the high-value detainees (see below).

A. Saddam's Prison Release and the Resulting Lack of Prisons: In fall 2002, Saddam decided to release all the prisoners, political and criminal, in Iraq. Presuming that more than half of the prisoners were criminals, they likely led to the looting and pillaging of Baghdad following its fall in April 2003. The vacuum of law enforcement authority created by the sudden fall of the city was quickly filled by thugs bent on chaos and destruction, including the destruction of their own criminal and courthouse records. Many Iraqis who felt entitled to some compensation for their suffering during Saddam's regime decided to dismantle existing law-purposed buildings, including prisons. The resulting lack of available incarceration facilities created significant difficulties for the detention of criminals as a police force was stood up. With the court system and courthouses significantly damaged, no outlet valve existed for those criminally detained. The pressure upon the entire justice system and rule of law reached boiling points throughout Iraq during the early period of occupation. Only the heroic efforts of Iraqi lawyers and many Coalition JAs reestablished a reasonably efficient system of justice in Iraq.

B. Abu Ghraib Dilemma: Abu Ghraib was the "Dark Hole" of Iraq. Notorious for its executions and political prison population, it merited becoming a museum more than continuing as a prison. The complete absence of viable prisons in Iraq left little room for a decision other than its continued use as it was intended, incarceration. LTC Warner chaired the detainee and prisoner meetings weekly at CPA and was heavily involved with MAJ Jacobsen and the JRATs who worked the judicial system to facilitate the orderly and swift disposition of the court system, trying to release the pressure on the prison populations. The 12th JAs departed Iraq proper in early September before trouble stirred at Abu Ghraib.

Abu Ghraib wasn't intended to be an interrogation facility, but an insurgency mounted during the long, hot summer of 2003 resulted in a high-stakes demand for intelligence on insurgent operations. By September, military intelligence and extreme interrogation operations commenced there, the ramifications of which surfaced catastrophically in the months thereafter.

C. ICRC Inspections and Overcrowding: LTC Warner also served as ICRC liaison for CJTF-7 for detainee and prison affairs as well as for mortuary remains return and identification issues, returning EPW-patient issues, Iraqi-POWs-held-in-Iran issues, missing-relative inquiries and detainee issues. He met weekly with the ICRC to address detainee issues. Also, as part of Ministry of Health counsel, LTC Warner met multiple times with the ICRC protection coordinator and chief surgeon and coordinated the CFLCC positions on ICRC issues.

D. Tracking the Detainees: "How many ways can you spell Mohamed?" This phrase was often heard in connection with administratively accounting for the huge number of detainees in Coalition custody. The three main categories of detainees were prisoners of war, security internees, and criminal detainees. High-value detainees could fall into any of the three categories. We had thousands of detainees in the prison camps at Camp Cropper, Umm Qasr (renamed Camp Bucca), and Abu Ghraib, as well as in myriad other prisons, holding cells, compounds, or police station facilities throughout Iraq. Without judicial or detention-board outlet valves, the number of criminal detainees continued to mount, as did the pressure from the ministries and the Iraqi people to do something with them. Just releasing them was not an option. Nor was holding them forever, thus running afoul of the Geneva Conventions. Thus, we instituted detainee review boards and detention criteria to adjudicate the status and stay of the detainees. We even held a JAG "all-hands" review—Operation Clean Sweep—calling in all available JAGs and paralegals in Iraq to review the detainee files, if any, to determine whether there was sufficient evidence to recommend continued detention, immediate release, or prosecution.

Keeping track of who was where, for what reason, and for how long was a recurring nightmare. Detainees seldom had identification cards. If they had criminal pasts or records, those records no longer existed. Almost everyone had a clean slate, whether deserved or not.

Almost everyone was named Muhammed in one of their four names, so tracking the names was next to impossible. But the families and friends of detainees certainly were entitled to know where their kin were being held, for what reason, and for how long. The ICRC and other nongovernmental organizations (NGOs) certainly wanted to know those answers and know them now. So too did we, for that matter. We had to field many inquiries from Amnesty International and the ICRC on detainee issues and details. LTC Warner served as the Coalition detainee liaison with the ICRC, chairing the weekly detention meetings with all stakeholders in the system: police; justice; corrections; military police; intelligence; and US/Coalition-division SJAs. Technology failed us dramatically early on. However, we eventually put a system in place to meet the needs in part. Detention is hard. Ample resources and dedicated personnel from a variety of disciplines, especially judge advocates, are needed for success.

11. <u>Combined Joint Task Force-7, Baghdad, Iraq</u>
- Deputy SJA, CJTF-7 (Coalition Provisional Authority)

As deputy to CJTF-7 SJA, Coalition Provisional Authority, LTC Warner served as legal advisor to the commanding general and CJTF-7 staff. He was responsible for prison and detainee operations and served as liaison with CPA Ministry of Justice, serving on action committees responsible for command and ministry briefings and all phases of operations of CJTF-7 from its inception in Iraq in April 2003 until 1 September. LTC Warner served as deputy to COL Marc Warren, SJA, CJTF-7, for all SJA functions and responsibilities involving the CPA. He prepared briefings and reports for and provided legal analysis of myriad operational, security, and stabilization issues and situations involving the Coalition forces' occupation of Iraq and its obligations under international law to the CJTF-7 commander LTG Ricardo Sanchez and his staff as well as to Ambassador Paul Bremer and his staff.

A. The Authority: As the Coalition forces transitioned to Phase IV Post-Hostilities operations following the fall of Baghdad, the

Office of Humanitarian Assistance (ORHA), led by LTG (Ret.) Jay Garner, moved into Iraq and headquartered in Baghdad. ORHA was part of CFLCC and thus reported to Washington through LTG David McKiernan and then through CENTCOM and GEN Tommy Franks. ORHA was the occupational authority in Iraq until mid-May when suddenly the president and the secretary of defense sent in Special Envoy L. Paul "Jerry" Bremer to take over from LTG (Ret.) Garner as head of the new Coalition Provisional Authority (CPA). ORHA had started down a different path from that taken by Ambassador Bremer, who reported directly to SECDEF and POTUS.

ORHA under LTG (Ret.) Garner had planned to continue to restart government ministries with what was already in place until those leaders could be properly vetted ("de-Ba'athified") and also planned to keep the defeated Iraqi Army intact. LTG (Ret.) Garner, and many of his ORHA key staffers, left Iraq for good on the last day of May 2003. CPA and AMB Bremer were now the clear authority in Iraq. Their first order of business was to disband the Iraqi Army and put its thousands of soldiers on the streets without pay. They also moved to immediately declare the three highest levels of Ba'athists ineligible for governmental service. These two particular CPA orders would have dire, long-term consequences.

B. The Ministry of Justice: We worked closely with the ORHA and CPA general counsel's office, led by Col. Mike Murphy and COL(P) Scott Castle respectively, on virtually every issue involving the ministries and Iraqi governance and justice. LTC Warner became the CFLCC and CJTF-7 representative to the ORHA and CPA Ministry of Justice teams led by MG Campbell and Clint Williamson. JAGs from the 12th, LTC Warner and later MAJ Jacobsen and MAJ Wadsworth, also served on the V Corps Judicial Reconstruction Assistance Team (JRATS) in standing up and reestablishing the courts throughout Iraq, coordinating criminal cases to put before the court, and assisting in all matters pertaining to the courts. In addition, LTC Warner briefed and assisted the CPA judicial assessment teams of US federal judges and prosecutors who had volunteered to come to Iraq for several weeks in order to evaluate the court system and vet judges throughout Iraq.

C. Uday and Qusay: The killing of Saddam's sons Uday and Qusay in July 2003 marked a banner day for the Coalition forces in Iraq and for Iraqis in general. JAGs quickly became involved in the announcement of the killings; weighed in on whether the CPA could show photos of the dead sons to prove they were, in fact, dead under the Geneva Convention; ensured the use of positive identification methods; and even negotiated the burial of the remains. These tasks took many turns and required significant negotiations with the Red Crescent, the only organization willing to accept their remains.

D. Multinational ROE Synchronization: Throughout the fight and post-hostilities in Iraq, a critical component of order and preservation was a common set of rules of engagement (ROE). Unfortunately, ROE is owned by commanders and is determined by their nations. Countries that were part of the Coalition had differing views on concepts of self-defense and on whether they could conduct more than defensive operations in Iraq. For example, was deadly force allowed for protection of Coalition property or just for personal protection, and if so, what comprised deadly force? Could a soldier use warning shots? Should a soldier fire to prevent theft or other violence on Iraqis? So, a patchwork system of ROE developed over the months of 2003 in the assigned sectors of Iraq. Significant coordination, communication, and even negotiation became necessary to homogenize the ROE effort.

12. The Office of General Counsel, Coalition Provisional Authority, Baghdad, Iraq
   - Assistant Counsel to the Office of General Counsel, CPA
   - NCOIC, Office of General Counsel, CPA

MAJ Owen Lewis moved to Baghdad in June 2003 to serve as the assistant general counsel to the Coalition Provisional Authority in the Office of General Counsel. He became an integral member of the OGC and drafted or assisted in the preparation of numerous Coalition Provisional Authority legal instruments, including regulations, orders, and memoranda. MAJ Lewis played a significant role in the development of policies and procedures for contracting; use of the Development Fund for Iraq; the disciplinary system for the New Iraqi Army; the formation of the Iraqi Civil Defense Corps; and economic initiatives centering around foreign investment and privatization of Iraqi enterprises. He also devised a preliminary claims program to address combat-related claims in the event funding is made available under the Iraqi Relief and Reconstruction Fund. He drafted and coordinated the issuance of the Trade Bank of Iraq, civil confiscation, and Central Bank independence orders. MAJ Lewis also addressed issues of occupation and international law, including the application of Iraqi law related to CPA initiatives.

SSG Beverly Smith moved to Baghdad in June 2003 as NCOIC of the Office of General Counsel, Coalition Provisional Authority. She developed, implemented, and maintained tracking systems for all legal instruments generated by OGC, ensuring that orders, regulations, and memoranda were issued and public notices effected. She also coordinated electronic management and filing of all legal work product of OGC and publication and translation of the Iraqi Official Gazette, which served as the public notice of all CPA legal orders and proclamations. SFC Smith supervised other enlisted members of the OGC and developed templates for the consistency of all legal instruments and coordinated with SJA, CJTF-7 to maximize interoffice coordination.

Key topics of the Office of General Counsel to the CPA included the following:

A. Orders, Proclamations and Decrees, and the OGC: Following GEN Franks' "Message to the Iraqi People," the CPA issued regulations, orders, and memoranda. These enactments had the force of law. The CPA remains the primary rule-making body within Iraq. While local commanders issued some local orders and pronouncements as situations dictated, the primary law-making function was reserved to the CPA. These enactments are the vehicle the CPA uses to change existing Iraqi law to implement its policies.

B. Commercial Policies: The authorization of foreign direct investment in Iraq was a subject of significant debate. It is widely believed that business investment is the only means to address Iraq's substantial unemployment situation. Pre-war investment laws and the Iraqi Constitution limited foreign investment in Iraq. Certain Arab nationals were permitted to make investments in Iraq and to hold stock in Iraqi companies, but most foreigners were precluded from owning stock or making investments in Iraq. The constitution also provides that only Iraqis may own real estate. Many Iraqis are suspicious of outsiders and do not favor foreign investment. Existing Iraqi law reflects that notion. While the former regime authorized certain foreign companies to operate in Iraq, these arrangements were solidified by bribes and fraud. Ultimately, the CPA promulgated an order providing for "national treatment" of foreign investors. Generally, under the CPA order, foreigners may now invest in Iraq in the same manner as Iraqis except in owning real estate.

C. The Iraqi Trade Bank, Central Bank Independence, and the Bank Laws: Iraq's pre-war banking system lacked the capability to support international trade transactions. The Central Bank was subject to the directives of other government agencies as its board members were composed of the heads of other government agencies, including the Ministry of Finance. This required the Central Bank to make loans to other government agencies. Many banks were state-owned enterprises. The US Treasury Department, the International Monetary Fund, and other international agencies assisted in the development of laws to reform the banking system. The Office of General Counsel served as a coordination point for these initiatives.

D. The Iraqi Development Fund and Commanders' Discretionary Funds: The authorization to use "vested, seized, and found" Iraqi assets in support of the reconstruction of Iraq gave commanders unprecedented access to a flexible funding mechanism. The CPA made funds available to commanders to support local reconstruction efforts. The program originally consisted of one $25,000 grant to brigade commanders. The program was remarkably successful in speeding reconstruction at the local level. Courthouses and police stations were repaired without red-tape delays, enabling the reestablishment of the rule of law, thus quashing unchecked chaos and tempers in their areas of operations. When the program was greatly expanded, increased funding was made available. These assets were not subject to US government contracting rules, thus creating a great deal of flexibility. As the program was rolled out quickly, few guidelines were in place. In many commands, JAs were called upon to act as fund managers. They reviewed projects, acted as payment officers, fostered competition, and worked to minimize fraud.

E. Security Forces: In the complex situation following the war, the need was great for forces to provide security at fixed sites. A number of forces with distinct but overlapping missions were created to address the security needs of the Iraqi people. This resulted in competition for resources, including weapons, training and vehicles. Ample military police and security contractors trained in facility and infrastructure security need to be deployed to meet the needs.

1. The New Iraqi Army was created following the disbanding of the Iraqi Army. From a legal perspective this represented a significant challenge as none of the existing legal structures could be used. First, CPA orders establishing the force and basic administrative rules were published. The New Iraqi Army also needed a system of military discipline. The pre-war code of military discipline was a complex separate system with military lawyers and military judges. The new system relies on the civilian criminal court system for the adjudication of serious offenses with a simple system of nonjudicial punishment to address minor offenses.

2. Iraqi Civilian Defense Corps: The Iraqi Civil Defense Corps is one of the security forces that will take on greater security responsibilities. With a mission similar to that assigned to our National Guard in the US—protection and securing of property and people in the community—the ICDC is trained by Coalition forces, provides fixed-site security, conducts joint patrols with Coalition forces, and is intended to support the "Iraqification" of security efforts.

3. Facility Protection Service: The Facility Protection Service is a fixed-site security force under the supervision of Iraqi ministries. This force is distinct from the police, ICDC, and NIA in that it solely provides fixed-site security.

F. Civil Forfeiture: Pre-war Iraqi law authorized the confiscation of property used in crimes following a conviction. However, the growing problem of oil theft and smuggling, as well as theft and damage of electrical infrastructure, necessitated the creation of a system similar to the US drug forfeiture laws authorizing the confiscation of property independent of a conviction. Like that of the US, the Iraqi constitution provides for compensation of the unjust seizure of property. The problem was made more complex by the absence of *in rem* jurisdiction in Iraq. Thus, the CPA promulgated an order authorizing the seizure of property used in offenses involving the theft or damage of infrastructure or natural resources, followed by a hearing after the publication of a notice. The process has been used to seize trucks and boats involved in the theft and smuggling of oil.

13. High-Value Detainees, CJTF-7, Baghdad, Iraq

- OIC, Article 5 Tribunals for High-Value Detainee Screening Operations

MAJ Perry Wadsworth was selected by the SJA, V Corps to be the OIC of high-value detainee tribunals and processing. He developed the CJTF-7 process for making status determinations under the Geneva Conventions for prisoners of war and for civilians, respectively, including the development of both a screening procedure and an

Article 5 tribunal procedure. Article 5 tribunals determine the status of a detainee—whether they are security internees or prisoners of war. Each category requires different treatment and has separate rights during custody. The problem is that the regime and the Ba'ath Party all held "military rank," so were they enemy soldiers or civilian officials? It is similar to deciding whether our postmaster general or surgeon general are military men with the rank of "general" or civilians with that title only. MAJ Wadsworth also created new procedures in regard to the classified nature of high-value detainees. He screened over 100 high-value detainees, including predominantly black-list members, ranging from #4 to #241. He, along with other members of the 12th LSO team (MAJ Lenski, MAJ Lewis, MAJ Summers, MAJ Jacobsen and LTC Warner), conducted Article 5 tribunals with approximately fifty high-value detainees, including those formerly at the highest levels of Iraq's regime and governmental infrastructure. These HVDs included deputy prime ministers, revolutionary command council members, cabinet ministers, directors and scientists of programs for weapons of mass destruction, presidential advisors, ambassadors, presidential diwan, governors, Ba'ath Party command and leadership, family members of Saddam Hussein, intelligence service agents, and assassins.

MAJ Wadsworth was responsible for coordinating the administration and allocation of resources, to include facilities, interpreters, classified files, and evidence from intelligence and military police units. These tribunals required extensive questioning and dialogue with the HVDs within the compound of the Special Confinement Facility, Baghdad, Iraq. MAJ Wadsworth also conducted over thirty Article 5 tribunals for detainees accused of serious crimes against Coalition forces. He trained and incorporated judge advocates and paralegals from multiple CJTF-7 units into the Article 5 tribunal process.

MAJ Wadsworth also researched and established civilian/ security internee procedures in accordance with Geneva Convention for the Protections of Civilian Persons, 12 August 1949 (GC). He was responsible for maintaining CJTF-7 compliance with the Geneva Conventions by providing over seventy-five high-value detainees with their Article 78 rights. He also developed court/board for Article 78 GC appeals and six-month reviews.

14. <u>Special Prosecution Task Force, Baghdad, Iraq</u>

- Judge Advocates, Special Prosecution Task Force, Ministry of Justice, CPA

In order to provide a forum to prosecute political and unique crimes of national import in Iraq, the Central Criminal Court of Iraq (CCCI) was devised by members of the Ministry of Justice, OGC (CPA) and OSJA, CJTF-7, including LTC Warner. The CCCI was sort of a self- contained federal court system comprised of fifteen judges and five prosecutors in a trial and appellate court hierarchy that could ride circuit and cross traditional jurisdictional boundaries across Iraq. It also may serve as the foundation forum for the eventual trial of atrocities and crimes against humanity committed by the former regime. The Special Prosecution Task Force (SPTF) was in turn developed to select and prepare cases to be tried before the CCCI. LTC Warner and MAJ Jacobsen were charter judge advocates of the SPTF. The SPTF soon became a fairly robust prosecution team that enabled the first trial in the CCCI and a slew of oil-smuggling prosecutions in the south.

A. Central Criminal Court of Iraq Cases: The Central Criminal Court of Iraq (CCCI) was created by CPA Ministry of Justice team, including CPA general counsel and CJTF-7's LTC Warner, as a special court system similar to the US federal system. It was comprised of respected Iraqi trial judges and prosecutors who would ride circuit throughout Iraq and try cases of national import (for example, the trial of Saddam Hussein and his regime's leadership) or those of political or national security consequence (for example, oil smuggling or cases involving violence against the Coalition). Appeal would be directly to the Court of Cassation.

The first trial involved insurgent arms smuggling in Red Crescent vehicles! The cases were selected and prepared by the Special Prosecution Task Force that included LTC Warner, and by the CJTF-7 JRATs, led by MAJ Jacobson of 12th JAG and MAJ Juan Pyfrom of V Corps, and were ultimately tried by the Iraqi CCCI prosecutors. Consistent with the due process, fairness, and justice written into the CCCI, engagement of defense attorneys was mandated early in the proceedings. JAGs assisted in the marshalling and coordination of evidence for trial by the Iraqis for the CCCI cases. These early cases included the successful prosecution of oil smugglers from *Navstar I* and other culpable ship captains and mates arrested during Operation Sweeney Todd and riverine operations in the Shaat and in the Arabian Sea. The potential prosecution of those responsible for the death of the Grand Ayatollah in Najaf was also part of the CCCI docket.[18]

B. Oil Smuggling and the *Navstar I* Tanker Confiscation: In early August 2003, Special Prosecution Task Force (SPTF) members COL Mike Kelly (AUS) of the OGC, CPA; LTC Warner of the OSJA, CJTF-7; and Capt Brian Cooke (USMC), of the CPA MOJ, boarded the *Navstar I* GP 3 oil tanker in the waters off the Port of Umm Qasr, Iraq, to commence investigation of diesel-fuel bunkering into the *Navstar I* in Iraqi waters of the Khawr Az Zubayr and the Abu Flous. Prior investigative actions included meeting with local Iraqi judges to review requirements for investigative hearings and sworn statements of the crew. We assembled local Iraqi police and Royal Military Police assets to assist in securing the crew and evidence.

The SPTF interviewed the Ukrainian crew of twenty and prepared sworn statements for over fifteen hours on board. Critical evidence was uncovered, including hidden logs, falsified documents, and evidence of a major oil-smuggling ring, setting the conditions for the eventual successful prosecution of the captain and first mate, who are now spending ten years in an Iraqi prison contemplating how to come up with over $2.5 million in restitution. As a result,

---

18 Saddam Hussein was eventually tried and convicted in the CCCI.

over 3,500 metric tons of diesel fuel was returned to the Iraqis, a 130-meter tanker vessel formed the nucleus of the new Iraqi merchant marine, and the tracking of twenty-eight other smuggling vessels commenced. A solid foundation for further pursuit of oil smugglers was built. Operation Sweeney soon followed.

C. Operation Sweeney and Joint Operations in the South: As a result of the *Navstar I* success, a joint British and American Navy and Marine operation was conceived. LTC Warner and the British command legal officer served as legal advisors to planners for Operation Sweeney, a joint anti-smuggling effort that engaged the 13th Marine Expeditionary Force and the combined British assets in patrolling the Aw Faw Peninsula and the waters of the Shatt Al Arab in southern Iraq. The operation required careful harmonization of conflicting rules of engagement of the British and American forces involved. The resulting operations conducted in late September and early October 2003 resulted in over seventy-five arrests and seizure of twenty full barges, fifteen empty barges, eight oil boats, thirty-six petroleum tankers, and nine pickups containing fuel, and ten fuel pumps. These confiscations and prosecutions have mortally damaged historic smuggling operatives and operations in the region.

15. Conclusion and Lessons Learned

Flexibility is paramount. During deployments, reservists must be prepared to serve in any role in the office. Good judgment and generalist training is essential. Team members were called upon to provide services in all JA disciplines and many areas that are not traditional JA functions, such as those involving prisons, piracy, prisoners of war, detention operations, healthcare systems, other governmental agencies, international agencies, and nongovernmental organizations. All team members must be prepared to do what it takes—not all of the roles will be glamorous, but they are all necessary. Be prepared to accept assignments that best make use of your skills and experience, but do not be surprised to be placed in positions that test your skills training.

Understand the legal system of the country you will be operating in and learn translations of key laws early on. The Iraqi legal system is highly developed. Iraq has a large body of intelligent jurists who understand the rule of law and who are ready to debate its application. Some of the Iraqi laws had been translated, but many of the amendments had not. Iraq publishes laws in the "Gazette." They are not codified in the same manner as are US laws. The problem is like using the Federal Register to find the Code of Federal Regulation provisions. We often operated without a complete understanding of existing Iraqi law. The existing law must be used to shape policy decisions most effectively. As a JA, you can expect to be asked about the law of the nation you are in as though you were at home. Locate as many accurate translations as you can in advance and study them.

The judge advocates of the 12th LSO team quickly became part of the One Army Team in the prosecution of COBRA II and Operation Iraqi Freedom. The team was fortunate to be the first LSO team in theater before the war commenced. This created opportunities for the 12th LSO team members to carry out meaningful assignments throughout the theater of operations. The unique tasks assigned to the team were all successfully accomplished. Although the team was immediately dispersed in a variety of tasks throughout CFLCC and CJTF-7 with the result that each member has his or her own unique set of lessons learned, the team remained remarkably coherent and unified in effort throughout the deployment. As COL Goetzke, CFLCC SJA, notes, the members of the 12th LSO team nobly "dropped their plow-lines and answered the call."

12th JAG Detachment: UIC: WR1EYI (12th Legal Support Organization, 13000 Jackson Blvd, Ft. Jackson, SC 29207-6070):
LTC Kirk G. Warner
MAJ Sebastian P. Lenski
MAJ Lake Summers
MAJ Alvin Perry Wadsworth, Jr.

MAJ Owen D. Lewis

MAJ Craig Jacobsen

SFC Beverly Smith

SSG Amanda Eisman

Judge advocates from the 12th JAG atop the Republican Palace, Green Zone, Baghdad, which served as the Coalition Provisional Authority headquarters, August 2003. (Left to Right: MAJ Perry Wadsworth, MAJ Craig Jacobsen, MAJ Lake Summers, LTC Warner, MAJ Owen Lewis and SFC Beverly Smith) Four giant busts of Saddam in Roman headgear gaze over Baghdad.

SELECTED OIF ISSUES ADDRESSED

- Palestine embassy raid
- Zubaidi and Ubaidi detention and release
- Free Iraqi Freedom Fighters (FIFF) issues (age, arming, discipline)
- Argentine journalist remains
- Children injuries and evacuation out of Iraq
- Mass-grave issues
- Medical evacuation of Iraqis into Kuwait

- Badr Corps issues
- MEK issues
- Voluntary blood samples from EPWs for immunizations analysis
- Property dispute resolution from Arabization and Ba'athist confiscation
- Perfidy and use of human shields
- Escapees disguised as corpses
- HVD status hearings
- Real estate records issues
- Intl. Atomic Energy Agency Inspection Team—Tawaitha Nuclear Site
- Kurd leader's son's medical evacuation to Germany
- Media regulation on incitement to violence
- Weapons control policy
- War trophy policy and requests for trophies
- Remains to Syria
- Prison and detainee issues
- Increased insurance for contractors
- Claims issues and solatia
- DIA top 55 list PAO issues
- Akbar —the Muslim issue—101st Airborne
- Gold bar issues
- Detainee cards
- Flying the US Flag in occupied territory
- Tearing down statues of Saddam
- Saddam prisoner pardon
- Article 5 issues
- Central Criminal Court of Iraq issues
- Office of Transitional Justice issues
- De-Ba'athification and renunciation issues
- Reconciliation issues
- Contracts to purchase newspapers

- Investigations of the Palestine Hotel, friendly-fire incidents (Patriots), HMMV rollover
- Squatters in government buildings
- Missionaries across the border
- Convoy attack in hot pursuit over Syrian border and reception party
- Docketing of Iraqi-on-Iraqi criminal detainees for court
- Translation of all criminal files and arrest records
- Arming of the New Iraqi Army
- US citizen arrested in Iraq for murder and detained
- Turkish Special Forces colonel plotting political assassination
- PKP compound north of Mozul
- ICRC issues with electronic tracking and publication of detainee list
- Joint fact-finding board on Turkish detainees in Kirkuk
- Recruiting EPWs to NIA and Iraqi Civil Defense Corps
- Targeting regime statues/symbols
- Shutting down Iraqi newspaper for inciting violence against the Coalition
- Military commissions vs. general courts-martial
- Palestinian-detainee issues
- Juvenile-detainee handling and adjudication issues
- Rules for use of force by contract personal-security detachments
- Use of non-lethal weapons
- Prison squatter and displaced marsh Arabs
- Tobacco to detainees
- KMEK Radio shutdown at MEK compound
- General Order No. 2 (Iraqi non-fraternization and ban on marriage)
- Oil-smuggling regulations, customs court and ROE for joint operations
- Photos of HVDs/POWs

- Release of photos of Uday/Qusay
- Disposition of remains of Uday/Qusay
- Disposition of leg bone and orthopedic plate for forensic ID of Uday
- Saudi refugees and borders/customs issues
- Plan for handling HVD #1 (Saddam Hussein)
- Harvesting of sperm from KIAs for spouses/parents
- Effect of artificial reproduction (frozen sperm/embryos) from KIAs on survivor benefits
- TOC hit by mortars
- *Navstar I* oil-smuggling prosecution and confiscation issues
- Civil vs. administrative forfeiture/confiscation order
- UK journalists and UK soldiers POW executions and trials
- Contract requests for trailers, women's bras and panties, paving roads, and CG's pen
- Mortar attack on detention compound
- Organized crime prosecution
- Child kidnapping and prostitution
- UN bombing and mortal remains
- Red Crescent truck trial before Central Criminal Court
- Rules of engagement for riverine operations
- Prosecution and arrest of Sadr in An Najaf
- Bombing in An Najaf—medical treatment by US facilities

ACKNOWLEDGMENTS

"My human habits of greed, lust, impatience, vanity, sloth, and foolishness tend to hobble my idealism."
—William Dietrich, *The Emerald Storm* (2012)

Idealism aside, the reality is that I owe thanks to many encountered on this journey. In addition to my life's main battle buddy, Diane ("Household Six"), and my good friends, family, and law-firm mates, my key battle buddies, mentors, and teammates during this journey to Iraq and back were the best JAGs, officers, and paralegals in the world, listed below by their rank at the time. Since 2003, each has gone on to higher roles in their remarkable service to our nation. In turn, each is owed our eternal praise and commendation. We were a proud conspiracy of doers.

The 12th JAG/LSO Team: MAJ Sebastian (Phil) Lenski, MAJ Lake Summers, MAJ Alvin (Perry) Wadsworth, MAJ Craig (Jake) Jacobsen, MAJ Owen Lewis, SFC Beverly Smith, and SSG Amanda Eisman. This team was simply superb.

Our 12th LSO backbone at home: COL Dan Shearouse, LTC Joe Zima, MSG Ruth Blackmon, our mother hen, and our brothers and sisters of the 12th LSO.

CFLCC/US Third Army: COL Richard (Flash) Gordon and COL Karl Goetzke, both of whom believed in us; LTC Don Perritt, Maj Kevin Chenail, SGM Chris Zaworsky, and many others.

V Corps/CJTF-7: COL Marc Warren, the greatest boss and roomie ever; LTC Corey Bradley, LTC Jeff Nance, MAJ P. J. Perrone, CPT Ryan Dowdy, CPT Travis Hall, and the many great V Corps JRATs, JAGs and paralegals. And to COL David Brown, the CJTF7 DCOS.

Other key partners, enablers, and derring-doers: the inspiring leaders of CFLCC, CJTF-7 and ORHA/CPA, including LTG David McKiernan, LtGen James Conroy, LTG Ricardo Sanchez, MG J. D. Thurman, MG William Webster, MG Donald Campbell (ORHA/CPA), Clint Williamson (ORHA/CPA), COL(P) Scott Castle (CPA); the great COL Mike Kelly (Australian Forces); LTC Rich Whitaker, MAJ Susan Arnold and MAJ Paul Wilson (101st ABN (AA) Division); LTC Mark Martins, LTC Sharon Riley and MAJ Walter (Skip) Hudson (1st Armored Division); LTC Flora Darpino (4th Infantry Division); Col Don Armedo (I MEF); LTC Tom Ayres (82nd ABN Division); and the 250,000-plus other dedicated and brave ground-pounders: the men and women of CFLCC, CJTF-7, CPA, and the British 1st Armored Division. And a hearty thanks to COL David Hayden (XVIII ABN Corps), who let us sleep in his office at Ft. Bragg . . . although many others have done so before!

To our dear translator Fatima Fileefl: a special thanks. You helped us fathom the nearly unfathomable.

And finally, a shout-out to Kayani: Thanks for the ice cream, man. I'll find you a gas mask next time! Until then, we will buddy-breathe.

GLOSSARY OF TERMS AND ACRONYMS

AA: Air Assault

ABN: Airborne

Abrams: M1A2 Abrams third-generation main battle tank

AD: Armored Division

ADA: Air Defense Artillery

ADACG: arrival and departure airfield control group

ADOCS: Automated Deep Operations Coordination System

AO: area of operation

ARCENT: US Army Central Command

Article 5 Tribunal: detainee status determination proceeding under the Geneva Conventions

Article 32: UCMJ hearing to assess appropriateness of prosecution

ATACMS: Army Tactical Missile System (surface-to-surface)

Blue-on-blue: friendly-fire incident

Bradley: M2/M3 Bradley Tracked Armored Fighting Vehicle

BUA: battle update assessment

CA: Civil Affairs

CALCM: conventional air-launched cruise missile

CCCI: Central Criminal Court of Iraq

CDE: chemical defense equipment

CENTCOM: US Central Command

CFLCC: Coalition (or Combined) Forces Land Component Command (US Third Army)

CID: Criminal Investigation Division

CIF: central issuance facility

CJTF-7: Combined Joint Task Force-7

CMOC: civil-military operations center

COIC: Current Operations and Intelligence Center

Conex: standard intermodal shipping container

CONUS: continental United States

CPA: Coalition Provisional Authority

CRC: combat readiness center

CTT: common task training

DA: Department of the Army

DCU: Desert Camouflage Uniform

DFAC: dining facility

DIA: Defense Intelligence Agency

DSJA: deputy staff judge advocate

EECP: early entry command post

EPW: enemy prisoner of war

FIFF: Free Iraqi Freedom Fighters

FORSCOM: US Forces Command

FRAGO: fragmentary order

FUOPS: Future Operations

Green Ramp: Pope AFB air departure waiting area

GWOT: Global War on Terrorism

HUMINT: human intelligence

HMMWV or "Humvee": High Mobility Multi-purpose
    Wheeled Vehicle

ICRC: International Committee of the Red Cross

IED: improvised explosive device

ITO: installation transportation officer

JTF: joint task force

JRATs: Judicial Reconstruction Assistance Team members (V Corps)

JSLIST: Joint Service Lightweight Integrated Suit Technology

JSOTF: joint special operations task force

JOC: joint operations center

ID: Infantry Division

IZ: Iraq

JAs or JAGs: judge advocate generals

JDAM: Joint Direct Attack Munition

LAR: Light Armored Reconnaissance

LCE: load-carrying equipment

LOW: law of war

LSO: Legal Services Organization

MARDIV: Marine Division

MEDCOM: Medical Command

MEF: Marine Expeditionary Force

MOPP: Mission Oriented Protective Posture

MRE: Meals Ready-to-Eat

MSR: main supply route

MWR: Morale, Welfare, and Recreation

NBC: nuclear, biological and chemical

OCONUS: outside Continental United States

OPLAN: operations plan

OPLAW: operations law

OPORD: operations order

ORHA: Office of Reconstruction and Humanitarian Assistance

PGM: precision-guided munition

POA: Public Affairs officer

Pogey Bait: any snack food that does not fall under typical field rations

PSYOP: Psychological Operations

RDL: rucksack deployable law office and law library

Recon: reconnaissance

ROE: rules of engagement

RPG: rocket-propelled grenade

SA: situational awareness

SECDEF: secretary of defense

SCUD: Series of Soviet tactical ballistic missiles

SIPRNet: Secret Internet Protocol Router Network

SITREP: situation report

SJA: staff judge advocate

SOF: Special Operations Forces

SRC: Soldier Readiness Center

TBMs: tactical ballistic missiles

TI: Target identification

TJAG: the judge advocate general

TLAM: Tomahawk land attack missile

TPFDD: Time-Phased Force Deployment Data

TOC: Tactical Operations Center

TSC: Theater Support Command

TSIRT: theater specific individual requirements training

TST: time-sensitive target

UCMJ: Uniform Code of Military Justice

USARC: US Army Reserve Command

UXO: unexploded ordinance

VBIED: vehicle-borne improved explosive device

Z: Zulu time (Greenwich Mean Time, the universal time used to coordinate all operations)

Seated in captain's chair on bridge of NAVSTAR I following seizure and confiscation by CPA in August 2003, Umm Qasr, Iraq. Finally, Captain Kirk! Where is Mr. Spock when you really need him?

ABOUT THE AUTHOR

Kirk Warner retired as a senior army judge advocate colonel after thirty-three years of military service. He is a partner and senior litigator with the Smith Anderson law firm in Raleigh, North Carolina. Following his service in Iraq, he became deputy legal counsel to three Chairmen of the Joint Chiefs of Staff, staff judge advocate of the Army Reserve's Training Command with its three divisions, and the first commander of the 134th Legal Operations Detachment. In addition to five graduate degrees, he is a graduate of the US Army War College, Joint Forces Staff College, and the Army Command and General Staff College. Kirk lives in Raleigh, North Carolina, with his wife, Diane, and their dog, Wally. He still answers his phone.